Early Sino-American Relations, 1841–1912

A Westview Replica Edition

Copyright © 1977 by Westview Press, Inc.

Published in 1977 in the United States of America by

Westview Press, Inc.
1898 Flatiron Court
Boulder, Colorado 80301
Frederick A. Praeger, Publisher and Editorial Director

Library of Congress Cataloging in Publication Data

Swisher, Earl, 1902-1975.
  Early Sino-American relations, 1841-1912.

  (A Westview replica edition)
  Bibliography: p.
  1. United States--Foreign relations--China--Collected works.
2. China--Foreign relations--United States--Collected works.
I. Rea, Kenneth W. II. Title.
E183.8.C5S895   1977   327.73'051   77-13252
ISBN 0-89158-305-X

Printed and bound in the United States of America

In memory of Earl Swisher
(1902-1975)

Early Sino-American Relations, 1841–1912

The Collected Articles of Earl Swisher

edited by Kenneth W. Rea

Westview Press
Boulder, Colorado

Westview Replica Editions

This book is a Westview Replica Edition. The concept of Replica Editions is a response to the crisis in academic and informational publishing. Library budgets for books have been severely curtailed; economic pressures on the university presses and the few private publishing companies primarily interested in scholarly manuscripts have severely limited the capacity of the industry to properly serve the academic and research communities. Many manuscripts dealing with important subjects, often representing the highest level of scholarship, are today not economically viable publishing projects. Or, if they are accepted for publication, they are often subject to lead times ranging from one to three years. Scholars are understandably frustrated when they realize that their first-class research cannot be published within a reasonable time frame, if at all.

Westview Replica Editions seem to us one feasible and practical solution to the crisis. The concept is simple. We accept a manuscript in camera-ready form and move it immediately into the production process. The responsibility for textual and copy editing lies with the author or sponsoring organization. If necessary we will advise the author on proper preparation of footnotes and bibliography. The manuscript is acceptable as typed for a thesis or dissertation or prepared in any other clearly organized and readable way, though we prefer it typed according to our specifications. The end result is a book produced by lithography and bound in hard covers. Edition sizes range from 200 to 600 copies. We will include among Westview Replica Editions only works of outstanding scholarly quality or of great informational value and we will exercise our usual editorial standards and quality control.

Early Sino-American Relations, 1841-1912:
The Collected Articles of Earl Swisher
edited by Kenneth W. Rea

In this collection of seven essays, Sino-American relations
from 1841 through 1912 are examined by one of America's fore-
most authorities on the topic. Relying heavily on Chinese
material and concentrating on the Chinese perspective, Professor Swisher introduces new material and analyzes selected
aspects of these relations in detail.

Earl Swisher, widely recognized as an authority on
Chinese affairs, received a doctorate in Chinese history from
Harvard University, after which he returned to teach at the
University of Colorado, where he had completed his earlier
studies. He retired from the university as a professor emeritus
in 1971.

Kenneth W. Rea holds a doctorate in history from the
University of Colorado and is currently professor of history
at Louisiana Tech University.

CONTENTS

PREFACE   xi

1 EARLY FORMULATION OF CHINA'S FOREIGN
  POLICY   1

2 BEGINNINGS OF WESTERNIZATION   25

3 THE MOST-FAVORED-NATION POLICY   37

4 THE TREATY OF WANGHIA   56

5 EXTRATERRITORIALITY AND THE WABASH CASE   108

6 THE CHARACTER OF AMERICAN TRADE WITH
  CHINA, 1844-1860   117

7 ATTITUDES OF CHINESE OFFICIALS TOWARD
  THE UNITED STATES, 1841-1861   135

8 CHINESE 'BARBARIAN EXPERTS' IN EARLY
  SINO-AMERICAN RELATIONS   152

9 CHINESE REPRESENTATION IN THE UNITED
  STATES, 1861-1912   163

  NOTES   204

PREFACE

This volume, a companion to Canton in Revolution, concentrates on Earl Swisher's pioneering research in early Sino-American relations. From 1935 until his retirement in 1971, Swisher taught history at the University of Colorado and for many years served as the director of its Asian studies program. His interest in China began when he accepted a teaching appointment at Canton Christian College (Lingnan University) in 1924. After four years in China, he returned to the United States and completed his graduate studies at the University of Colorado and Harvard University. A gifted linguist who mastered Chinese, Japanese and several other languages, Swisher made a major contribution to the study of Sino-American relations. In the 1930s and 1940s, he translated and edited documents dealing with China's early relations with the United States. This work formed the basis of his dissertation at Harvard. After further research in Peking, the documents themselves were published under the title, China's Management of the American Barbarians, a monograph which has proven to be a major source for American scholars seeking a clearer and more meaningful understanding of Chinese policy toward the United States. The following articles, some of which are now published for the first time, shed additional light on this policy.

For this volume, I am deeply indebted to Ms. Robin Swisher Turcotte for making Professor Swisher's papers available. I wish to express my appreciation to Professors Joyce Lebra, John Brewer, Wiley Hilburn and Yawsoon Sim for their encouragement and assistance. Dean Paul J. Pennington and Professor W. Y. Thompson, of Louisiana Tech University, deserve my special thanks for their support of this project, as does Ms. Glenda Hammons who helped prepare the manuscript.

xi

Finally, this book would not have been possible without the patient understanding of my wife, Rebecca Rea, and my sons, Michael and Christopher.

K. W. R.

CHAPTER 1
EARLY FORMULATION OF CHINA'S FOREIGN POLICY

The earliest discussion of Chinese policy toward the United States to appear in the official records of China occurs in a memorial dated February 6, 1841 (the date of official reception in the Palace at Peking). The memorial was presented by I-li-pu,[1] then governor general of Liang-chiang and imperial commissioner in charge of military affairs to deal with the English who had occupied Ting-hai, on Chusan island, Chekiang province. I-li-pu was a Manchu of the Bordered Yellow Bannerman, who, although a collateral relative of the reigning Manchu house and thus entitled to wear the Red Girdle, had gone through the Chinese academic discipline to become a chin-shih in 1801 and member of the Hanlin Academy. After some service in the capital, he served as magistrate on the southwest frontier in Yunnan province and in 1819 was commended to the throne as proficient in "controlling tribal chieftains and managing Burmese bandits" and recommended for promotion. Later as governor of Yunnan he became associated with Juan Yuan,[2] whom he succeeded as governor general of Yunnan-Kweichow. In 1839 he was transferred to Chekiang where the frontier problems involved the ocean routes and the English instead of Burma and the tribesmen.

In his memorial of 1841, I-li-pu took up the barbarian problem as it had developed in Canton and Chekiang, quoting at length a letter from the venerable and respected Juan Yuan, already seventy-eight sui (probably seventy-seven by Western computation). Juan Yuan was one of the most distinguished men in China at the time this letter was written. A native of Kiangsu province,[3] he became chin-shih in 1789 and bachelor of the Hanlin Academy, inaugurating a long career as an ideal exponent of the Chinese cultural and official system; a scholar who applied himself

1

alternately or concurrently to creative writing, to research, and to official duties of the most varied nature. He suppressed piracy on the Chekiang coasts; he undertook educational reform and promotion; he demonstrated his filial piety and his loyalty to his friends, even at the risk of imperial censure; he edited, wrote, or compiled works on ancient inscriptions, biography and anthology and prepared a new edition of a T'ang dynasty thesaurus.

As early as 1818, as governor general of Liang-kuang, Juan Yuan reported confidentially to the throne on precautions to be taken against the English, pointing out that China should avoid meeting them on the sea, where they were strong, but should take advantage of their devotion to trade and their lack of land forces, utilizing the weapons of stoppage of trade, cutting off of foodstuffs, and finally, of firing on them when they venture to land. In dealing rigorously with the English, who "fear strength and scorn weakness" and pointed out the possibility of securing the approbation of "the merchants of other countries who would all realize that they defied our prohibitions, rather than our lightly picking a quarrel with them." The occasion for these extensive remarks on policy toward England may have been the recent unpleasantnesses connected with the Amherst Embassy in 1816 and 1817, when Captain Maxwell of H. M. S. Alceste had entered the Bogue, been fired on from the forts and in turn fired on the Chinese forts guarding the entrance to the river, beyond which foreign ships of war were not supposed to go.[4]

In 1832 Juan Yuan had occasion to investigate the traffic in opium by barbarian ships and removed one of the hong merchants who was security for the ships dealing in the drug. He also attempted to regulate the trade of the English receiving ships at Lintin Island, where illegal transfers were made.[5] In 1826 he was transferred to the post of governor general of Yun-kuei where he resumed his activity against the Burmese border ruffians. On the occasion of his seventieth birthday, in 1833, the emperor conferred honors and gifts on him, and two years later he was recalled to Peking to serve as grand secretary. In 1837 and again in 1838, Juan Yuan acted as regent while the emperor was on tour, but he was then old and ill and asked to retire. He was allowed to retire with the rank of grand secretary and half his salary.

At the time of the present memorial Juan Yuan was presumably in retirement and passing to his former colleague, I-li-pu, the advice and experience of more than fifty years of official life. That he was still vigorous is indicated by the fact that in this year he made the journey to Peking to pay his respects on the occasion of the emperor's sixtieth birthday. Juan Yuan was given further honors and full salary in 1846 and died three years later at eighty-six *sui*.

The third person involved in the memorial is Ch'i-shan, a Manchu Solid Yellow Bannerman, hereditary marquis of the first grade. Unlike I-li-pu, he entered official life on account of birth, rather than through civil service examination, beginning his career in 1806. Described by the emperor as clear-headed and capable, able to endure hard work and ill-will, he was appointed governor general of Liang-chiang in 1825. His rather turbulent career contains only two items which bear on the foreign impact: he recommended the use of rifles instead of spears and bows and arrows in the army, and formulated rules for the prevention of opium smuggling at Tientsin, noting that it was the English who opposed and delayed compliance.

In 1839, when English ships came to Tientsin, it was Ch'i-shan who persuaded them to return to Canton, and for this service he was commended and ordered to Kwangtung as imperial commissioner "to investigate and act." In Canton he recognized the hopeless position of the Chinese forces pitted against the English and made the fatal error of conceding them Hong Kong, recommending to the throne that a settlement be reached with them before further damage and bloodshed. The indignant Rescript said, in part:

> We, the Sovereign, regard the world as insufficient for the people, so much more that which the nation has; yet Ch'i-shan dared to give away Hong Kong, dared to allow trade and even more so bold as to ask us to confer extraordinary favors; moreover he rashly said that this territory was unimportant, that armaments were not good enough to rely on, military strength insecure, and popular morale unreliable, speaking traitorously under coercion. What kind of bowels has he, to ignor Favor, betray his country and exhaust utterly his better nature?[6]

3

He was ordered deprived of office and brought in irons to Peking for trial and all his property confiscated by the government. When the full account of the British capture of Canton and occupation of Hong Kong reached Peking, the blame was placed on Ch'i-shan and the princes and ministers passed sentence of beheading. He was released by Imperial Favor and sent to Chekiang garrison to redeem himself.[7]

In the letter quoted by I-li-pu, Juan Yuan notes that Ch'i-shan has not been able to curb the barbarians in Canton and then proceeds to comment on foreign policy:

> I have long known that of the various countries trading at Canton, besides England, the United States is the largest and most powerful. In this country the ground is level and rice plentiful. The English barbarians look to her for supplies and do not dare offend her. But the American barbarians at Canton have customarily been peaceable, not obstinate like the English barbarians. If we treat the American barbarian courteously and abolish their customs duties, and also take the trade of the English barbarians and give it to the American barbarians, then the American barbarians will be sure to be grateful for Heavenly Favor and energetically oppose the English barbarians. Moreover, the ships and cannon of the English barbarians have mostly been acquired by hire or seizure from other foreign states. If the American barbarians are made use of by us, then other countries will learn of it and it will not be difficult to dispose of them.

Juan Yuan goes on to say that while this policy will probably not stop the English, without allies they will wear themselves out and then China can step in and expel them. He explains to I-li-pu that he is old and ill and does not trust himself to memorialize the plan.

I-li-pu, recognizing the superior force of the English and their pressing demands, sees merit in Juan Yuan's plan.

> If we borrow the strength of the American barbarians in order to curb the English barbarians,

4

it would seem that the effort would be halved and the result doubled.

Although in view of the greatness of the Heavenly Court, to borrow the help of the outside barbarians may not seem to be proper handling, still in the books of strategy there is the theory of 'attack and get terms' and the technique of 'using barbarians to curb barbarians.' From Han and T'ang times onward it is recorded in history, not once but many times, that such has been done without loss of dignity. Moreover, considering the two propositions of conciliating the English barbarians or utilizing the American barbarians, still the latter is better than the former. It would seem that the device of Juan Yuan is still not without perspicacity. The only questions are whether or not the American barbarians can curb the English barbarians; whether or not they are willing to be used by us.

I-li-pu protects himself in submitting his proposal by explaining that he is not sure of its wisdom, particularly as Juan Yuan has been away from Canton for many years and barbarian affairs have undergone changes. Nevertheless he commends it to the emperor's judgment and, should he approve, asks that it be committed to Ch'i-shan at Canton for execution.[8]

When I-liang, governor of Kwangtung and concurrently in charge of Canton customs, memorialized (received February 10, 1841) that customs had fallen off and that not only the English and Indians had stopped trading, but also "the ships of other countries have been obstructed by the English barbarians and are unable to enter port," the court detected the means of bringing influence to bear on the Americans. The Imperial Rescript to I-liang's memorial said:

Kwangtung legally authorized the various barbarians to trade. The respectful and obedient states naturally should trade as usual. The English barbarians are overbearing and tyrannical and have interfered with the livelihood of other countries. Are those states willing resignedly to lose their profits? (We) hereby charge Ch'i-shan, Jung-wen and Ch'i Kung on their respective arrivals at Canton, to investigate carefully the attitudes of the various

5

countries, whether or not they are resentful of
the English barbarians' interference with their
livelihood or have any resentment toward the
Heavenly Court for not yet being able to draw
them in and pacify them, causing them to be neglected and lose their trade, and memorialize
according to the facts.[9]

Ch'i-shan also memorialized that the American
merchants were under the impression that China was
in the market for foreign ships for war purposes. He
had the hong merchants disillusion them on this score
but pointed out that their troubles were all caused
by the English. He advocated trading with the Americans in order to keep them quiet, make them resentful toward the English and grateful toward China.
"Thus while they would not be used by us, there would
not be any danger of their siding with evil and abet-
ting treason."[10]

Another memorialist on foreign policy in 1841
was Yu-ch'ien, at this time imperial commissioner,
governor of Kiangsu. Yu-ch'ien was a Mongol Bordered
Red Bannerman, of the Po-lo-t'e tribe, whose ances-
tors for three generations had distinguished themselves in the Manchu military service on the northwest frontier as well as in China proper. He was
originally named Yu-t'ai and under that name became
a chin-shih in 1817 and a bachelor in the Hanlin
Academy. He served in various capacities in the Peking government until 1826, when he was appointed to
a prefecture in Hupeh. As the financial commissioner
of Hunan[11] had the same name, the governor general
memorialized asking to change the new appointee's
name to Yu-ch'ien. In 1839, he received appointment
as judicial commissioner of Kiangsu, acting concurrently as governor. In the following year, while
he was acting governor general of Liang-chiang, the
English occupation of Ting-hai, on the island of
Chusan, took place.[12] Yu-ch'ien took charge of the
defense at Pao-shan, north of Shanghai, on the Yangtze estuary, later retiring to Shanghai. He memorialized on strategy for the recovery of Ting-hai pre-
posing to take advantage of the mobility of Chinese
infantry, as opposed to the cumbersome English artil-
lery; and the light draft of Chinese fishing craft,
as opposed to the large British vessels which could
not maneuver in the shallow waters. He urged the
necessity of taking the offensive immediately and
making a bold move to restore the morale of the
government troops.

In 1841, he was imperial commissioner. In the meantime, I-li-pu had arranged an armistice and the evacuation of Ting-hai by the British, but the emperor did not accept the terms. I-li-pu was recalled to Peking for punishment and Yu-ch'ien named to act as governor general of Liang-kiang in his stead. He was to take charge of the reoccupation of Ting-hai by Chinese troops. Yu-ch'ien rebuilt the defenses and reported that he was confident he could withstand a British attack. The British renewed their campaign in August and recaptured Ting-hai on October 1. Yu-ch'ien fought to hold Chen-hai, on the mainland opposite Ting-hai, and when Pottinger's forces captured it on October 10,[13] Yu-ch'ien "threw himself into the water to preserve his honor," and committed suicide.[14]

Early in 1841 (memorial received on March 21), just after his appointment as imperial commissioner, Yu-ch'ien presented his views on the military and diplomatic situation:

To continue, these marine volunteers are all vagabonds. In Kwangtung they are called 'rascals'. To use them against the barbarians would be like using poison to counteract poison. In case they are wounded or killed there will be no regrets; thus there will be no injury to the Heavenly prestige and, at the same time, a local evil can be removed.

Furthermore, I have ascertained that the various foreign countries, because the English rebels have stirred up trouble and trade as become slack, are all thoroughly angry and resentful. The strength of such countries as Europe, the United States, and France is separately equal to that of the rebels. It is not worth while for the Heavenly Court to issue an Edict ordering them to render help, but in a proclamation offering rewards, there is no harm in making clear that no matter whether they be soldiers or people, marine volunteers, Chinese traitors, or barbarians of the various countries, all are authorized to kill rebels and claim rewards, and also to issue a manifesto informing the various countries 'that the Great Emperor as Sovereign over all under Heaven, looks upon Chinese and outsiders with the same benevolence. Those who obey He soothes; those who rebel He

7

chastizes. England is rebellious and has resisted authority and troops have been sent to punish her. You other countries are not involved, and are all allowed to trade as usual. If the English rebels brazenly dare to use force to stop you or interfere with your livelihood, you other countries are authorized to fire upon them on the high seas or separately to use warships to attack their country, or anything else you can do.' Thus the minds of the various countries can be pacified and also the gall of the rebel barbarians overcome. Furthermore, (we can) secretly summon the capable and dependable among the Hong merchants and order them, acting as though this were their own idea, to make use of the policy of converting their spies (to our own uses), to meet emergencies as they arise, and to play them off and egg them on, causing them to destroy one another. Our army can merely remain quiet and depend on their activity, until the said (English) barbarians are left isolated and in embarrassed circumstances. The government troops and marine volunteers can then take advantage of their weakened condition to attack them. Such an insignificant rebel can easily be eradicated with one stroke of the drum.[15]

The Rescript expressed confidence in the ability of the land forces to expel the British, once they came ashore, but sent Yu-ch'ien's proposal to offer rewards to General I-shan to use or not as he saw fit.[16] Such proclamations had already been issued in Canton as early as July 1840 and were repeated in February 1841.[17]

In the meantime, Assistant Military General Yang Fang was in charge of military operations at Canton. Yang Fang, a native of Kweichow, was a military career man. He showed courage and ability as a common soldier and was chosen from the ranks for promotion. After some twenty-five years of military service in west and southwest China, with various promotions, he took part, 1827-1830, in a large expedition into Kashgaria. He distinguished himself and was rewarded by the emperor, being made hereditary marquis of the second grade, Grand Tutor to the Heir Apparent, privileged to ride horseback in the Forbidden City, given gifts of clothing and

ginseng, was invited to dine with the emperor, and
on his sixtieth birthday given an imperial autographed
scroll. His fortunes suffered a setback in 1830 and
he was degraded and recalled from Kashgaria. In 1833-
1835 he served, with varying success, in campaigns
against the "barbarians", native tribesmen, in Honan
and Hopei. In 1841, when the English "rebelled against
Heaven and defied reason," and I-shan was appointed
Rebel Quelling General, Yang Fang was made one of two
assistant military generals and ordered to proceed to
Canton and make up for the losses suffered under
Ch'i-shan.[18]

Yang Fang memorialized (April 6, 1841) that
American trade had been interrupted by the hostilities
and that Warren Delano, Jr., American vice consul, had
requested the renewal of trade, both for his nationals
and for British civilians. Yang Fang sent the Canton
prefect, with an interpreter, to interview Delano
and reports his statement of the American position as
follows:

The English barbarians having been attacked
and expelled, we do not venture to make further
requests, but consider the taking up of arms
and rebelling against authority are the evil
doings of the English barbarians. Our merchant
ships have never dared to participate in stirring
up trouble but on account of it, have been
obstructed for more than a year and unable to
trade. That their merchants have been implicated
by the military leaders of their own country is
not worthy of sympathy, but we, the United
States and other countries, have been respectful
and obedient and have not dared illegally to
sell prchibited goods. For the receipt of the
Great Emperor's gracious permission to trade as
usual, we are extremely grateful. But since
our arrival at Canton last year, we have been
implicated by England and unable to get into
(Huang-)pu to discharge cargo, to the end that
goods have been ruined and trade decimated.
We acknowledge the Heavenly Courts commisseration.
Now we find that the English barbarian merchants
are in a critical situation. Could you not in
this way, after attacking and driving out their
warships, for the time being allow their merchant
vessels to trade without discrimination so that
the various countries would not incur the hatred
of England and escape being hindered or implicated?

Besides, with the English merchant vessels at
(Huang-) pu, her warships would have them to
consider and would not dare start trouble. This
would seem to be a way of subduing them.

Yang Fang sent word that

although what the barbarian said was reasonable,
he did not fully realize that the English barbarians had fomented rebellion and committed
murderous acts, that her guilt was onerous and
great, and that actually she had cut herself
off from the Heavenly Court. Now the Great
Emperor has ordered the army out and specially
declared the Heavenly punishment. Although he
says that the barbarian merchants have not
helped the rebels, they are after all Englishmen
so how dare they request to trade.[19]

Having thus replied to Delano, Yang Fang proceeds to
plead his case to the emperor, saying that since the
English had restored Ting-hai, peace could probably
be restored by granting the right to trade according
to the old regulations. He also said that a pledge
not to deal in opium had been presented. He concludes:

But I have been ordered to lead troops and only
know that military affairs are paramount. By
no means because the various countries con-
tinuously make requests (Vermilion Comment: These
are clearly subversive plots of the English
rebels.) will I relax the morale of the army. .
. . As to the statement that the barbarian
traders have also had no share in causing
trouble and by letting their merchant ships
enter port we can curb and reduce the barbarian
troops, I have secretly inquired and openly
investigated and apparently this is not without
foundation. And from the point of view of
military strategy, there are also occasions
for 'letting go as a means of grasping.' If
we stubbornly resist the barbarian hordes, it
is feared it will lead to general disappointment
and perhaps (we should) use finesse to control
them.[20]

The Rescript to this memorial reflects the attitude
of the interlinear notes made by the emperor (Vermilion
Comments): that these requests by Americans are a
part of a British ruse to divert China from military

activities. Yang Fang is warned not to allow the English to slip out of Canton into the outer ocean and thus escape the punishment that awaits them. He and the other generals are "to cut off their rear, close in on all sides, and recover Hong Kong."[21]

A week later Yang Fang joined Manchu General A-ching-a and Governor I-liang in a memorial reporting that the Americans were jubilant over the resumption of trade while the British merchants were looking on enviously and hopefully.[22] The Rescript approved the opening of trade to American merchants but again repudiated their good offices on behalf of the British.[23]

About the first of April (memorial received in Peking on April 18, 1841; last date mentioned in the memorial, March 31.), Yang Fang and I-liang again memorialized regarding Consul Delano's request for trade on behalf of the Indiamen which, as the emperor pointed out, were the principal carriers of opium. The request, advanced by the United States, France, and other countries, was supported by the argument

> that India, although a dependency of the English barbarians, is more than twenty thousand li from England, nor did it join her in causing trouble. (Vermilion Comment: The following details should not be discussed now. We know only one word, 'Attack!' Besides, they are entirely untrustworthy.) At this time the trading ships of the other countries have all entered port and it seems inappropriate for India to be forced into the corner to show discrimination. Even (Charles) Elliot made a statement to the American consul, saying that the India merchants had no connection with England's resort to arms; that the English ships of the mother country were willing to await the Imperial Edicts and would not dare enter port hastily, only India had innocently suffered and had her goods tied up and actually this was discourteous to them; so he had the request made on their behalf to have their trade opened along with the others.

> We find that India is a dependency of Great Britain. Previously we memorialized fully in the case of the Hong Kong blockade. Now we have investigated carefully the Indian barbarian merchants and they have not participated

in causing trouble. It is fitting that in
dealing with the obedient and the rebellious
we consider the course of accommodation.
Moreover (underlined in Vermilion), according to the report of the Hong merchants, among
the Indian merchant ships were nine cargoes of
foreign rice, amounting to something over
30,000 piculs (2000 tons). Kwangtung, being
cut up with hill and sea and the grain production
not being large, has always depended on supplies
of Saigon and foreign (Indian or Siamese) rice.
(Vermilion Comment: This is the source of opium.
Whom are you deceiving? On reading this, we are
angry in the extreme!) Now the Indian barbarian merchants have always imported rice.
That they are not also harboring evil in their
hearts (underlined in Vermilion [line not shown]),
can still be believed. Moreover, there is real
benefit to the sustenance of the people and in
this way the populace can be pacified. It
seems that to allow the India merchant ships one
and all to unload, extending the Sage Sovereign's
gracious kindness to those from afar, would at
the same time diminish the strength of England's
following.[24]

When Yang Fang and I-liang pressed their arguments
for extending trading privileges to the Indian and
English ships, the emperor charged them with yielding
to pressure as Ch'i-shan had done. One Vermilion
Comment was: "We see that you two men desire to
follow Ch'i-shan's precedent. Therefore A-ching-a
did not attach his name." At the end of the memorial
the emperor wrote: "If trade were the solution of the
problem why would it be necessary to transfer and
dispatch generals and troops in this way; and why
did We need to arrest Ch'i-shan? These observations
are entirely wrong and edicts will be issued at
once."[25] An edict of the same date charges Yang Fang
and I-liang with idleness, procrastination, and
"deliberate obstruction and demoralization of the
army's morale." They were both ordered turned over
to the Board for trial and punishment.[26] The situation
was discussed and the issue made clear; first, that
the court approved allowing the neutral nations to
trade; second, that it was not ready to allow the
Indian merchants to trade because it was not deceived
by the argument that they were carrying rice but was
convinced that they were dealing in opium and the
officials were conniving in this trade; and third,

that the court wanted an aggressive military campaign to expel the English, and that they expected I-shan and Lung-wen were to carry it out where Yang Fang and I-liang had failed. "No reference to the word 'commerce' will be tolerated nor any idle loss of opportunities. . . . I-shan and the others . . . are charged forthwith to have the commanders order troops distributed for attack and to be sure that not a single rebel sail returns on getting word of the danger. If the barbarian ships hear the rumors and hide far away and we expend our military strength in vain, only the said generals will be held to account. Tremble!"[27]

The two new arrivals on the Canton scene were both Manchus, but men of very different character. I-shan was an Imperial Clansman, descendant in the fourth generation of Hsun-chun Prince Yun-t'i and was attached to the Manchu Bordered Blue Banner. He campaigned in Kashgaria and Ili and in 1837 was made Tartar General of Ili. In 1841 he was appointed Rebel Quelling General to lead the combined military forces in Kwangtung against the English.[28] Lung-wen was a member of the I-erh-kan Collateral Clan, a Manchu Solid Red Bannerman, and a chin-shih of 1808. With one brief exception, when he filled out a term as Imperial Resident of Tibet, he served in the court at Peking usually in some high judicial capacity. His biographer says that when he accompanied I-shan to Canton "their views were so incompatible that he became ill, despondent, and embittered unto death."[29]

I-shan and Lung-wen stopped at Shao-chou, now Chu-chiang, on the North River near the Hunan frontier some 100 miles north of Canton, to await the arrival of Governor General Ch'i Kung who was coming to Canton by way of Mei-ling Pass from Kiangsi. They memorialized on the military situation, the views, apparently, being those of the militant I-shan. They reported the gathering of forces from the provinces around Canton and also the occupation by the English of the Bocca Tigris and Dutch Folly forts at Canton, following the repudiation by both English and Chinese of the convention arranged between Ch'i-shan and Captain Elliot. "On February 26th Captain Elliot notified that 'the batteries of the Boca Tigris have this day fallen to her Majesty's forces. Several hundred prisoners have been captured, the enemy is in flight in all directions, and no loss reported up to this time on our side.' On the same day Commodore Bremer notified that merchant ships were 'permitted to repair to the Bogue, and will be allowed to proceed higher, as soon as it is ascertained that the river is clear of all obstructions.' The ships of war advanced at once, and on the 27th a battery below Whampoa was destroyed, the ship <u>Cambridge</u> blown up, and a flotilla of forty war-junks <u>dispersed</u>. On March 2nd the light-draft ships reached Canton."[30]

I-shan's appraisal of this situation follows:

At that time the Americans were asking to trade. The high officials in Canton temporarily put them off and encouraged them by promising to memorialize their request. Now the rebel barbarian warships are not willing to withdraw into the outer ocean and are still at Huang-pu (Whampoa) in reserve. They let it be known that after we arrived at Canton, they would immediately request a settlement. (<u>Vermilion</u> Comment: Detestable to the extreme!) We on hearing this, were filled with grief. We personally consider that since the beginning of the rebel barbarians' defection, they have seized forts and wounded our commanders. Wherever their ferociousness reaches, is it true that no one dare resist it? On the whole, it is rather that heretofore we have proposed conciliation, voluntarily removed barriers, causing them to take advantage of the opening to penetrate deeply and press at our gates. Those ministers acting as circumstances required, could follow expediency, but we have received (imperial) command to attack. How dare we hesitate or equivocate and idly lose an opportunity, thus betraying our trust. (<u>Vermilion Comment</u>: Take care that there be no weak, careless, or unprincipled conduct! We are wholly dependent on you.) But troops can hardly be collected hastily and ammunition has not yet arrived. If on our arrival at Canton, we were to refuse trade, the barbarians would certainly attack the city with all their strength. If there should be any unexpected danger and rescue be too late, then, wishing to protect Canton, we would on the contrary be hastening its loss. Now the enemy's determination ought not to be further fostered (pointed with Vermilion); national prestige (<u>Vermilion Comment</u>: Quite right.) ought not to be <u>further injured</u> (pointed with Vermilion). We must devise thoroughly complete plans, in accord with our

Sage Instructions. At this time the governor general, Ch'i Kung, is crossing the Mei-ling Range. We are halting temporarily at Shao-chou and have despatched a letter to the said governor general to hasten here for a conference, to collect government troops from all regions, to occupy all the land routes and strategic places, to station troops for defense, to urge the collection of powder and secretly devise implements for defense and attack, prepare ambushes everywhere, encourage volunteers and use them in unexpected ways, to attack sharply the inner anchorages, causing the rebel barbarians to lose courage, and in addition to defend the various inlets of the river in order to show that we are always on guard. It is reported that the barbarian ships' stores are depleted and an immediate battle would be to their advantage. This is nothing more than anxiety to force the sale of goods to supply their needs. If we strengthen our walls and purge the countryside, then the Chinese traitors will have no profit to covet. When their adherents are cut off, then (we can) send crack troops to take their rear, lower rafts to fill up the river, join land and marine (forces) to capture and seize by different routes so that not a single barbarian sail will return (home), in order to manifest Heavenly punishment and gratify men's minds.

Vermilion Comment: These views are very proper. We only await the news of victory with the greatest impatience.[31]

Yang Fang was waiting in Canton for their arrival. He reported ten-odd English ships anchored at various places outside the Bogue, moving about here and there. "They sail around, delay, and merely hope along with the United States and other countries to receive (Imperial) Favor." He complained that "the sores on my legs have again broken out, but I did not dare on this account to evade at all my responsibilities," and was hopeful that military preparations were adequate "without a chance in ten thousand of failure."[32] On March 5, he went into the city on horseback and his description reveals a rather sorry situation.

The streets are narrow and were crowded with people. Suddenly a Chinese traitor seized my

15

left arm and almost unhorsed me. (<u>Vermilion</u>
<u>Comment</u>: Odious.) He was in due time <u>seized</u>.
On being questioned he made no other complaint,
merely acknowledging his fault in confused
words. I immediately ordered that his head be
hung up and exposed--by killing one man, to
strike fear into the hearts of the populace.

After six days, the rebels pressed the gates
of the capital. Inside the city, orders were
carried out and prohibitions enforced. The
Chinese traitors held their breath. The small
boats plying their trade in the Canton River,
were very numerous. On March 18 and 19, two
days and three nights, when the rebel ships were
anchored at Pai-hao T'an,[33] I because there were
no wood supplies, hastened the work on one
hundred fire-boats and two large bamboo fire
rafts. I originally intended to release them,
lighted, with the tide, but the said three-
masted barbarian warships and armed steamers
were anchored at wide intervals, each protected
by three-masted warships, and more than a thousand
small boats of the Chinese traitors were going
about over a radius of five or six li. (<u>Vermilion</u>
<u>Comment</u>: Odious to the extreme!) <u>Elliot</u> (<u>underlined</u>
<u>in Vermilion</u>) stayed at night on a patrol boat,
and on seeing the flames would certainly have
withdrawn, and the fire would not have served its
purpose. So, on account of the request of the
United States, I temporarily restrained them and
led them on, in order to wait for the collection
of troops from the rear and to plan for defense
and attack.

But there has long been the rumor that the marine
forces received three hundred dollars for each
empty cannon shot. I have investigated the
death in the field of Kuan T'ien-p'ei[34] because
the officers did not dare to force the soldiers
to fire the cannon (<u>Vermilion Comment</u>: Such
utter uselessness. As a rule the military and
civil officials are all like wooden idols.) Kuan
T'ien-p'ei himself took a fuse, but the mouth of
the cannon already had water coming out. Thus
the degenerate practice of soldiers and people
yielding to bribery will hardly bear inquiry. If
we do not cleanse their hearts and wash their
faces, repair the strings, and get out of the
rut, it will be very hard to effect reform.

As to curbing the Chinese traitors, I propose
to post proclamations setting forth the
dangers. After the governor of Kwangsi, Liang
Chang-chu, has sent wooden rafts and large
stakes, and the means of attack are prepared,
I shall again issue proclamations to curb
the traitors' hearts and break the rebels'
courage.[35]

I-shan and Lung-wen finally reached Canton,
April 14, and immediately reviewed the situation
in a memorial received in Peking on May 11. They
were especially concerned about neutral shipping
and the loss of customs revenues since the beginning
of hostilities. They found that normally, Portugal,
the United States, France, Holland, Spain, Cambodia,
Denmark, Sweden, Prussia, Austria, England, and
India traded at Canton; that from April 27 to June 30,
1840, only nineteen merchant ships, American and
Spanish, entered port, and after that time, none at
all, being obstructed by the British hostilities.

The English barbarians are imperious and
domineering. The strength of the said
countries is not sufficient to restrain
them and they are all very resentful. On
February 26, of the present year, when the
English barbarians without authorization
entered Hu-men and attacked and destroyed
the Wu-yung guard station, the barbarian
ships went direct to Huang-pu (Whampoa).
Therefore the merchant vessels of the
United States, France, and India, which
were formerly allowed to trade, to the
number of forty-two vessels, were able to
follow the British warships and enter port.
They then requested trade on behalf of the
English barbarians.[36] Yang Fang, together
with Governor I-liang, has thoroughly
investigated the situation, and memorialized
clearly to continue to allow the respectful
and obedient countries to trade as before.
The said barbarians all gladly honor Imperial
Grace and dare not be disappointed with the
Heavenly Court. We have had the reports of
the interpreters examined and they are all
in agreement. Now, although trade has been
opened, the substantial buyers have all
fled, and those doing business are extremely
few. We have already issued proclamations

17

ordering their speedy return, that all
peaceful firms could trade with the
respectful and obedient countries as usual,
with no need for fear or doubt. In the
last few days more are returning to their
occupations, and the popular temper is a
little more stable.[37]

The Americans and the English were not the only
Western peoples with whom the Chinese officials had
to deal. King Louis-Philippe sent a mission to China
headed by Dubois de Jancigny aboard the frigate
Erigone. The Erigone sailed from Brest on April 28,
1841 and proceeded to Canton where France was
represented only by a merchant consul, an Englishman
named Lancelot Dent.[38] The mission came up to Canton,
with two French priests as interpreters, and asked
to meet the officials, saying, according to the
Chinese record, that they had military matters to
discuss that could not be committed to intermediaries.
General I-shan met them on board a Chinese junk some
ten li below Canton. Jancigny said that France was
"profoundly grateful for the Heavenly Court's generous
favors; that the king, . . . on hearing that the
English barbarians had taken up arms against China,
feared that the commercial ships of his country would
be implicated, and thereupon, sent them to provide
protection, and in addition ordered them on their
arrival here to act as intermediaries for the settlement of the dispute."

I-shan replied:

That your country has long been respectful
and obedient, the Great Emperor is thorougly
aware. The English rebels are so obstinate
and unregenerate, so reckless and overbearing,
that in the future your several countries are
sure to be injured by them. The king of your
country has sent you here with ships-of-war;
if you are really able to exert yourselves to
reciprocate, I, the general-in-chief and others,
will certainly adhere the facts and memorialize
the Great Emperor to treat you with unusual
kindness and grant special favors.

According to their statement: 'We and the
English barbarians, although we are enemy
states, have now recently made peace and,
with no pretext to rely on, we cannot act

18

rashly. If we attack them without reason, we fear that other countries will be resentful. Would it not be better to conclude the affair and stop the fighting, and make an early settlement of it?'

On hearing this, we asked them what method they had of concluding the affair. According to their statement, they were willing to negotiate with the English barbarians and if they agreed, that would be the end of it; if they did not agree, then they would have a pretext for taking up arms against them.'

We informed them that as the English barbarians had repeatedly defied authority and were now encroaching upon Ningpo, Ting-hai, and other places, they had caused the Emperor to be angry and to select and commission awe-inspiring generals and military governors of various districts to lead the government troops of the various provinces to proceed to deal with them. At this time how could the present general and others dare on their own authority to authorize them to negotiate?

We received their statement:

'Since Your Excellencies do not dare memorialize, we shall first go out on the high seas and negotiate with the English barbarian leaders. If there are any developments, we will come back and report.'

Then we distributed gifts of various kinds and thereafter the said officers and priests took their leave for the high seas.

Further, according to investigations of the local police, the rebel barbarian officer, Pottinger, during the twelfth month of last year (January 11-February 10, 1842), secretly returned from Chekiang to Hong Kong.[39] Furthermore, they found that the French officers came to Hong Kong and had two personal interviews with the rebel barbarians. We subsequently received the report of the Hsiang-shan (now Chung-shan) assistant district magistrate residing at Macao, Chang Yu, that the French priest Yu-ch'ao and others had reported personally that the military officers now had important business and on February 25 had set sail for the Philippines, going to look after the warships. They left word for Jancigny to go to Canton to petition in reply. On March 16, Jancigny arrived at the factory and presented a memorandum, still under the pretext of concluding peace, hoping to be given the English rebels' wharf. We investigated their activities: it seems that the English rebels recently made peace with them and the French barbarians thought to share in the gains and also thought to share in the territory; hence the mediation on their behalf. The barbarians are by nature full of cunning. Although the said military officers are apparently respectful and obedient, how do we know they will not avail themselves of this to spy out conditions in the interior or otherwise cause trouble? Since at present the said barbarians, along with the barbarian merchants of the United States and other countries, have access to the Canton factories and carry on trade as usual and now with no reason seek peace, it is impossible not to be suspicious. Accordingly, we employed polite words to reject (their proposal) and also informed them that they should not help the rebels (lest) jade and stone be both destroyed; that if they could exert themselves on China's behalf, the Great Emperor would certainly bestow favors on their country.[40]

An Imperial Rescript to this memorial instructed I-shan to tell the French: "Your country has always been respectful and obedient and naturally will be allowed to trade as usual. If you are really able to exert yourselves on behalf of the Heavenly Court, the Great Emperor must naturally be highly pleased. As to protecting yourselves from being thrown into confusion by the English barbarians or having a pretext for taking up arms, China rightfully is not concerned."[41]

A little later Niu-chien, governor general of Liang-chiang, reported a French warship anchored outside Woosung, the port of Shanghai, on July 31. The captain asked for an interview and the Shanghai tao-t'ai met him outside the city. He reportedly also asked on behalf of the English permission to establish an English representative in Peking, the same as Russia; and permission to proceed up the

Yangtze to confer with Pottinger whom they hoped to
induce to cease hostilities. The request for
representation at Peking was dismissed as being
impracticable and a Ch'ien-lung edict of 1793, on
the occasion of the Macartney mission, cited. As
to mediation, the French captain was told that
hostilities had already ceased and that the signing
of a treaty with England was imminent (August 29),
so there was no need of his going up the Yangtze.
On August 13, the tao-t'ai reported that the French
seized a grain transport ("sand" boat), saying they
were going to Nanking, and sailed away. Niu-chien
then gives his views on foreign policy as regards
the French:

Now we find that France in the former Ming
dynasty (1368-1644) was most powerful. In
firearms, the Frank type was then introduced
into China from that country. In recent years
she has been comparatively weaker. At Canton
they trade and pay duties and have been regarded
as respectful and cautious. Now they come to
the Yangtze in ships nominally to urge the
English to cease hostilities, actually, we
fear, to take advantage of the time before the
fighting has ceased. As to the said barbarian
leader's going out and mediating, it is hard
to be sure that it is not because he plans
to appear friendly to the Heavenly Court in the
hope of getting a pretext for making demands.
(Vermilion Comment: Actually, it is hard to
determine.) But we have learned that England
dominates the high seas and all the foreigners
recognize her leadership in all respects. If
this country obeys the Heavenly Court, the
other countries all keep quiet. Therefore,
on the occasion when the English barbarians
requested trade, I joined Imperial Commissioner
Ch'i-ying in a memorial requesting Imperial
Favor, it was primarily to relieve the anxiety
of the predicament of the interior and also
to nip the opportunism of all the barbarians
in the bud. Now Cecille (the French captain)
is in command of only one warship and will by
no means dare to assume perverse or unrestrained
airs. As Canton allows them to trade he is not
likely to be willing to forfeit their livelihood
by making greedy demands unadvisedly. He was
merely in a hopeful frame of mind and therefore
tried an experiment.

21

Niu-chien thus concludes that he will have no
difficulty in disposing of Cecille if he appears
at Nanking and of persuading him to return to
Canton. In case the French demur, he will have
Pottinger, who is now anxious to please in order
to get his treaty, to send the French away.[42]
When Pottinger was consulted, he assured Niu-
chien's representative that he "would not find
it hard to explain to them and induce them to
return."[43] The Imperial Rescript approved Niu-
chien's action and charged Ch'i-ying, who was
proceeding to Nanking to assist in the negotiation
of a treaty with Pottinger, to inform Cecille "that
his mediating for peace to stop hostilities shows
fully his country's respectful and obedient intent,
but now that England has already made peace with
China (truce declared on August 14, English terms
accepted on August 17; the Rescript is dated
August 24) and will never resume hostilities, the
said barbarian leader should quickly return to
Kwangtung and carry on trade as usual." The Rescript
continues:

> As to the matter of England setting up a bar-
> barian official in Peking to handle her affairs,
> formerly in the Ch'ien-lung period (1736-1796)
> it was not possible to carry this out. Now in
> the three matters in which the English bar-
> barians request Imperial Favor (i.e., the
> British terms laid down at Nanking), they were
> unwilling to allude to it, and besides, as this
> does not concern the said country (France), it
> is naturally unnecessary to give rise to
> additional complications. In this way give
> explicit instructions in such a way that the
> said barbarians will have to turn sail and go
> away.

> We further charge them to send deputies to
> notify Pottinger: 'China is now at peace with
> your country, having discussed the terms in
> detail and ceased hostilities forever. Now
> the French barbarian leader has come despite
> obstacles, declaring that he will urge your
> country to make peace. Actually what is his
> point of view? If it is sincere, then explain
> to him that now you are already at peace with
> China and will not bother the barbarian leader
> to state your case for you. Take care to make
> Cecille understand this and quickly sail back

home. Still more if Cecille's coming was
nothing but a desire to get profits out of
this, you should devise means to admonish
him and to destroy his illusions so as not
to cause him to interfere and disrupt
matters.'[44]

Thus down to April 1842, several general
tendencies and specific policies had become apparent
in China's foreign policy:

1. A general application of the old Chinese
device of using barbarians to curb barbarians. China
hoped by a judicious distribution and withholding
of favors to keep the various countries pitted against
one another and prevent the necessity of meeting them
all at once.

2. The hope that the United States, as the
principal commercial rival of England, could be
utilized to thwart England.

3. The belief that the hostilities of England,
which blocked commerce and destroyed property, would
anger the United States and lead her to turn her
military and naval strength against England.

4. The assumption that most-favored-treatment
would be given to the United States, whose merchants
had always been obedient and tractable. It was
unquestioningly accepted that the normal trade
privileges had been taken from the neutral countries
by the English, not by the Chinese. Why should the
peaceful countries be punished and the war-like ones
rewarded?

5. The reluctance, although not the impossibility,
on the part of the Chinese to form a military or
diplomatic alliance with the United States.

6. The tendency, somewhat vague but already
apparent, to place the United States slightly above
the other barbarian countries, as somewhat more
tractable, less aggressive, and less dangerous,
particularly than England and probably also than
France.

7. The possibility, soon abandoned under the
glare of imperial disapproval, of enlisting the help
of France as an ally or an intermediary.

8. The beginnings of a tendency on the part of China to recognize in England, not only China's most formidable enemy, but also the leading Western state which could keep the other countries under control.

9. The recurrent hope that each settlement was final and that having accepted this set of compromising terms, all China's troubles with barbarians were to be over for ten thousand years.

10. The belief that all defeats and resulting concessions of trade and residence were minor; that China and the Chinese court was unshaken so long as access to Peking was not conceded. This was a matter of primary concern during the period of the Cushing negotiations and continued to be down to 1860 when it was rudely shattered by the march of British and French troops into the Forbidden City.

CHAPTER 2
BEGINNINGS OF WESTERNIZATION

China's first recognition of Western superiority in the fields of naval engineering and armament
came as a result of the success of British arms
between 1839 and 1842. The Chinese who came in
contact with the West at Canton, the Bocca Tigris,
Macao, and Hong Kong came to realize that Western
ships were more seaworthy, faster, and more impreg-
nable to cannon fire, and particularly that the
amazing new "fire-wheelers" on steamers were capable of a mobility, irrespective of wind, that the
lumbering Chinese junks could not equal. A present-
day Chinese writer says that "the leaders of the
Opium War in the forties, practically none of whom
had at that time any real knowledge of the West,
driven by the sheer necessity of war, were willing
to learn from the 'barbarians', and to adopt their
means of armament. Their efforts unconsciously
opened up, for weal or for woe, the great possibilities of the moderization of China."[1]

This whole interesting development is reflected
in the memorials and rescripts of this period but
it will be treated merely as it affects the interests and the policies of the United States.
American traders had become the principal commercial
rivals of the English and during the period of the
war with England the United States was the principal neutral power in China. Naturally it was to the
United States that China turned for ships, armaments, and knowledge of this Western magic that
worked such destruction on China's coasts and rivers
and turned even the stoutest Manchu garrisons into
fleeing mobs or useless martyrs.

Commissioner Lin Tse-hsu came to Canton in 1839 determined to put an end to the opium evil and prosecuted his campaign with vigor and considerable ability. Because of his bold defiance of the English and his destruction of 20,283 chests of opium, he was regarded by the English as the archdisciple of anti-foreignism in China. But this same Lin Tse-hsu was one of the first Chinese to advocate the sincerest kind of pro-foreignism: the imitation of Western methods.

Lin Tse-hsu was a native of Fukien province on the eastern seaboard north of Canton. He was a chin-shih of 1811 and began the usual official career; he served in the capital until 1820 and then in the provinces, with the usual six years out for mourning after the death of his mother and father in 1824 and 1827, respectively. In 1837 he was made governor general of Hu-kuang (Hunan and Hupeh provinces), where he interested himself in the opium problem. He memorialized that the use of opium was spreading rapidly into those interior provinces and advocated a rigorous program of suppression by confiscating opium and opium equipment, by punishing smugglers, dealers, manufacturers, and smokers, and by disseminating information on prescriptions and methods of breaking the habit once acquired. The emperor was so impressed with his zeal that he made him an imperial commissioner and authorized him to proceed to Canton to end the opium evil once and for all. His vigorous action in Canton in 1839, is well-known in Western annals. He then proceeded with an equally vigorous but less effective program of defense and resistance against the British. The emperor approved his opium crusade but when he failed to curb the English, charged him with maladministration. He was tried by the Boards and removed from office late in 1840. The following year he was sent to Chekiang to redeem himself but the persistent British victories were against him and in the summer of 1841, he was again degraded, deprived of ministerial rank and banished to Ili, on the Siberia-Mongolian frontier. His exile was delayed by an imperial order to assist in flood control work on the Yellow River, but when the emergency was met he proceeded to Ili where he remained until 1845. He was then called back to Peking and served in various posts in Shensi, Kansu, and Yunnan with vigor and distinction. In 1849, he resigned on account of illness and returned home. He was not allowed the rest he had earned. The next year the Taiping Rebillion reached alarming proportions in Kwangsi. The emperor ordered Lin Tse-hsu to that province as governor and empowered him to take complete charge of the campaign to suppress the Long-haired rebels. The aged campaigner set out from his home in late winter of 1850 but died in Ch'ao-chou, Kwangtung, before he reached his last post.[2]

Although the formal biographies and official papers of Lin Tse-hsu give a clear picture of an unusually energetic and resourceful public servant, they give slight indication of the pioneer of Westernization which he appears to have been. His interest in the West is attested by the Hai Kuo T'u Chih (Illustrated Record of Maritime Nations), the authorship and editorship of which is shared by his close associate, Wei Yuan, published in 1844. According to the latter, Commissioner Lin utilized his time in Canton, 1839-1841, to gather information about foreign countries, and to purchase and translate foreign newspapers and books.[3] The Hai Kuo T'u Chih is primarily a work on the geography of the Western world, translated from the materials Commissioner Lin obtained at Canton, but "it contains, at the beginning, four essays on the Policies for Maritime Defense, and at the end has several chuan devoted to Western armaments, steamships, modern mechanical inventions, and astronomy. It seems to be the first elaborate attempt by a Chinese to spread the knowledge of Western things by a direct translation from foreign sources."[4] Lin Tse-hsu also patronized Western medicine, as represented in Canton by the American medical missionary, Dr. Peter Parker, "bought more than two hundred foreign guns from every country in the West" for the Bocca Tigris,[5] and built improved types of warjunks from European models purchased in Canton.[6]

This implied recognition of the superiority of Western ships and gunnery is brought to the imperial attention in a memorial of Chin Ying-lin received August 21, 1842. Chin Ying-lin, a native of Chekiang province, was a chin-shih of 1826. He served in various judicial offices and in 1842 was made Sub-director of the Court of Judicature and Revision in Peking.[7] He represents the academic type of Chinese official, devoted to historical and literary studies at the capital, without the broadening experience of service in the provinces. He had no experience either with Westerners or with Western ships and guns. His natural reaction to the foreign novelties is that they are all wrong and that they are not new anyway. He begins his memorial in the following manner:

> I consider that the ruthlessness of the rebel barbarians is entirely attributable to the weakness and unmanliness of our marines, hence the defeats. I venture to think that what the said barbarians rely on is ships. Last year, Canton bought a ship from the United States. On taking it apart and examining it, the wood was very hard, covered with five layers of leather, in addition to copper and iron coverings, also in five or six layers, making a thickness of something over a foot (14.1 English inches), placed on a wooden frame. Thus cannon balls even though large could hardly shatter it. The masts were of very hard wood and the tops could bear a number of men; the cannon could shoot a great distance, thus causing people to be very afraid of them.

He considers these by-products of China and goes on to describe shipbuilding and ships drawn from Chinese literature, pointing out that there is nothing new to China and that the barbarians have merely capitalized on Chinese ideas. He describes twelve types of ships and boats, all of which should be provided in order to meet the barbarian on the sea. These 1842 models would include the "mother and son" boat; a "ships-chained-together" model; a "tower-boat"; a "fast galley", a large warjunk 366 feet long, carrying 2000 men and provided with four banks of oars, "on the top horses can be driven; on the prow is painted a strange beast to scare the River God"; a "sea-gull" model; a "covered-shed" type, covered with rawhide and protected by copper plates, and so forth. He also discusses tactics to take advantage of the limitations of the barbarian ships. Included is the helpful hint that "around the rebel ships, there is always noxious smoke; licorice and brown sugar held in the mouth gives immediate relief." The memorial concludes optimistically:

> Now the rebel barbarians from the time
> they presented tribute in the Chia-ch'ing
> era (1796-1821), have been arrogant in
> their language and draw maps everywhere
> they go. They have harbored mischief in
> their hearts for a long time. Having
> provocation, they rebel; without pro-
> vocation, they also rebel. Now their
> low and cowardly nature is worse than
> before. If we restrain them with
> temporary measures, how can it endure?
> If we sleep on firewood and taste bile,
> eat late and go without rest, what has
> been lost will be recovered and success
> will not be slow in coming. If we are
> unsparing of time, keep a steadfast heart,
> do not shun heavy expense nor cling to
> 'rules of grammar', the insignificant
> barbarians will not be worthy of being
> conquered. [8]

The Imperial Rescript ordered Chin Ying-lin's
memorial sent to Canton for consideration and
study, authorizing the officials to buy up supplies
of strong wood for shipbuilding, to hasten the
work, and send up to the throne copies of all charts
and designs. But more significantly the Rescript
added that "if among the Hong merchants of the said
province there are any thoroughly familiar with the
methods of building ships and able to devise means
of buying barbarian ships" the Canton officials
were to seek them out and give them encouragement.

This memorial indicates first, that even an
academic court official was aware of the serious-
ness of the British naval threat to China and urged
the adoption of an extensive and expensive naval
building program to meet it; second, that it was
the hong merchants and the provincial officials at
Canton who understood and appreciated the advantages
of Western ships and armaments and who had already
taken steps to secure these advantages for China;
and third, that the emperor and the court were
aware both of the emergency and of the possibility
of adopting Western instruments to meet it.

The Canton officials, headed by Barbarian-
Pacifying-General I-shan, and including Governor

Liang Pao-ch'ang, and Kwangtung Commander-in-Chief
of Marine Forces Wu Chien-hsun, replied to the
Rescript and Chin Ying-lin's transmitted memorial
in a memorial received at Peking, October 28, 1842.
They discussed the ships being built at Canton with
private funds raised by subscription among the hong
merchants.

In the meantime, Commodore Lawrence Kearny
had arrived in China, reaching Macao on March 22,
1842 and proceeding to Whampoa on April 13. The
account given by General I-shan and others,
including Admiral Wu Chien-hsun, who went on board
Kearny's flagship, Constellation, indicate clearly
the important role the American neutrals played in
influencing Chinese opinion in favor of
Westernization. Their memorial reads:

> During the summer of the present year,
> two American warships protecting
> American trade came to Whampoa. . . .
> The barbarians of the said ships notified
> the interpreters that 'our foreign warships
> are strong and large; if the officials of
> the Heavenly Court wish to come on board
> and inspect them, they are entirely free to
> visit.'
>
> At that time the brigade general of
> Nan-shao-Lien, Ma Tien-chia, and the
> acting grain intendant, Hsi-la-pen, were
> going to the eastern district to inspect
> volunteers, so together with Wu Chien
> and others, they went on board their ships.
> The said military leader presented a
> small (model?) boat and an atlas of his
> country and we made them exceptional
> gifts in order to show a conciliatory
> attitude. Then they made a detailed
> inspection. The said warship is divided
> into two decks, top and bottom, set with
> forty-odd cannon, all on ingenious
> carriages. They made trial shots, turning
> them around with great dexterity. The
> most versatile feature was that the main
> mast fore and aft were all in three
> sections, as were also the sails. If they
> encounter a heavy wind they lower the top
> sections of the sail and mast. Compared
> to the masts of our ships which are in

one piece, they seem particularly suitable. For instance, if there is a north
wind and you are sailing from south to
north, this is a head wind and is called
tacking. Our ships are slow and clumsy and
in tacking go back and forth like a shuttle.
The barbarian ships turn their sails
smartly and proceed by heading a little
obliquely into the wind. Our ships have
always used wooden anchors and coir rope.
If they met a strong current or big waves
and dropped anchor, it would not reach the
bottom. These barbarian ships make theirs
entirely of iron which is more efficacious.
We should seek out skillfull workmen and
build ships on the model of these ships.

We all examined and consulted together.
The rebel barbarians rely on the strength
of their ships and the effectiveness of
their cannon. Since our warships cannot go out into the high seas and engage
them in battle, they act wantonly without
fear. The undergraduate Fang Hsiung-fei
says that for the quota warships, the price
was very low and that the contractors, unwilling to incur losses, used thin boards
and few nails so they could hardly withstand wind and wave. This is the actual
situation.

As to the methods of building ships which
the said sub-director (i.e., Chin Ying-lin)
spoke of: 'to be unsparing of time, to
keep a steadfast heart, not to shun heavy
expense, nor cling to rules of grammar',
these are particularly apt. Now if we
seek to determine the most useful ships,
it is certain we must make them after the
model of the barbarian ships, then we
may be equal to the said barbarians. But
the largest barbarian ships with cannon
on three decks can carry more than
seventy large guns, the hulk is about two
hundred feet long, and we would find some
difficulty in building them. Now we propose taking their middle-sized as a model
and build accordingly.

We . . . also transmitted orders to the Canton customs superintendent (Hoppo), Wen-feng, [9] to instruct the Hong merchants to buy barbarian ships. Later according to the said superintendent's report, in turn quoting the statement of the Hong merchants. 'At present the barbarian ships at Whampoa have all come to Canton loaded with goods and, as before, must go back with goods loaded in the original ships and are not for sale. We are waiting to find out if, of the ships coming to Whampoa, there are any strong ones which are for sale and then devise means of purchasing them.'

Now as to the battleship built by P'an Shih-ch'eng, the actual price is figured to be 19,000 taels. The said superintendent is willing to contribute from his salary, paying for it in installments, and not necessitating using funds from the treasury. This should also be reported to the Throne. Furthermore, in building ships we find that we must insist on good workmanship and sound materials and not in the least begrudge heavy expenditure. We must first build thirty large type battleships and then thirty or forty small ships. These will serve as auxiliaries to the large ships and will also serve to patrol the seas. The expenditure will actually be very great.

We have taken counsel together and propose that the Canton war junks now due to be built for the regular building period be temporarily held up in the hope that the saving for one year is not a large amount. We shall wait until we have secured funds and then memorialize as to procedure.[10]

This must go down as one of the most clear-cut and constructive, not to say daring, memorials of the whole period down to 1861. The ship referred to as built by P'an Shih-ch'eng was completed in 1841. It was build after an American model, retaining, however, the native type of masts and sails. It was built of foreign materials, even foreign wood, and the bottom was covered with copper. It was an ocean-going vessel, one hundred thirty-three feet long and carried three hundred men.[11] The builder, P'an Shih-ch'eng,[12] was a pioneer in this hybrid type of ship. He later built three more ships after this model. He was probably a hong merchant and has been tentatively identified as the one referred to in contemporary Western records as Tinqua.[13]

The Imperial Rescript showed both approval and intelligent interest:

> We consider that in the matter of maritime defense, . . . the building of ships and the manufacture of cannon are vital. The building of warships by the various provinces is actually a mere sham and of no use in meeting an emergency. This is extremely infuriating. Now as to ships which are being built, we shall certainly not go so far as to cling blindly to the old types which are of nominal rather than actual value. The proposal to stop the building and repair the war junks and instead to build battleships, closely conforms to Our intention and We charge all to act according to the proposal. But in the large sea-going ships the cannon are fired from mounts; when the charge explodes and the force necessarily goes toward the back buffer, how can there be a level muzzle? According to the memorial of the said governor general and others, gunners are already skilled and proficient. (We) charge them to memorialize again and in full detail on the matter of the method of firing.

> According to the memorial, the ship built by P'an Shih-ch'eng is sound and practical. As to subsequent shipbuilding, (We) charge the said officials to give him full charge and above all, the officials not be allowed to interfere and as before result in carelessness and graft. The necessary wages are authorized to be paid by the officials. Moreover, there must be no limitation as to time, so as to enable him liesurely to do sound work and exert his utmost skill.

Battleships are already being built; moreover firearms and munitions, whether they are
to be increased or diminished, need not conform
rigidly to old regulations. On the whole,
excellence and utility are the criteria.[14]

Subsequently, the same memorialists report that
a prominent Cantonese citizen named P'an Shih-jung
engaged barbarian artisans and built a small steamship
but that it was not very successful. The explanation
offered was that steamers were too complex for native
workmen to manipulate, that the cost was great, and
that it was doubtful whether China should hire barbarian artisans to build them or buy them already
built. In the same memorial they report that P'an
Shih-ch'eng, in the summer of 1842, "raising money
himself and not sparing expense, engaged an American
barbarian official, Jen-lei-ssu, living in an out-of-
the-way, quiet monastery, to concoct explosives.
Moreover, he was skilled in making mines. According
to the statement of the said citizen, a mine built by
him is particularly ingenious and efficacious. We
have already sent men to learn his skill. In the
future, after they have completed, if the experiments
are successful, the said citizen will himself send a
man to forward them to the capital and await their
inspection."[15]

The Rescript vetoed the construction or purchase
of steamers on the ground of their impracticability
when tried out at Canton. P'an Shih-ch'eng's explosives, however, if the experiments proved successful,
were to be sent to Peking for examination.[16]

The hong merchants at Canton responded to the
appeal to buy Western ships. Two of them, Wu Ping-chien
and P'an Cheng-wei, raised subscriptions and bought
one American and one Spanish ship. Ch'i Kung said of
these ships: "We find on inspection that the timber is
solid and rather fit for service, only the ships are
a bit small and are also rather old."[17]

Later (memorial received December 12), Ch'i Kung
reported that on October 20, he had received a communication from an American by the name of Ball[18]
who said that he was skilled in astronomy and
mathematics and asked permission to go to Peking
and enter government service. Ch'i Kung felt that
as the foreigners who had served in Peking, presumably referring to the last European mathemati-
cian and astronomers who left Peking in 1821, had

been dismissed, there was little use in forwarding
the request.[19] The court concurred in Ch'i Kung's
decision without comment.[20]

The American Jen-lei-ssu was probably Lieutenant
J. G. Reynolds of the United States Marines stationed
on the U. S. F. _Constellation_, whom P'an Shih-ch'eng
engaged to conduct experiments with "water thunder."
The experiment was held in a Taoist temple not far
from Canton. Its success convinced P'an Shih-ch'eng
of its military potential: "The 'water thunder' is
so effective that it will blow up any kind of foreign
ship. . . . It only takes a few days to make one
'water thunder' at a cost of 4000 _taels_ each. If
each province would spend 4000 _taels_ to make one
hundred 'water thunders', which would be able to
attack one hundred enemy ships, this would be the
most effective way to control the barbarians."[21]

These official notices indicate a considerable
activity among laymen and officials in Canton in
learning about and building Western ships and
armament in 1841 and 1842. They show that the court
was fully informed, not only of the ideas, but also
of the technical details through charts and diagrams,
and that the court was on the whole favorable to the
utilization of the new methods and new equipment.
It seems clear that the failure of these hopeful
beginnings to usher in an era of reform in China can
be attributed to two things, one immediate, the
other inherent in the Chinese system. As to the
first, the interest and approval of the court at
least in the new experiments were due to the imminent
dangers of the war. With the conclusion of peace
and the resumption of trade, the pressure was
relieved and the matter was promptly dropped, as far
as Chinese officialdom was concerned. More fundamentally, however, the failure was due to the
hopelessly decentralized Chinese system. The court
had neither the funds nor the machinery to carry out
expensive and complicated undertakings. As indicated
in the documents, the ships were built by private
subscription; hong merchants were urged to contribute
money or to purchase ships themselves; provincial
officials contributed their salaries, or funds were
diverted from routine channels but these were meagre.
The emperor could encourage, the governor general
could exhort, the _tao-t'ai_ could plead, but none of
them could do anything.

35

For Chinese-American relations, this phase is significant. It is clear that Kearny and his officers were willing to demonstrate goodwill in concrete form by showing the Chinese the advantages of Western ships and armament and by assisting them to learn their manufacture and use. The Chinese were equally willing to learn and profit. Here was a nascent opportunity for Chinese--American cooperation and friendship--stillborn because the termination of hostilities turned American attention to acquiring the advantages won by the English and turned China's attention away from her foreign danger. But even had the war continued or the gesture been made earlier, there was little opportunity for effective contact of such good offices when the Americans were on the ocean frontier and the court exercised such vague control over its periphery.

CHAPTER 3
THE MOST-FAVORED-NATION POLICY

The first official reaction of the United
States to the opening of hostilities between China
and Great Britain was the sending of a squadron to
Chinese waters to protect American commercial
interests and "to prevent and punish the smuggling
of opium into China either by Americans or under
cover of the American flag." The squadron consisted of two vessels, the frigate Constellation
and the ship Boston. In command was placed
Commodore Lawrence Kearny, of Irish extraction,
native of Perth Amboy, New Jersey, and a career
man in the navy. He had seen thirty-three years
of active naval service, in the War of 1812, in
chasing pirates in the West Indies, and in the
Mediterranean, before he was given the assignment
to the Far East, which was to constitute the peak
of his naval service.[1]

Commodore Kearny arrived in Macao on March 22,
1842, when the Opium War was moving toward its final
stages. On April 11, he left Macao, proceeded up
the river past Bocca Tigris and on the 13th anchored
at Whampoa. He communicated with the governor
general, Ch'i Kung, concerning grievances of
Americans against the Chinese soldiery, and a few
days later a group of Chinese officials visited the
Constellation.[2] Kearny was in Hong Kong in September
when news of the signing of the Treaty of Nanking
arrived. On October 8, he addressed Ch'i Kung
asking for most-favored-nation treatment for
American merchants; Ch'i Kung received the letter on
the 13th and replied with the famous "dry-stick"
letter, implying that the interests of the Americans
would not be ignored by China.[3] In reporting the

37

incident to the throne Ch'i Kung said:

> On October 13, 1842, a letter was trans-
> mitted to me from the American barbarian
> leader Kearny. Its object was to request
> a memorial on his behalf asking for
> Imperial favor allowing the barbarian
> merchants of that country to trade in the
> same way as the barbarian merchants of
> England. I immediately took counsel with
> Rebel-Pacifying-General I-shan and Governor
> Liang Pao-liang and in reply ordered him to
> wait until the Imperial Commissioner reaches
> Canton, when it will be considered jointly and
> again be taken up and disposed of.
>
> Further, I learn that the American barbarians
> have always been fairly respectful and obe-
> dient and even now there is no unreasonable
> language. But barbarians are by nature
> extremely treacherous. Besides . . . there
> is the affair of the barbarian leader Kearny's
> communication regarding trade. He is still
> watching and hoping. I shall visit until
> Imperial Commissioner I-li-pu reaches
> Canton to weigh the situation with him,
> consider carefully, and then memorialize
> in full.[4]

The Imperial Rescript, dated December 12,
indicates that the court was hardly aware of the
situation. It would seem that the Treaty of Nanking
had made very slight impression on the emperor or
the officials in Peking.

> As to the matter of the barbarian leader
> Kearny's communication regarding trade,
> (We) charge I-li-pu and the others to
> investigate carefully and post prohibitions
> in order to show (our) sympathy. If they
> dare to covet the establishment of ports
> and such, be sure to stop them with earnest
> and sincere orders. Let there be no com-
> promising. On the whole (We) consider that
> in commiserating those from afar, to show
> that the fixed laws of the Heavenly Court
> permit no fomenting of trouble is essen-
> tial.[5]

Thus the first suggestion to the court to extend the privileges secured to the British by the Treaty of Nanking to the American merchants met with slight consideration. In the light of developments in the next few weeks, however, this pronouncement of the court should probably be regarded as a conventional and cautious repetition of a form which had become habitual, rather than as a considered expression of policy. The actual policy of extending the privileges of the new ports and the benefits of the new tariff to the American merchants was formulated by various provincial officials.

In a memorial received at Peking on December 15, 1842, Ch'i-ying, at this time governor general of Liang-kiang and who will be treated at greater length in connection with his negotiations with Cushing, memorialized that one of his officials reported that an American vessel was already applying for trade privileges at Ningpo. The local tao-t'ai told the American captain, circumspectly, "that, although the English barbarians had received an Imperial Edict authorizing them to trade, since the regulations were not drawn up, they were not yet trading; that the said country, having customarily traded at Kwangtung, must as before go back to Kwangtung." The Flowery Flag barbarians accepted this reasonable explanation and "immediately go their sails and rigging in order and on the 29th (November), weighed anchor and got under way." Ch'i-ying approved the tao-t'ai's cautious policy and reported that he was proceeding to Shanghai where he would watch out for the American vessel if it should go from Ningpo to Shanghai.[6]

The Rescript to this memorial was in the same tone. "If they make any demands, notify them that as their country has traded at Kwangtung for a long time, they should naturally return to Kwangtung province and trade as of old; that the laws of the Heavenly Court, being established, cannot suffer the least change. It is essential to show restrictive control."[7]

In a memorial received ten days later, governor of Chekiang, Liu Yun-k'o,[8] reported the same incident with more specific details. The governor had the local tao-t'ai make sure that the vessel did not carry on any illegal trade with the natives, who were admittedly interested in the foreign goods.[9]

I-li-pu was en route to Canton as imperial commissioner when he was acquainted with Kearny's request. He took up the matter in earnest, in accordance with imperial instructions, and made the first concrete proposal of a Chinese policy. He had helped negotiate the Treaty of Nanking and was conversant with the circumstances. He wrote in response:

I venture to refer to the establishment of additional ports and the coming of all foreign ships alike to trade. Previously at Nanking, the barbarian chief Pottinger said that in case the various countries came to Fukien, Chekiang, and the various places to trade, whenever China was willing to give her consent, the said chief would by no means stop them in order to seek exclusive gains. Thus there is the view that he has already secretly invited the other countries to come and trade. Moreover, American ships have already made requests in Chekiang; now they are also petitioning in Kwangtung. Previously, when France went to Ningpo, her general purpose was also for trade. If we allow only England to establish additional trading ports and do not also allow other countries to come trade in the same way, it is feared that as their ships and dress are not very different it will be hard to distinguish clearly. Moreover, it is feared that prohibition would give rise to complications and perversely cause the various countries to complain on account of England. Furthermore, it is feared that if England joins them and all alike come to trade, it will be hard for us to prevent them and, perversely, the kindness would derive from the barbarian leader. Then the various countries would be well disposed toward England and resentful toward China. This would also be erroneous reckoning. On this matter, I only wait until after I arrive at Canton to discuss thoroughly and properly with the governor and governor general.

Moreover, I must come to an understanding
with Pottinger; then the discussion can be
terminated, a joint memorial be (prepared)
asking for an Edict, and action taken
accordingly. [10]

The court was dubious but receptive to
I-li-pu's proposal to extend the benefits of the
Treaty of Nanking to other countries on a most-
favored-nation basis. The fear was that England
might object and cause further trouble for China,
which was the last thing the court desired. The
Rescript said, in part:

What I-li-pu memoralizes is not without
insight. But if we suddenly allow them
to trade on the same basis, it is hard to
guarantee that England will not, on
account of having to share her gains with
other countries, cause further trouble.
We charge I-li-pu, when he meets and
confers with the said chief (Pottinger),
to discuss it in extenso and settle it
properly. Above all we hope that the
concord will last for a long time and not
give rise to mutual jealousy and quarreling.
This will be the greatest good.[11]

I-li-pu, old and tired, had formulated China's
policy of extending most-favored-nation treatment
to all the Western countries indiscriminately. But
the man to rise to this occasion to become in a
very real sense, China's first foreign minister was
Ch'i-ying. To him, foreign affairs became a study,
a theory, an opportunity, an absorbing game, and
the principal interest in his life. One of the
first to recognize that these troubles on the
ocean frontier were of great significance to China,
he made the temperament of the foreigners, the
minutiae of trade, and the maneuvering of diplomacy,
his concern. Ch'i-ying was born an Imperial
Clansman, a descendant of Hsien-tsu or Nurhachi, the
founder of the Manchu dynasty. He was a Solid Blue
Bannerman. His father Lu-k'ang was a grand secretary and he grew up in the court with princes for
playmates, slipping into official life without the
routine of examinations and slow promotions. He
served for one term as superintendent of
Shanhaikwan, where the Great Wall comes down to the

sea, between China and Manchuria, and a short time
in Kirin province. But most of the posts he held
over a period of thirty years were in and around
Peking. In 1838, however, he was appointed Tartar
General of Mukden and came into contact with one of
the burning questions of the day: the smuggling of
opium. In 1840 and 1841, British warships cruised
about Lu-shun (Port Arthur) and Shanhaikwan.
Ch'i-ying carried out coast surveys, memorialized
on maritime defense, but never closed battle with
the English intruders. In the spring of 1842, he
was made Tartar General of Canton and soon after
made imperial commissioner, specially charged with
maritime affairs in Chekiang. When the important
ports on the coast and on the Yangtze had fallen to
the British, Ch'i-ying memorialized urging conciliation and took a leading part in the negotiation
of the Treaty of Nanking. With peace restored, he
was appointed governor general of Liang-chiang, in
which post he was at the time Commodore Kearny
petitioned for most-favored-nation treatment, and
American traders began to try the new ports opened
to the British by the Treaty of Nanking. In April
1843, he was again made imperial commissioner and
ordered to Canton to assist I-li-pu in the negotiation of the trade regulations, tariff schedule
and supplementary treaty with the British envoy,
Pottinger. When the negotiations were concluded,
he returned to his post as governor general of
Liang-chiang.[12]

It is obvious from his official biography that
foreign affairs occupied a large place in the life
of Ch'i-ying; it becomes also clear that he is
China's first career man in the "foreign office"
in modern times. This is borne out in a number of
ways. In the first place, he recognized the
importance of relations with the Western countries
and gave his best thought to adjusting them favorably. He studied the records and conditions in
Kwangtung and along the east coast and saw in their
true perspective the positions of Great Britain and
the United States as primary and secondary commercial powers. He saw the need for a Chinese policy
toward the United States. He was not above giving
serious consideration to economic factors, recognizing
the importance of the customs and the increased opportunities for China in customs honestly administered.
He was anxious to encourage trade by removing

obstacles and annoyances. To these problems he
brought an objective point of view and an inquiring
mind. When the Americans quoted prices of ginseng
and bulk lead, he sent out into the market to buy
some and see if they were telling the truth. He
was able to see the whole eastern seaboard as a
commercial and economic unit, disregarding port
rivalries and provincial jealousy. Trained in the
court and aware of its prejudices, he was able to
present the unpleasant facts of humiliation and
defeat at the hands of the barbarians, in the least
offensive way, not to deceive the court but to get
approval for what he regarded as an essential program. There is little genuine statesmanship apparent in Ch'i-ying's memorials. He is shrewd, cagey,
intelligent, ambitious, but not particularly constructive or farseeing. In positive policy, his
program boils down to something like the ancient
formula to divide and rule, to use barbarians to
curb barbarians, to scatter the barbarians at five
ports rather than concentrating them at one, and to
prevent the various national groups from being
united by common grievances in opposition to China.

At the same time, Ch'i-ying, now under appointment to Canton to assist in the negotiations with
Pottinger and anxious to be the arbiter in foreign
affairs, came to the same conclusion independently.
Using much the same reasoning and facts as I-li-pu,
he goes to considerable pains to build up his case:

> . . . during the 7th month (August 6-
> September 5), when I discussed pacifi-
> cation with the English barbarians would
> imitate them; so I questioned the English
> barbarian and afterwards received his reply
> 'that all the countries of the outer ocean
> were allowed to trade at Canton and England
> would not seek (Imperial) favor on their
> behalf, but if the Great Emperor graciously
> allowed other countries also to go to Fukien,
> Chekiang, and Kiangsu to trade, England
> would not begrudge them in the least; that
> access of the various countries to Hong
> Kong would also be unimpeded.' But when I
> shall have discussed it thoroughly and
> sympathetically with I-li-pu after reaching
> Canton, we shall investigate the attitudes
> of the various barbarians, reconsider, and
> request an Edict for our guidance.

Now the United States has gone to the
two provinces of Kwangtung and Chekiang
and requested to trade. As to the
benefits and evils involved, I venture to
address my Emperor. Now where profit is,
there men are sure to rush after it. In
the K'ang-hsi period (1667-1723) the
English barbarians originally built a
wharf at Ting-hai. Because the duties
were troublesome and heavy and the
trading sparse, they could not count on
any profit and went back to Kwangtung.
For more than one hundred years, in
Kwangtung province, evils stopped and
conditions were good. The various barbarians appeared respectful and throughout showed no domineering, untractable
attitude. It was only after many years
that evils developed. The hardships
and burdens of the various barbarians
became unbearable and they cherished
resentment in their hearts. The English
barbarians thereupon took the lead in
causing troubles which have reached the
present extremity. The rest of the
barbarians, although outwardly respectful
and obedient, in reality sat by to see who
won or lost. If we were able to overcome
the English barbarians, then they would
take the profits of the English barbarians
for themselves; if it were otherwise, then
they would throw in their lot with the
English barbarians, adhere to and join
with them, and their profit would still
be there.

For instance, when the English barbarians
first defied authority, their battle ships were
not numerous. Later on they increased day
by day until they finally numbered a
hundred and several tens of vessels. The
said barbarians, separated (from China)
by oceans several tens of thousands of li
wide--how can it be said to be easy to
mobilize and despatch (forces)? If it is
said that they are not in collusion with
other barbarians and secretly being
helped, I certainly dare not put much
confidence in it. Now the English barbarians have already got what they want

44

but the other barbarians are still in
Kwangtung, neglected and harassed.
Observing from a different angle, I
fear that in their hearts they feel
some injustice. The various barbarians
have helped the English barbarians; how
can the English barbarians fail to help
the other barbarians? This is an
inevitable consequence. Even if the
said barbarians do not dare openly to
oppose authority but, adhering to the
English barbarians, secretly go to the
various ports to trade, then how are we
going to keep watch over them? Thus
the English barbarians can in the end
gain the gratitude of the other barbarians and secretly seize the lever of
our country's wealth. The various barbarians not being able to expect favor from
the Heavenly Court will be bound to the
English barbarians hand and foot. Consequently the cohesion of barbarian to barbarian will be daily closer while the
estrangement between the barbarians and
ourselves will become daily wider. The
English barbarians alone were enough to
cause damage to the frontiers; how much
more so all the barbarians if we cause
them to unite? This is also necessarily
a matter for thorough consideration and
deep concern. If it is said that by
diligently removing accumulated evils and
giving all a new start, the various
barbarians would trade peacefully at
Canton and not be led erroneously to
harbor expectations, this is truly the policy
of clearing roots and purging sources. But
the roots of the evil are already deep and
can hardly be pulled up suddenly. In
addition, it is feared that after the evil
clumps have been removed, then the former
illegal exactions will be regarded as
something required by custom. Just like
the port of Amoy in Fukien, originally a
place where foreign merchant ships trading
to the interior congregated, later because
the illegal exactions were troublesome
and heavy and which, though repeatedly
forbidden, the more they were forbidden
the worse they became, eventually the

foreign Hongs failed and foreign trade was stopped. Fortunately the native merchants were able to go wherever they wanted and did not cause trouble. As to the barbarian merchants, they legally had a definite port and could not go a foot or an inch beyond. Men have the same feelings; how would they be willing to accept this complacently? This is what I have thought of on clear nights, unable to keep from worrying nervously. Thinking it over and over, if the United States and other countries also wish to establish separate wharves in Fukien, Chekiang, and Kiangsu for themselves, we certainly should use strict language to stop them in order to show control. In case the English barbarians take the wharves in Fukien, Chekiang, and Kiangsu for themselves and are unwilling to let other countries trade, then there will be occasion for fighting among themselves. Then we could 'take their strategen to effect our plans.' Now the said barbarians are after all willing to compromise and the other barbarians would also gladly follow. When a system is worn out it should be changed. If in dealing with them we scrupulously preserve the old regulations, it will cause many pricked fingers and is not as good as leading them advantageously according to circumstances and treating all with equal kindness. If the United States and other countries are determined to trade with Fukien, Chekiang, and Kiangsu, it would seem that we could allow them likewise to draw up regulations and let them go there at will. But outside of this there should be no coveting, nor should they be allowed to establish individual wharves in Fukien, Chekiang, and Kiangsu. Although the customs receipts in Kwangtung province would not be without curtailment, still in Fukien, Chekiang, and Kiangsu they would be augmented. What is drawn from one is poured into the other and national revenue would not be affected. Moreover, Fukien, Chekiang, and Kiangsu

province have already admitted the
English barbarian ships which are
congregated in one place and scatter
them in five places, their strength
would be dissipated and their relations
estranged. In the matter managing and
curbing outside barbarians, this is not
necessarily a bad plan.[13]

The Rescript gave a tentative approval of
Ch'i-ying's reasoning and charged him to consult
fully with I-li-pu and devise a "perfect plan."[14]

The reasoning that it would be difficult to
distinguish between English, American, French, and
other national ships is borne out by a memorial of
Liu Yun-k'o. He reports that two barbarian ships
anchored before Shih-p'u, on the Chekiang seaboard.
The captains paid their respects to the local sub-
prefect and requested pilots to guide them to
Teng-chou, on the north coast of Shantung. This
request aroused the suspicions of Chinese officials.
But whether the petitioners were "English barbarian
officials or Americans or Frenchmen is rather hard
to determine." Their request was refused and all
officials along the coast warned against receiving
or assisting them or others.[15] The Rescript said
that whether the ships were English, American, or
French, Pottinger should be held responsible and
should order them back to Canton.[16]

Meanwhile at Canton, I-li-pu, Ch'i Kung and
Liang Pao-ch'ang were discussing commercial regulations with England. Although I-li-pu favorably disposed toward the most-favored-nation policy
and Kearny was still in Chinese waters, the matter
had not been officially broached to the negotiators.
I-li-pu wrote:

As to the United States and France, since
I, I-li-pu, arrived at Canton, they have
made no request to go to the various ports
to trade. It must be that, because the
English customs regulations are still not
clearly established, they are maintaining
an attitude of watchful hoping. We beg
leave to wait and observe the temper of
the barbarians and act according to
circumstances.[17]

To which the court, apparently convinced by the arguments of I-li-pu and Ch'i-ying, replied with what in Chinese documents must be interpreted as carte blanche to I-li-pu. In case they did ask to trade after the customs regulations were agreed upon with Pottinger, he was to "examine the situation and manage with the greatest safety in order to fulfill his commission."[18] This was I-li-pu's final contribution to the most-favored-nation negotiations, for his colleagues memoralized (received at Peking, March 22, 1843) that he died of illness on March 4.[19] One biography implies that his illness was aggravated by discouragement and melancholy due to disturbed conditions in Canton and the perversity of the barbarians.[20]

Ch'i-ying, still in the capacity of governor general of Liang-chiang, was watching the movements of two American and one French ship, laden with cloth, moving about in Ting-hai waters. His concern was to be sure that they had no hostile intentions, to prevent their trading, and to induce them to return to Canton.[21] Ch'i Kung was assured that the British warships would not proceed to Shantung and that the American and French trading vessels had returned to Canton.[22]

American ships were pushing north to inaugurate the trade ensured to the British and from which it was assumed they would not be excluded. On March 3, two American ships came to Woosung, hoping to proceed to Shanghai to trade. The local officials told them that the tariff schedule was not agreed upon nor were wharves built and it would be inconvenient to trade. They tarried at the mouth of the river for a few days, making repairs on their ships, and then departed. On the 15th another American ship appeared and was sent away. On April 11, "again a barbarian ship, taking advantage of the wind and a favorable tide, sailed from Wu-sung to the outskirts of the city wall of Shanghai. The said local officials went aboard and found on inquiry that it was a 'Flowery Flag', that is, American ship laden with goods, and coming here from the Philippines to trade. The said officials explained that they still had no notice regarding the customs agreement. The said barbarians agreed to return to Kwangtung and wait for word. On the

15th they sailed away." The English officials at
Ting-hai were also concerned that neither English
or other merchant ships be allowed to trade until
due arrangements were completed and sent a steamer
to Shanghai to reenforce the orders of the Chinese
officials.[23]

In May, the two American ships returned to
Woosung, along with three English merchant vessels.
By this time, the Chinese officials were more fully
informed and notified them explicitly that the commercial regulations under negotiation with Pottinger
at Canton were not completed, so they could not be
allowed to trade. Apparently the acting tao-t'ai of
Shanghai had been rather ambiguous in his orders to
the foreign merchants who came in March and some
trading had taken place. The unfortunate tao-t'ai
was impeached and the emperor commented in vermilion
at the end of the memorial: "Removal from office is
not enough. There must be a rigorous trial. If
there are other reprehensible circumstances then he
should be indicted according to the facts. Punishing one, warns a hundred. Take care that there is
no indulgence."[24] The memorial as well as the
Rescript abandoned the former thesis that the American and other non-English merchants should resume
trade under the old regulations at Canton and merely
stated that they should wait until the new tariff
and trade regulations were published before they
commenced trade at the new ports. By inference,
most-favored-nation treatment was already conceded.

In a memorial received at Peking on July 30,
1843, Ch'i-ying (now succeeding I-li-pu at Canton)
asked for official confirmation of this policy. He
said, "again as to the United States and France,
I have now received a request to proceed according
to the newly completed regulations. I beg leave,
together with the governor general and governor,
after the regulations are ascertained, to make a
clear agreement with them and handle it as a special
case."[25] The Rescript gave the requisite authorization[26] and the regulations and tariff schedule proceeded to treat the trade with all foreign countries
alike, with no discrimination in favor of the
British.[27]

A little later a long memorial, received on
September 23, 1843, was presented reviewing the whole
foreign trade situation. Although this memorial
is presented under the names of all the high Canton

officials, including the governor general, the governor, and the hoppo, the author is obviously Imperial Commissioner Ch'i-ying:

> We humbly observe that ships of the various countries come to Canton, but those of England and her dependency, India, are most numerous. Next, those of the United States are nearly as many. Besides these, only Holland has from three or four up to ten-odd merchant ships a year; France, Spain, Denmark, Sweden, Prussia, Austria, and Belgium sometimes have ships coming, sometimes not; sometimes many, sometimes few. In general, each country has from one or two up to not more than five or six. Now the British commercial regulations have been concluded. As to the wharves at Shanghai and other places, they also dare not monopolize their advantages. Moreover, as Ting-hai and other places all have had American merchant vessels anchored along with those of the English barbarians, eagerly looking foward to the opening of trade, naturally trade should be discussed first with the United States.

> However, previously at the yamen of Your official Ch'i Kung, they presented a letter of the barbarian leader Kearny who during the third month (March 31-April 30), before I arrived, sailed back to his country. There was only an acting consul, (Edward) King, at Canton in charge of trading affairs. Again, in my presence he petitioned asking to trade according to the new regulations. We, leading them to advantage according to circumstances and exemplifying Imperial kindness, have allowed them to trade and pay duties according to the new regulations in the five ports in Fukien, Kwangtung, and Chekiang, in order to show conciliation.

> Now, according to the sincerely grateful petition of the said barbarians, it is stated that the imports include foreign ginseng and bulk lead produced in the said country. Formerly, because of the duties were so troublesome and heavy, there was often considerable smuggling. Now, although irregular exactions were eliminated, still the newly established duty on superior

foreign ginseng is thirty-eight <u>taels</u> for
each hundred catties, on inferior
foreign ginseng, three <u>taels</u> five mace
for each hundred catties; the duty on lead
and pewter is four mace for each hundred
catties, that figured on the selling
price this is forty or fifty per cent and
the said merchants would not only realize
no profit but would suffer losses. They
asked that taking five per cent as a
standard, the duty on superior foreign
ginseng be four <u>taels</u> per hundred catties,
on inferior foreign ginseng, two <u>taels</u>,
seven mace per hundred catties; on bulk
lead, two mace per hundred catties.
Since the customs schedule had been
determined and reported in memorial and
as this initial request for revision of
the said barbarian chief, if imitated by
many of the other countries would be a
rather unseemly procedure, we forthwith
expressed our disapproval.

Afterwards, we received another petition
from the said barbarian stating that
foreign ginseng originally was not divided
into superior and inferior. Figuring each
hundred catties to be half each superior
and inferior, it should temporarily conform
to the new rule and, like bulk lead, pay
the duties according to verified facts,
but that at present the ships of the said
country have not all arrived; after the
barbarian chief arrived, he would order
them to settle the matter.

Having reason to fear that his words
were neither true nor complete, we
immediately sent trusties into the
market to buy (samples). Superior
grade foreign ginseng cost one <u>tael</u>,
four mace per catty. Figuring one
hundred catties, it would be one hundred
forty <u>taels</u>. Furthermore, we found
on careful investigation that one price
of foreign ginseng was high or low
depending on whether the importation
was large or small. At times when it
is cheap a catty is not worth more than
about one <u>tael</u>. What the said barbarian
requested was not presumptuous or

exacting. Moreover we found that the
annual importation of superior grade
foreign ginseng was not more than four
hundred-odd piculs; of inferior grade
foreign ginseng, not more than a
thousand piculs; of bulk lead, not more
than two hundred-odd piculs. Thus to
reduce the duty as they requested would
only amount to an annual loss of a few
thousand taels. Considering that heavy
duties would cause smuggling and moreover
provide occasion for complaints, is it
not better, magnanimously to collect
duties according to verified facts and
avoid giving rise to fresh complications?
But now France and the other countries
still not having reached an agreement, it
is not appropriate to inaugurate the
system. We beg leave to consider the case
as a whole, reach a decision, and separately
memorialize asking for an Edict.

The memorialists then take up the commercial problems of France, Holland, and Italy, which is
strangely identified with Macao. They conclude
their memorial:

All in all, the various countries of the
West take trade as their life. The
Heavenly Court's secret in restraining
and curbing is entirely in maintaining
absolute equality and should not be concerned with exacting demands. If we
sedulously preserve general propriety,
then the refractory temper being unrestrained will defeat itself. Moreover,
the results we could get from taking a
little would be the same as if we took
much. But we, not always avoiding
animosity, have abolished irregular
exactions in order to relieve the
barbarians' suffering and increased the
tariff in order to enrich the national
revenue, all in the hope of Chinese-
barbarian concord and perpetual friendly
relations and in order respectfully to
supplement our Sovereign's supreme
purpose of pacifying the ocean frontiers.
Vermilion Comment: Do not be concerned
with the immediate present. Above all

it is important to consider what is
large and what is distant. After it
is settled, memorialize fully.[28]

Ch'i-ying and the other officials at Canton
then reported (memorial received September 23, 1843)
that the negotiations were completed and Canton
opened to trade under the new regulations on
July 27. In the first six weeks of trade, July 27
to September 3, fifty-three English and American
ships had entered port and customs collections of
more than 129,000 taels showed an increase over the
corresponding period of the previous year. Both
Chinese and foreign merchants appeared pleased with
the new arrangement. Ch'i-ying, however, recognized at the outset that the new regulations, with
fixed duties and definite port rules, imposed new
responsibilities on China. The rough-and-ready
system of bickering, gratuities, bribes, and smuggling had not imposed heavy duties on the hoppo, but
now an extensive organization for collecting duties
and preventing smuggling was called for. The vast
horde of hangers-on who had profited from the old
system must find legitimate occupation under the
new. "Now the irregular exactions are entirely
abolished and they are reduced to working on empty
stomachs. Under the circumstances we cannot but
provide their expenses in order, by filling their
mouths, to stop corrupt practices."[29] A revolution
had occurred in a small corner of China's life and
Ch'i-ying at least recognized what had happened. The
court acquiesced in the inauguration of the new
system without recognizing the significance. Its
only concern was that there be no more barbarian
trouble on the ocean frontiers.[30] The court did,
however, recognize the true nature of most-favored-
nation clause inserted by the Britich themselves in
the Supplimentary Treaty, signed October 8, 1843.[31]

The last vestige of the old order was shattered
when Ch'i-ying stepped fully into the role of
foreign minister, received the American counsel in
an interview and opened the way for direct and personal intercourse. In reporting this to the throne,
Ch'i-ying made clear that the old days of dealing
through the hong merchants was past. The interview,
attended also by the other high officials at Canton,
took place in a public hall outside the city wall.
This meeting also prepares for the next development
in Sino-American relations, as Consul Forbes took
the occasion to notify Ch'i-ying that the United

States had appointed an envoy to come to China, where he intended to negotiate a treaty and to visit Peking. To Ch'i-ying and certainly to the court, this was further evidence that if you gave these barbarians a foot they took a mile.[32]

Although Commodore Kearny's request was made at an opportune time and brought the matter of extension of trading privileges to the attention of the Chinese officials, it would appear from the documents reaching the court that it did little more than this. His request was directed to Ch'i Kung who, as governor general of Liang-kuang, was a Chinese official primarily concerned with military affairs. His career gives no indication of interest in foreign policy or friendliness towards the United States. What has been called his "dry stick" letter, in reply to Commodore Kearny's request for most-favored-nation treatment, is the principal grounds for the claim that Kearny secured this status for the United States. Ch'i Kung's statement, according to the official translation, was "decidedly it shall not be permitted that the American merchants shall come to have merely a dry stick." Ch'i Kung was not commissioned to negotiate, any more than was Kearny, and his reply must be interpreted to be non-committal evasion. Nor did Ch'i Kung present a case for Kearny and ask for or recieve an edict extending the trade privileges. Moreover, it is clear that during the course of the war, China formulated a policy of extending favors to the United States as a means of preventing a united front of Western powers aganist her. This was done as early as 1841. Kearny's request then, transmitted to Peking without argument or support, did not evoke any edict extending privileges to the United States.

The court referred the matter to I-li-pu, then en route to Canton as imperial commissioner to nego- tiate supplementary commercial matters with Pottinger. Before he reached Canton he formulated a clear case for most-favored-nation treatment as the best policy China could pursue and the only one practical or operational. His only qualification of this policy was that England might object, but he recalled the assurance of Pottinger at Nanking that England would not claim exclusive privileges. Nevertheless, I-li-pu felt that he should secure reaffirmation from Pottinger before China should

commit herself to it, lest future troubles result.
After I-li-pu arrived at Canton, Kearny did not
press his claims, either in person or by letter.
I-li-pu died while negotiations were in progress.

The full credit for China's policy of extending
most-favored-nation treatment to the United States,
as well as to all other countries trading to China,
goes rightfully to Ch'i-ying. This because
Ch'i-ying, after considerable experience and no
little serious study of foreign affairs, worked
out a well-reasoned policy for China. Ch'i-ying
formulated his policy while he was still in
Chekiang and without any contact with Kearny or
other Americans. It was based on what he considered China's best interests. This he presented
as a Chinese policy for dealing with Western powers,
not a particular policy toward the United States,
although he recognized that the United States was
the principal commercial country besides Great
Britain. After Ch'i-ying reached Canton and took
up the negotiations where I-li-pu had left off, he
completed the commercial regulations. He had
already formulated his policy and finding that the
British, as they promised in Nanking, made no
objection proceeded with the approval of the court
to extend their application to all foreign ships
trading to China simultaneously. King, the acting
American consul made a formal request, but this in
no way influenced Ch'i-ying's decision. Kearny
was not on hand to press the case of the United
States nor was it not necessary. China had
determined on most-favored-nation treatment as a
matter of policy for her own protection, for her
best self-interest, and as the only practicable
procedure.

CHAPTER 4
THE TREATY OF WANGHIA

The close of the war and the conclusion of the Treaty of Nanking brought Chinese affairs to the attention of the United States. President Tyler, in his message to Congress, December 30, 1842, cited the British treaty opening four new ports and commented that it provided "neither for the admission nor the exlusion of the ships of other nations. It would seem, therefore, that with every other nation having commercial intercourse with China to seek to make proper arrangements for itself with the government of that Empire in this respect." He remarked on the large and growing trade with China, and the prospect of extending the American market in the interior. He noted that on account of the inaccessibility of the court at Peking, the British treaty did not contemplate regular diplomatic representation there. He recommended the appointment of a commissioner to reside in China to watch over American interests.[1]

The new tariff schedule drawn up by Pottinger and Ch'i-ying was published in America in 1843 and it was assumed without question that it would apply to American commerce without the conclusion of any formal agreement between the United States and China.[2]

American businessmen were not entirely optimistic about the results of the war. It was recalled that one of the causes of the war was "the fact that China had not the means of paying for that which they had already purchased." The debts of the hong merchants were cited and it was asserted that the opium trade was draining China of specie and improvishing the country; that American trade must be based on the introduction of American manufactures and that the prospect for this was not cheerful. "Of all nations on the face of the earth, the Chinese are the most backward in adopting the fashions and habits of foreigners. They are industrious, emulative, and ingenious. Their manufacturing skill and experience are unsurpassed. Hence if trade becomes extended, it is likely to flow mostly into a demand for raw materials. Cotton piece goods and long cloths may be supplied, to some extent, from New England . . . but . . . China has first to be enlarged by moral influences."[3]

The proposal for a treaty with China was made in a report to the House of Representatives by John Quincy Adams on January 24, 1843, advising the appropriation of $40,000 for a mission to secure "the future relations of intercourse between the United States and the Empire of China upon a footing of national equality and reciprocity." The long report bears the clear imprint of Adams' personal opinion in regard to the first Anglo-Chinese war.[4] Forbearing to advance any opinion on the opium question he said the issue in the war was "in root and substance, for equal rights of independent nations against the insolent and absurd assumption of despotic supremacy." He observed that Great Britain has gained trading rights in China as a result of the war and predicted that the spell being once broken, the honor, the interest, and pride of the emperor will all be prompted to concede in peace and amity, to other nations, the same equality of access to his government which has been extorted from him by British arms."[5] Adams' interpretation of the war was not typical. The prevailing opinion is better expressed by Francis Wharton:

> That the war which has led to her
> humiliation was both unjust and un-
> Christian, it has been within our
> power to exhibit more than once in
> this magazine. China has a perfect
> right to regulate the character of her
> imports, as either of the countries
> with whom she trades; and we can
> imagine no more glaring violation of
> the law of nations, than the successful
> attempt which has been made to cram
> down her throat, by force, an article
> which she had deliberately refused to

receive. Undoubtedly, the bearing of
the Chinese government was preposterous,
and the aspect of Chinese institutions
to a stranger, ludicrous in the extreme;
but we cannot discover in what way the
conceit and ignorance of the Chinese
authorities can be considered as sufficient
to justify the summary remedies which
have been adopted. Neither the inequality
of the imperial tariff nor the arrogance
of the imperial manners, were legitimate
causes of invasion; and however beneficial
in its remote consequences the unsealing
of the Chinese ports may be, we cannot
but regret it should have been conceived
in crime and consumated in violence.[6]

The bill was then introduced into the House of
Representatives. There were some objections that
the appropriation was excessive but these were
overridden and the bill passed the House 96 to 59.[7]

The selection of the envoy was a matter of
purely domestic politics--Daniel Webster was
retiring from the State Department.[8] Edward Everett,
Minister to the Court of St. James, was appointed
to go to China in order to allow Webster to go to
London. Everett declined, despite Webster's long
personal letter to him, and Caleb Cushing was at
once proposed by Webster the very day of the
latter's retirement from the Cabinet. The nomi-
nation was made during the Congressional recess,
so that the Senate could not block it, and before
Congress convened, Cushing had sailed for the Far
East.[9] John Quincy Adams aptly noted in his diary
for July 3, 1843:

He (Cushing) had not made his court to
Captain Tyler in vain. His obsequiousness
and sacrifice of principles lost him the
favor of his constituents, who repudiated
him at the recent elections; but Mr. Tyler
had more precious favors in his gift, and
has lavished them in profusion on Cushing.

Thus the first appropriation for a Chinese
mission was fat from the Congressional pork barrel
and the first appointment, a presidential plum,
reserved for a loyal henchman who had sacrificed
his political position for his chief. Nevertheless,

it was a good choice. Cushing was a capable man of wide interests, a competent lawyer. His biographer remarks: "In general, the public was pleased. Even Cushing's enemies were glad to have him out of the country for a year; and his friends felt that he had found at last a fortunate issue out of his many tribulations."[10]

Caleb Cushing was born in Newburyport, Massachusetts, in 1800. His father was a captain of a trading ship to India whose business was ruined by the embargo and the War of 1812. Cushing was a precocious child; he entered Harvard at thirteen. He was graduated in the class of 1817, elected Phi-Beta Kappa, and tied George Bancroft for second honors. Of that happy age when a well-informed and educated man could write scholarly monographs on any subject assigned to him by an editor, Cushing was a typical exponent. He became a regular contributor to the North American Review, published a translation on maritime law (R. J. Pothier, On Maritime Contracts of Letting to Hire, Boston, 1821), wrote a history of Newburyport (History and Present State of the Town of Newburyport, 1826), and wrote articles for the Annual Register.

He was elected to the House in 1834 and served four terms there, serving on the Committee on Foreign Affairs with John Quincy Adams. During his third term he took occasion to deny any intention on the part of the Committee on Foreign Affairs to associate the United States with Great Britain in forcing on China "the odious traffic in opium."[11] He began a serious study of Chinese problems and called on Martin Van Buren to send to the House the correspondence with China. As his antecedents would indicate he was chiefly interested in trade.

Cushing was a Whig and when the young Republicans began to assume leadership at Washington, he remained loyal to the unpopular minority group, associated personally with the president and was known as Captain Tyler's Corporals' Guard. At the close of his last term in the House, Tyler twice appointed him Secretary of the Treasury but the Senate rejected the appointment both times. His appointment to the Chinese post was accomplished by a political ruse.[12]

Cushing had written to President Tyler in 1842 proposing a special mission to China which should be informal enough to enable it to treat either with the court in Peking directly or, if that were not permitted, with the provincial authorities. He suggested that the Chinese might favor a treaty with the United States to save them from a "condition of being an exclusive monopoly in the hands of England." He added that if the envoy should succeed in negotiating a treaty, "he might proceed thence for the same purpose to Japan."[13] Cushing's position with regard to Great Britain's Chinese policy was unequivocal. He said in the House at the opening of the Opium War:

> God forbid that I should entertain
> the idea of cooperating with the
> British government in the purpose . . .
> of upholding the base cupidity and
> violence, and high-handed infraction
> of all law, human and divine, which
> have characterized the operations of
> the British, individually and
> collectively, in the seas of China.[14]

After his appointment, Cushing conscientiously collected all the materials available on China, consulted China merchants in Washington and Boston, assembled newspaper clippings, and studied treatises on diplomacy and international law. In a speech delivered at Bunker Hill on the eve of his departure, he said:

> I have been intrusted with a commission
> of peace, and with the duty of bringing
> nearer together, if possible, the
> civilization of the Old and New
> Worlds--the Asiatic, European, and
> American continents. For though,
> of old, it was from the East that civili-
> zation and learning dawned upon the
> civilized world, yet now, by the refluent
> tide of letters, knowledge is being
> rolled back from the West to the East,
> and we have become the teachers of our
> teachers. I go to China, Sir, if I
> may so express myself, in behalf of
> civilization, and that, if possible, the
> doors of three hundred millions of
> Asiatic laborers may be opened to
> America.[15]

The official instructions were drawn up by
Webster and are not very enlightening. The mission
was charged "to secure the entry of American ships
and cargoes into those (five) ports on terms as
favorable as those which are enjoyed by English
merchants." It was to assure China that American
citizens would always abide by Chinese commercial
regulations but special care should be taken so
that the mission would not be construed as a tribute-
bearing one. As to proceeding to Peking, an
obligation which Cushing took very seriously,
Webster advised that this be insisted upon more
as a lever than as an object. Cushing was warned
against the kowtow, the bugbear of all Western
embassies to Eastern courts, but authorized to
pay the same marks of respect to the Emperor of
China as were paid to the Emperor of Russia. He
was always to keep before the eyes of the Chinese
"the high character, importance, and power of the
United States," emphasizing "the remoteness of the
United States from China, and still more the fact
that they have no colonial possessions in the
neighborhood." He was to insist upon most-favored-
nation treatment for the United States. The last
paragraph of the instructions was the most specific:
"It is hoped and trusted that you will succeed in
making a treaty such as has been concluded between
England and China; and if one containing fuller and
more regular stipulations could be entered into, it
would be conducting Chinese intercourse one step
further towards the principles which regulate the
public relations of the European and American
states."[16]

Cushing was provided with two sets of papers,
one as commissioner authorizing him to treat with
the governors of provinces or cities, or other
local authorities of China; the other as envoy
extraordinary and minister plenipotentiary, to be
presented at Peking, if he should reach the court
of the emperor.[17] He was given two letters signed
by Tyler, composed by Webster, and addressed to
the emperor.[18] Stripped of verbiage, the purpose
of the Cushing mission was to get a treaty like
that already obtained by England and to pick up
any other windfalls that might come its way.

Cushing's appointment was announced to
Imperial Commissioner Ch'i-ying, Governor General
Ch'i Kung, and Financial Commissioner Huang En-tung

by the new American consul, Paul S. Forbes, in
October 1843 (memorial received at Peking,
November 15, 1843). According to the memorial,

> The chief of the said country (the
> United States) had already separately
> delegated an envoy to come to Canton
> and intended to request in writing to
> proceed to Peking and respectfully
> regard the Heavenly countenance, as a
> means of expressing the sincerity of
> his esteem. Ocean winds being uncertain,
> he did not know when he would be able to
> arrive.
>
> We told him that his country (men) came
> from afar only for purposes of trade.
> Canton had long traded and in addition
> the other ports were also successively
> being opened. All matters were to be
> handled by the commissioner sent by the
> Great Emperor to Canton, together with the
> governor general, the governor, and the
> customs superintendent. If he had any-
> thing to say, he should make a factual
> report and await their decision. More-
> over, his country's previous respect
> and obedience had long since come to the
> attention of the Great Emperor and would
> be sure to receive condescending con-
> sideration. From his country to Canton
> he would already have traversed many
> oceans for over seventy thousand li. To go
> from Canton to Peking, counting the
> distance both ways, would be another ten
> thousand li and more. We certainly
> could not bear to have the envoy of the
> said country proceed by these circuitous
> routes to Peking and incur additional
> labor and expense. Even if the envoy
> went to Peking on matters of trade, he
> would be sure to receive an Edict of
> the Great Emperor ordering him to come
> back and resume discussions, and the
> laborious trip would have been in vain.
> The barbarian leader should, then,
> quickly stop and (we) as before would
> memorialize for him to inform the
> Emperor.

As to the said barbarian leader's residing
in China and supervising the trade of the
various ports, if he could constrain the
merchants to trade fairly and pay duties
according to the regulations without any
smuggling, (we) would naturally notify the
various ports to treat him courteously and
not cause him the least hardship.

The said barbarian leader replied that he
would not dare wantonly to make demands.
He would undertake to notify the envoy
to prevent his going to Peking, but as
he could not immediately receive the envoy's
reply, he dare not be positive. If in the
future the envoy should still come to
Canton and the Imperial Commissioner had
left, he would report to the high officials
of Kwangtung province and await their
decision.[19]

In the separate memorial, Ch'i-ying explained
that during the negotiation of the supplementary
treaty he incorporated a clause saying that other
countries would be allowed to go to the five ports
without discrimination. The British envoy made
no objection but added a most-favored-nation clause.
At first, Ch'i-ying was suspicious of this clause
but later decided that it was to cover the situation
now presented by Forbes. If the proposed American
mission were to be allowed to go to Peking, the
English should be accorded the same favor. He
wrote:

Unwilling to state it openly, England
in the statement added to the supplementary
treaty, understood clearly that there would
be a request of the United States to go
to Peking and secured a vantage point in
advance. Even if it were clear that there
was no mutual collusion, it is still an
artful experiment by the United States.
Furthermore, we ordered Huang En-tung and
others to select and delegate able officers
to explain carefully to the American barbarian leader and also to tell him not to
be duped by others. . . . England's
desire to make fraudulent use of Imperial
prestige to outshine neighboring countries
and induce the United States to act as
scapegoat, can already be clearly seen.[20]

The imperial edict in reply to this memorial agreed on the impossibility of an American envoy's coming to Peking and urged Ch'i-ying to talk him out of it by saying that the Heavenly Court soothed and restrained foreign countries but that no traditional regulations could be abrogated or changed. On this matter there was not to be the slightest equivocation.[21] Imperial Commissioner Ch'i-ying later memorialized (received at Peking on December 12, 1843) that his original fears were probably exaggerated. Forbes had only remarked casually that the envoy might go to Peking and when questioned further had agreed to stop him "but whether or not he could intercept him he dare not be positive. Also, he did not know when the said envoy would arrive." If he did come, however, Ch'i-ying was reassured that the local officials would be notified and there would be no irregularity.

> On examining the said barbarian Forbes, his language was sincere and ingenuous, his attitude was very respectful and obedient, not to be compared with (that of) overbearing, intractable people. Up to the present, there is still no news of the said envoy's coming to Canton. Whether or not he has already turned back or if they were only empty words to feel out the way, it is difficult to conjecture.

Ch'i-ying planned to leave Canton shortly and felt that the American problem was settled. If an envoy did arrive the governor general and governor could be counted on to "remove the covetousness of his heart and order him to return home in order to stop any ideas of other countries imitating him."[22] The imperial reply to this memorial elaborated the basis for refusal on the grounds of the fixity of Chinese laws, the fact that the Americans had never paid tribute, that the Chihli officials would not even allow the mission to come ashore and so the long voyage would have been made in vain.[23]

Thus the first flutter at the announcement by Forbes of the coming of the Cushing mission was caused by fear that the American envoy might insist on going to Peking. When this fear was quieted by the courteous manner, perhaps, as much as by the words of Consul Forbes, both the court and Ch'i-ying regarded the matter as closed.

Cushing reached Macao on February 24, 1844. On February 28, Ch'eng Yu-ts'ai, acting governor general of Liang-kuang and governor of Kwangtung, received a secret report from the provisional sub-prefect of Macao "that an American cruiser, having on board over five hundred barbarian troops and carrying sixty-four guns, on the twenty-fifth of the same month, anchored at Chiu-chou." Governor Ch'eng (Ching in the Cushing papers) continues in his memorial to the throne:

> Just when I was going to order an investi-
> gation, on March 2, I received a report
> from the consul saying that Cushing, an
> envoy of his country, had arrived in Kwang-
> tung. I, having assumed that the envoy who
> was to be sent by the said country had already
> been stopped by a letter of the said consul
> at our Minister Ch'i-ying's order, wondered
> why he still came--if it was that the said
> envoy had already set out so that he did not
> receive it. Immediately, I ordered the said
> consul to act in accordance with the original
> record. And also, since there was a physician
> of the said country, (Peter) Parker, who had
> long resided at Canton, was somewhat conversant
> with written Chinese, and seemed rather trust-
> worthy, I immediately delegated the magistrate
> of Yung-an hsien, Ch'ien Yen-kao, to instruct
> Parker to go to see Forbes and inquire into
> the motive of his coming in the face of
> orders to stop. Subsequently, according to
> the report of the said magistrate, he ques-
> tioned Forbes and the said envoy (Cushing)
> still sought to go to Peking for an audience
> with the Great Emperor and had no other mind.
> On being told of the repeated orders to
> desist, he said they had never reached
> him.
>
> Just as I was handling this, I again received
> word in barbarian character that the said
> envoy, Cushing, was sending the barbarian
> leader, O'Donnell, to Canton to ask through
> Consul Forbes for an interview. I find on
> examination the following Chinese translation:

'He has received the appointment of the
president of his country as Envoy
Extraordinary and Minister Plenipotentiary
of the United States of America, to come
to China and confer with ministers of
China on the terms of intercourse of the two
peoples and to conclude a treaty of amity.
He would proceed to Peking without delay
respectfully to present the president's
sealed letter containing various important
matters for the Great Emperor's honorable
inspection. Within one month, he would
go to Tientsin and the mouth of the Pei-ho.

I, inasmuch as the said envoy was far
away at Macao and had not come to Canton
to seek an interview and I had no means
of talking with him, immediately delegated
Financial Commissioner Huang En-t'ung,
on two occasions to explain clearly to
the various barbarian leaders the various
previous notices. And also in accord
with the previous Imperial Edict, again
questioned them, explaining the law and
enlightening by reason, by process of
making adroit explanations to intercept
them with appropriate language.

According to the said barbarian leaders'
reply, the envoy of their country had
received a plenary commission and traversed
eighty thousand li of ocean, taking nine
months to reach China, solely to ask
permission to go to Peking for an audience
and that actually this proceeded from the
utmost sincerity and he would be pleased
not to be impeded. They found his language
extremely respectful and obedient but his
purpose rather obstinate.

The said official again told them that if
they, having come from afar for a righteous
cause, should suddenly go by warship to
Tientsin, there would be some loss of
righteousness. Besides Tientsin was
hardly accessible by boat and the local
coastal (officials) could not allow them
to land. Thus first making a long voyage
with the certainty of being turned back
at Tientsin, how vain would be the trip!
The Great Emperor having always been

considerate, they would certainly not lightly
indulge in wanton activities or wilfully
commit improprieties. The various barbarian
leaders all seemed to accept this but
said that they could not make decisions.
Then they immediately went to Macao to
transmit the information minutely to
Cushing and again report back.

Then we looked in the barbarian document
for the so-called various items on
important matters to find what the matters
and items were. Previously when foreign
countries had matters of complaint, they
had to have the governor general or
governor memorialize for them according
to circumstances and could not directly
get Imperial attention. The said barbarian
leaders replied that they were entirely
friendly and well-intentioned and would not
dare make improper demands. The separate
items, we have not yet been able to
ascertain and dare not indicate carelessly.
In general they insist on going to the
north and on communicating with the
imperial commissioner. On inquiring two or
three times, all were in agreement.

I find that the United States has come to
Kwangtung to trade for more than a hundred
years and has not yet paid tribute. Now
the envoy, Cushing, requests to go to
Peking and also uses the title 'minister
plenipotentiary' and the words 'to discuss
regulations of intercourse and conclude a
treaty of amity.' His purpose to follow
the English barbarians and also his desire
to go beyond them are already entirely
apparent. The said country had traded up
to the present and been extremely peaceful,
never having the least pretext for quarreling.
Naturally there is no excuse for causing
trouble or other difficulties. But the
said envoy did not even come to Canton
and seek an interview. The barbarian ships
with favorable winds can reach Tientsin in
ten days. If Kwangtung province did not
report in a memorial and the ports in the
environs of the capital suddenly saw a
barbarian ship, some suspicions would be

67

aroused. Moreover, it is feared that if the barbarian temper were obstructed it might lead to trouble.

Considering that as barbarian affairs had just been settled and that present and past conditions were not alike, I was impelled to restrain temporarily and then consider maturely how to get them under control. Now I have already sent a perspicacious reply, repeatedly pointing out their error and refusing them in appropriate language. As before I used equivocal language to cause the said envoy to tarry in Kwangtung. Then the whole policy of holding in and giving leash can be conveniently worked out. I had a personal interview with Governor General Ch'i-Kung and our views entirely coincide. But barbarians are by nature impatient and without understanding of values. Whether or not they can be detained long is hard to predict with certainty. Besides investigating as time afforded and devising means to stop them, still waiting until the day when the said envoy replies again to report in a memorial, and immediately sending a flying message to the governor generals and governors of the various coastal provinces fully apprising them, I fittingly memoralized by four-hundred li post and also made a fair copy of the said envoy's letter and of my official reply and respectfully present them for Imperial scrutiny.

To continue. . . the said country has twenty-six regions comprising one country and consequently has the name of United States. What they call the president is their national executive.24

Ch'eng Yu-ts'ai, with whom Cushing dealt from February 28 until the arrival of Ch'i-ying, June 9, was a native of Hsin-chien, Kiangsi, chin-shih of 1811. He served in various provincial and metropolitan posts until 1827 when he was sent to Lan-chow, Kansu privince, as tao t'ai and participated in the campaign against the Mohammedan rebels of Kashgaria. In 1842, as governor of Kiangsu he incurred blame for the British advance up the Yangtze River and was degraded, but was appointed later in the same year governor of Kwangtung. Here he was associated with Governor General Ch'i Kung in defense projects and with Imperial Commissioner Ch'i-ying in drawing up the trade regulations at Canton.

After 1844, part of which time he was acting governor general of Liang-kuang, he served a troublous term as governor general of the rebel-infested provinces of Yunnan and Kweichow, then in Hu-kuang, where the Taipings were rapidly occupying the country. After the fall of Wuchang, capital of Hupeh, to the Taipings, during which his eldest son was killed, he asked for sick leave and was allowed to return home to recuperate. The following year, 1853, he was charged with accepting bribes during office and jeopardizing the Imperialist cause. He was exiled to Chinese Turkestan (Sinkiang). In 1857 he was allowed to return home but died after six months.[25]

In his dealings with Cushing, Ch'eng Yu-ts'ai appears to have been urbane and shrewd. His whole purpose, after failing either to stop the American envoy en route or to send him back after he reached Canton, was to detain him in the south. This he did by a carefully calculated policy of "holding in and giving leash", giving him enough rope to keep him interested but making sure that he was kept under control. While Cushing felt that a good deal was accomplished by this extended correspondence, particularly in saying harsh and undiplomatic things to the governor which he could not have said to Ch'i-ying, it is doubtful how much his ends were furthered thereby. Certainly Governor Ch'eng was entirely successful in his diplomacy, both in detaining Cushing and in pre-serving his own official position. His acts met with the complete approval of the court.

In a supplementary memorial, Ch'eng Yu-ts'ai reports his apprehensions that the French are also planning to send an envoy, which in view of France's negligible trade is regarded with sus-picion. He was afraid that a joint expedition to Tientsin was contemplated and his fears were con-firmed by the wealthy Cantonese P'an Shih-ch'eng. "I find," he wrote, "that American merchant ships are gathering like clouds, in numbers equal to those of England. The coming of their envoy to

Kwangtung could reasonably be expected. But the French coming to Canton to trade are very, very few. Now in sending an envoy on board a warship and anchoring in Kwangtung waters, their purpose must be based on something. But as the barbarian leaders of the said country have not yet made any requests, it is improper for me to stop them beforehand."[26]

The Imperial Rescript, issued the same day the above memorials were received, is matter-of-fact and explicit. There is no indication of alarm or of any serious consideration of alternative policies. No pressure nor persuasion was necessary to secure the appointment of a commissioner empowered to negotiate with Cushing and the "threat" to proceed to Peking was not regarded very seriously, although it would have been rigorously opposed if undertaken.

> What has been done is entirely satisfactory. Since America has never paid tribute, if (the envoy) were to arrive at Tientsin we should certainly have been ordered to return. The request to conclude the commercial regulations should certainly be discussed and settled as before with the commissioner of the original negotiations, and by no means should they on this account sail north to Tientsin and have specially appointed officials to negotiate with them. Now Ch'i-ying is notified and ordered to proceed post haste to Kwangtung. When the said governor shall have received this he must soon reach Canton. Before Ch'i-ying arrives, let Ch'eng Yu-ts'ai, together with Huang En-t'ung, notify the said barbarian that the commissioner of the original negotiations, Ch'i-ying, has been transferred to the post of governor general of Linag-kuang, is proceeding post haste to Kwangtung, and will arrive shortly. Order him to wait quietly in Kwangtung and by no means to engage in irresponsible actions.[27]

A supplementary edict instructed Ch'i-ying to proceed to Canton and act with Ch'eng Yu-ts'ai. It is explained that his appointment is due to the

fact that he is trusted by the various barbarians.
His only instructions are that he is to "explain
adroitly, control and curb, and not give rise to
further complications."[28] At the same time, orders
were sent to the Tientsin officials to warn them of
the possible approach of the American warships.
Should the American come, they were to notify the
governor general immediately and order the barbarians to await his arrival. "Since the said
country claims to be coming for an audience, by no
means open fire on them. What food and fresh
water they need, let them buy, but do not allow a
single man ashore." The governor general was merely
to inform them of Ch'i-ying's appointment and order
them to return to Canton to negotiate with him.
"As to their coming to Peking for an audience, say
that the Heavenly Court in pacifying and curbing
outside barbarians always follows old regulations
and that it is improper to memorialize the request
for them. Take care to explain adroitly and depend
on reason to cut them off. By no means leave the
least ambiquity."[29] Another supplement similarly
warned and instructed the provincial officials of
the various coastal provinces at whose ports the
American cruiser might call en route to Tientsin.[30]

Two weeks later, Ch'eng Yu-ts'ai memorialized
that on March 28, he had received a reply from
Cushing indicating a good deal of determination
to proceed to Peking and to negotiate a treaty,
the latter to be done with no one of lesser rank
than imperial commissioner. The governor is now
convinced that Cushing's purpose is "to outshine
the English barbarians and, like them, set up a
treaty in order to show superiority of treatment by
the Heavenly Court." The mere fact that the trade
regulations are now in force for the United States
as well as for Great Britain is not enough to
satisfy the American envoy. Governor Ch'eng,
therefore, took it upon himself to write privately
to Ch'i-ying of the probability of new negotiations in order to prepare him. He seems to have
taken it for granted that Ch'i-ying would be named
as the negotiator.[31] The Imperial Rescript reveals
some concern about Cushing's insistence on coming
to Peking and reenforces the arguments the Canton
officials are to use to dissuade him: that
negotiations can only be conducted by an imperial
commissioner, that Ch'i-ying has been granted the
official seal as imperial commissioner with the

exclusive control over barbarian affairs, that if they did come to the mouth of the Pei-ho, there would be no imperial commissioner there to negotiate and they would be compelled to order them back to Kwangtung, so "why should they make a laborious journey in vain?" To Cushing's suggestion that he was willing to proceed by land or by inland waterways, Huang En-t'ung was to say that "at this time the said country, no matter whether by way of the high seas or by inland waters can not be allowed to come to Peking."[32] The same re-iterations were made to Ch'i-ying in a supple-mentary edict and he was given explicit instructions on this one point.

> Let Ch'i-ying immediately proceed with redoubled speed. After reaching Kwang-tung, if the said country presents a letter proposing an Imperial Audience, say that China naturally has fixed regulations. There can be nothing con-trary to the law, and nothing can be added to it. If there are demands con-trary to propriety, on the one hand refuse them, saying that they could hardly be incorporated into a memorial, and on the other hand secretly report them in a memorial. This matter is to be handled entirely by the said governor general and he should take care that the arrangements be entirely satisfactory and free from contamination from beginning to end, so as not to give rise to further complications and so as to justify Our hopes.[33]

On this date, April 22, the Grand Secretariat was instructed to issue to Ch'i-ying the official seal of imperial commissioner, carrying authority to adjust all "residual matters relative to the trade of the various provinces," concurrent with his ordinary duties as governor general of Liang-kuang.[34]

Meanwhile, Governor Ch'eng was having dif-ficulty keeping Cushing at Macao until Ch'i-ying could arrive. He was also disturbed by Commodore Foxhall Parker's visit "of courtesy and civility" to Whampoa in the Brandywine. Governor Ch'eng memorialized (received at Peking on May 29, 1844):

I learned privately that the said country's
warship which went to the Philippines had
returned to Macao. Then I received
Cushing's despatch that the military chief
of the said ship, Parker, wished to come to
Whampoa. As Whampoa is an inland harbor
where the merchant ships of the various
countries trade and as warships cannot
enter the port unauthorized, I immediately
set forth the law clearly. After preparing
a despatch clearly forbidding it, to my
surprise the said warship on April 19,
entered the harbor and anchored at Shen-
ching, opposite Whampoa. Moreover, I
received a communication presented by the
military leader, Parker, that the said
ship came to port solely to restrain the
merchants and sailors and guard against
pirates and had no other motive whatever.
He also asked for an interview at my
yamen. I told him that warships could not
anchor inside the harbor, that the various
barbarian leaders never entered the city
for interviews, and ordered him to leave
immediately. I also sent a letter to
Cushing ordering him to restrain and stop
him. Just while copying and despatching
this, I received further word from
Cushing that as the said envoy had come
to Kwangtung, China should afford
courteous treatment. I considered that
as the envoy of the said country, Cushing,
was living far away in Macao there was
no way to meet him. Now Parker's ship
was anchored at Shen-ching, how dare I
deal with him personally. But the outside
barbarians are by nature impetuous and
rather suspicious. The said country has
never come to Court or paid tribute. With
the laws of the Heavenly Dynasty, they are
not yet fully acquainted. Therefore it
is impolite to accommodate too much and
increase their arrogance, yet we must
restrain them somewhat and open their path
to understanding. Now I have again explained
the customary prohibitions, enlightened
them with reason, and have prepared a
perspicuous document notifying them to act
accordingly.

73

This time Governor Ch'eng did not send copies of the various despatches for fear of annoying the emperor. He simply ordered the local naval commander to watch every movement of the Brandywine and to make a full report as soon as the vessel departed.[35]

Ch'i-ying reached Canton on or before June 9 (memorial received at Peking on June 23), having set out before the arrival of his official seal from the capital. He had reached Wu-chiang, some sixty miles southwest of Shanghai, before his credentials caught up with him. At Canton, after conferring with Ch'eng Yu-ts'ai and Huang En-t'ung, he prepared to take up negotiations with Cushing immediately.

> I, considering the barbarians are by
> nature somewhat impatient and that the
> said envoy had waited a long time, feared
> that on hearing of my arrival at Canton he
> would take ship and sail up the Canton
> river in hope of a conference, easily
> causing popular suspicion. If without
> waiting to assume office I immediately
> went to Macao, I also feared that false
> reports would quickly arise. I had a
> wholehearted discussion with Ch'eng
> Yu-ts'ai and, on the one hand, sent a
> communication to the said envoy informing
> him that I had reched Canton and would go
> without delay to Macao to confer with him,
> to quiet his heart in advance, and on the
> other hand took over the seal and the
> affairs of my post. After somewhat
> disposing of essential public business,
> taking Huang En-t'ung with me, I shall
> proceed to Macao. I shall order
> Huang En-t'ung to meet the said chief
> in advance to find out his reactions and
> devise means of controlling him.
> Furthermore, I personally announced the
> Imperial grace and earnestly en-
> lightened him. If he can be brought
> into our scheme, naturally he will not
> persist in asking to sail to the north.
> I shall negotiate separately and act
> carefully.[36]

This memorial elicited another statement of imperial instructions, not essentially different but indicating wherein the concern of the court lay. Ch'i-ying was first of all to "ascertain the said chief's position and devise means of controlling him. Afterwards in conference with him earnestly enlighten him. If he makes any requests, examine the importance of the matter, discuss it carefully in detail and take action, and send an express memorial in accord with the facts. By no means can other complications be allowed to develop."[37] These constitute the Chinese equivalent of full and discretionary powers and it would seem that an imperial commissioner with such powers and acting in the name of the emperor would be a fair equivalent of an envoy extraordinary and minister plenipotentiary. Were it not for the fact that the special functions of imperial commissioners were not limited to foreign affairs, it would be reasonable to translate Ch'in Ch'a Ta Ch'en as ambassador.

Ch'i-ying's first concern was the assistants to help him carry on the negotiations. Among the officials at Canton, the financial commissioner, Huang En-t'ung, and two minor officials, an expectant sub-prefect T'ung-lin and a degraded official on probation, Wu T'ing-hsi'en, had had some experience with the foreigners. En route to Canton at Nan-hsung, Kwangtung, he met with Chao Ch'ang-ling, a former prefect and expectant ministerial secretary, who had worked with Ch'i-ying at Canton during the negotiation of the supplementary treaty and trade regulations. He had found his ability extraordinary and his official reputation good, so he took him with him to assist with the American treaty. Ch'i-ying's principal technical concern was for suitable interpreters, as the Canton missionaries were usually familiar only with the local dialect.

> After arriving at Canton, I inquired
> fully of Huang En-t'ung regarding the
> American barbarians' difficulty of
> understanding. It is much greater than
> the English barbarians', because the
> English barbarians had (Robert) Morrison
> and others. Although they were artful
> and cunning they were somewhat conversant
> with Chinese written and spoken language,

and when there was business one
could discuss it with them. The
American barbarians have only Parker
and Bridgman who do not know many
Chinese characters. They are only
versed in Cantonese local dialect, with
the result that it is hard to understand
each other's point of view and a great
deal of energy is consumed. As it
immediately occurred to me that the
expectant tao-t'ai, P'an Shih-ch'eng,
who has long held a Board post and has
exceptional judgment, was born and
reared in Canton and is well versed in
the local dialect. Moreover, in the
adjustment of residual cases for
several years and because in the purchase
of barbarian cannon and the employment
of barbarian artisans to construct
torpedoes, he has become well acquainted
with a considerable number of American
merchants and is generally highly
respected by the barbarians of the said
country. Now the said official has not
yet put aside mourning. It was highly
expedient to take advantage of his
proximity and appoint him. So I
summoned him to this office and ordered
him, with Chao Ch'ang-ling and Huang
En-t'ung to assist me in handling
barbarian affairs.[38]

The Imperial Rescript approved Ch'i-ying's
preliminary negotiations but still showed
concern that no positive assurance was given that
Cushing would not come north, regarding "his
repeated use of the trip to the North as a threat
as rather cunning." Ch'i-ying was to reiterate
the arguments previously advanced to dissuade him
and to "be sure not to leave the tracks too conspicuous and cause the said barbarian envoy to
question our authority and further give rise to a
threatening attitude. This is of the utmost
importance. As soon as anything is decided upon,
immediately memorialize fully according to the
facts.

Five days later (received at Peking, July 22,
1844), Ch'i-ying reported the progress of his
negotiations with Cushing.

Your slave makes bold to report that
since last memorializing, the barbarian situation has taken a turn.
For several days, he, along with
Huang En-t'ung and the other
delegates, has sought to enlighten
them, following through what they do
understand to pierce their blindness,
leading from what they do believe to
dissipate their doubts. The said
barbarian envoy seems to have seen the
light for he has presented a despatch
saying that despite his originally
intending to go to Peking for an
audience, since receiving the Great
Emperor's Edict refusing this, he had
cogitated over and over the enlightening
conversations of the last few days and
was finally willing to abandon the trip
north, but hereafter, if other Western
countries had envoys visit Peking, his
country would insist on sending out an
envoy and would ask that he not again
be rejected; that as to commercial
regulations, he only insisted upon just
negotiations and if these could not be
concluded promptly, his request to
go north would be revived.

Your slave observes that in the despatch
presented by the said envoy he has agreed
to abandon entirely the trip north but
has brought in other countries to
preempt a vantage point in the future
and has also made the treaty a pretext
for slyly exerting pressure right now.
His mind is really cunning! But to
handle barbarians one has to squelch
their presumption before he can break
up their schemes. As the said
barbarian envoy regarded the treaty
as urgent, it was best to treat with
him, all the while agreeing and
repudiating, insisting on maintaining
the laws of the Heavenly Court, giving
full consideration to international
regulations, maintaining justice
comparatively uniformly, then it can
endure forever. Chinese-foreign harmony

77

cannot be in the least compromised
lest we be thrown into his wiles.
Therefore, along with Huang En-t'ung
and the other delegates, he argued
back and forth with them for several
days. Articles concerning trade were
made to conform to the regulations
fixed last year to avoid discrepancy.
Non-commercial clauses that were
included in last year's supplementary
treaty were also approved. As to new
clauses, not included but on matters
not difficult to carry out or unim-
portant, there was no harm just in
doing as he asked. Any new clauses
that were utterly incompatible
regulations not readily changed, were
all sternly rejected. The said envoy,
although not without repeated pro-
testations, bowed to reason and agreed
to most of them. There are only four
or five articles still not agreed upon.

It is again noted that the said
barbarian envoy said at the outset
that he had presidential credentials
and asked to proceed to Peking to present them in audience; when he gave up
going north, he did not divulge
specifically whether or not he would
hand over these credentials. When
the barbarian leaders, (Fletcher)
Webster and others, met Huang En-t'ung
they mentioned his intention to ask
His Majesty to send an official here
to receive the credentials, but
Huang En-t'ung orally rejected this.
During several days of treaty negotiation, the problem of dealing with
the credentials was probed, but the
envoy's expressions gave no
assurance that after the treaty was
concluded that he would not go north.
We cannot but guard against this in
advance.

The said envoy, during the present
negotiations, requested a metropolitan
cabinet office (Vermilion punctuation)
receive his country's communications,

following the precedent of Russia and
other countries. Analyzing his under-
lying motive, it is not certain that
it was not with a view of getting into
Peking to present his credentials.
Consequently, your slave firmly rejected
this (Vermilion Pencil: Right), but the
barbarian envoy kept repeating the request
untiringly.

Again, it is noted that the American
barbarians' interest is in commerce
and a treaty should in due course be
negotiated with them, but Chief Cushing
personally is rather crafty and our
precautions cannot be too elaborate
or detailed. If he is made to see
everything clearly and is prevented
from using the presentation of his
credentials as a pretext for reviving
his request to go north, your slave
is certainly not going to quibble
over details (Vermilion Pencil: Right).
So it is essential to conclude the treaty
with him.

It is noted that according to the text of
last year's negotiations with the English
barbarians, on the one hand, a copy was
made and memorialized, and on the other
hand, sealed copies were retained by
each party for reference, to preculde
the said barbarians' sprouting undue
apprehensions. If there is no positive
assurance (that they will not proceed
to Peking), when the treaty has been
concluded it still need not be approved
and sealed, in order to curb their
vain desires and keep them under
control.[40]

The edict in recognition of this memorial
urged Ch'i-ying to conclude the treaty, taking
care not to equivocate on the matter of coming to
Peking or to approve any provisions at variance
from the fixed laws of China. The main concern
was that the settlement be final, with no loose
ends to create future entanglements with the
barbarians. As to Cushing's request for a foreign
office at Peking to handle relations with the

United States, the edict gave two reasons why such
a thing was impossible: first, there never had been
such an institution; and second, there was no one in
Peking conversant with the written or spoken language of the United States, a fact which Cushing
must be aware of. Ch'i-ying was eminently right,
concluded the edict, "he should as before explain
to Cushing in detail, to open the springs of
his remorse and cut off his covetous thoughts."[41]

Finally, on or about July 7 (the treaty was
signed at Wang-hsia on July 3), Ch'i-ying was able
to memorialize that Cushing had finally handed over
his credentials, whereupon the treaty was promptly
concluded. Cushing had held out to the last for
the establishment of a foreign office in Peking
and Ch'i-ying had no assurance until he had
Cushing's "national letter" in his hands. To
obtain this end, he was willing to give assurance
that communications would be sent to Peking and
would receive imperial scrutiny.

> After several days' arguing back and
> forth, the said envoy finally agreed
> to the inclusion of a clause that in
> future whenever there were credentials,
> the Imperial Commissioner in charge of
> barbarian affairs, or the governor
> general of Liang-kuang, Min-che, or
> Liang-ciang, would be called upon to
> memorialize them. For the rest, the
> various commercial clauses which had
> not been agreed upon, were then agreed
> to one by one. Although the barbarian
> envoy had come into our control, so
> long as he was unwilling to hand over
> his credentials, your slave could not
> be one hundred percent sure. So again,
> along with Huang En-t'ung and the other
> delegates, he carefully quizzed him,
> utilizing the fact that they could be
> transmitted to break his stubborn
> views. The said envoy finally succumbed,
> unsuspecting, handling over the creden-
> tials he bore and a prepared paper.

This is the crux of the negotiations as far as the
Chinese were concerned; even the formal documents
reveal an almost audible sign of relief when these
credentials were no longer in Cushing's hands to be

used as a pretext for going north and demanding an audience. Ch'i-ying now realized that Cushing had distinguished the two matters all along: the negotiation of the treaty, which might be done with a properly accredited person in Canton; and the presentation of his papers from the president, which must if in any way possible be done at an imperial audience in Peking. Ch'i-ying elaborates:

> Reexamining the reason for the said barbarian's request to go north, it is not found in the treaty but in the credentials. In the very first despatch he sent the clue leaks out. Governor Ch'eng Yu-ts'ai has already had this copied and presented for Imperial scrutiny. His reasoning seems to be that the treaty could be concluded outside while the credentials must be carried in person to Peking. Therefore, so long as the credentials were undelivered, so long was the barbarian uneasy, and even though there was a comprehensive statement in the treaty, it was still uncertain whether he would go north or not. Now that the said envoy had handed over his credentials and asked that they be memorialized for him, and no longer looked forward to going to Peking, there was not the slightest hesitation. But barbarians by nature readily become suspicious and it was feared that if there were delay he would change his mind, so your slave had the treaty concluded, made a clear copy of the completed draft, and turned it over to the said barbarian envoy for translation into barbarian characters, and checked it back for discrepancies. Then he set a date, met the said barbarian envoy and sealed and signed it. He also entertained him at a banquet as evidence of favor and confidence. The said envoy was simply delighted. He is now at Macao, completely peaceable, which fact may somewhat alleviate Imperial concern.

> In addition, a copy of the treaty is being memorialized separately. The credentials, being in barbarian character, are not readily intelligible. To determine just what phraseology is used, your slave will

subsequently have his confidential
interpreter translate them into
Chinese. As to the method of presenting
them, after thorough discussion a request
will be submitted for an Edict and
action taken accordingly.

After meeting the said barbarian envoy
to seal the completed treaty, your
slave, along with Provincial Treasurer
Huang En-t'ung and the other delegates,
departed, returning to the provincial
capital, July 7.[42]

The actual negotiations of the Treaty of
Wang-hsia were brief. The first interview between
Ch'i-ying and Cushing was held on June 18 and the
treaty was signed July 3. Cushing had explained
that most of the differences between his treaty
and that of the British were due to the British
possession of Hong Kong. The United States did not
seek such a territorial base but hoped to secure
the same advantages for her nationals through special treaty provisions. No copy of this project is
in Cushing's despatches.[43] Cushing's resume of the
negotiations indicates a very simple procedure and
an uneventful series of discussions.[44] The
meetings were held both in Cushing's legation in
Macao and in the Chinese temple, dedicated as
Cushing says to the "Lady of Mercy" (Kuan-yin),
in which Ch'i-ying had established his official
residence. This was located in the village of
Wanghiya (Wang-hsia). After an exchange of official
visits between the two commissioners, the actual
discussion of terms, based on Cushing's project,
took place between Daniel Fletcher Webster,
Dr. Elijah Coleman Bridgman, and Dr. Peter Parker for
for the United States and Huang En-t'ung, Chao
Ch'ang-ling, and P'an Shih-ch'eng for China.
According to Cushing, these six "met together for a
number of days in succession, partly at my house in
Macao, and partly at Wang Sha, and discussed and
modified this project, . . . until it assumed the
form of the Treaty . . . . Meanwhile, on the 34th
Tsiyeng (Ch'i-ying) and myself had an interview
of business at the residence of the Legation, in
which interview the principles of the Treaty
and. . . incidental questions were briefly discussed."[45] One of the topics taken up personally
by the commissioners was Cushing's projected trip

to Peking. On this matter Ch'i-ying "avowed distinctly," wrote Cushing, "that he was not authorized either to obstruct or facilitate my proceeding to the Court, but that if I persisted in the purpose of going there, at this time, he had no power to continue the negotiation (sic) of the Treaty."[46] Cushing felt obliged to send a full account to the State Department of his reasons for abandoning the trip north, although his instructions were merely to use this as a lever for securing a treaty. The gist of Cushing's argument is that China's seclusion policy made Ch'i-ying adamant on the subject, that there was no department of foreign affairs in Peking if he did go, and that the opportunity of negotiating at Canton with so fair and competent a man as the imperial commissioner was too good to be jeopardized.

> The interests of the United States and
> China are commercial, not political,
> and it was the primary purpose of my
> mission to make satisfactory arrangements
> for the prosecution of our commerce with
> this Country under new and more favorable
> circumstances.

> All this was now within my reach. To
> sacrifice it, to run the risk of losing
> it altogether, and to peril our public
> peace as well as our commerce upon the
> question of being received at Peking
> was a proceeding, which, it seemed to
> me, neither my Government, nor any
> portion of the United States would
> justify or approve.[47]

All Cushing secured on the question of access to Peking was Ch'i-ying's agreement, contained in a note dated June 29, that:

> Hereafter if the ministers of Western
> nations are admitted to Peking, then
> the ministers of your honorable
> country in China will rightfully, with
> becoming etiquette, and without
> partiality, be received at the North.
> My August Sovereign treates all men
> with equal and perfect equity and will
> never make distinctions among the
> nations of the West, esteeming and

and favoring some more and others less.[48]

The other matter discussed between the two commissioners was the establishment of a separate ministry or bureau at Peking to handle correspondence with foreign governments. This was also rejected by Ch'i-ying. Cushing, however, felt he got a reasonable satisfactory equivalent in Articles 30 and 31 of the treaty which provided means for transmitting American correspondence to the court at any time and from any of the five ports.[49]

At the same time that Cushing was drafting his report to the State Department of the successful execution of his commission, Ch'i-ying discusses the negotiations in some detail.

It is noted that the said barbarian envoy originally presented a treaty comprising forty-seven articles. There were some impracticable matters, which he foolishly insisted upon; which there were vitally essential ones which he failed to set forth. Added to this, the meaning was crude and rustic, the phraseology was coarse and obscure, and the errors in it were too numerous to mention. Your slave, Ch'i-ying, along with the other delegates, day after day argued back and forth with him, now approving, now rejecting, now cutting, now adding to the various items, settling upon thirty-four articles. Those which his intelligence could grasp were explained in detail in order to break through his stupidity; those which affected legal institutes were strenuously opposed in order to check his vain expectations; while instances of obscure composition could not but be considerably edited and expressed simply and clearly to preclude any uncertainty. Altogether his draft was changed some four times before it was finally agreed upon.

It is noted that in the treaty originally presented there were altogether ten articles which could hardly be sanctioned but which he demanded insistently. For instance,

84

when the consuls at the various ports have
business they must report it to the governor
general or governor. (Article IV merely states
that consuls having grievances against local
officials can make representations 'to the
superior officers of the Chinese government.' Article XXIII provided that consuls
shall make annual reports to the respective
governors general but this is a commercial
rather than a legal function.) But the said
barbarian envoy had asked for a clause
permitting them to go directly to the
Censorate to state their case. In case
foreign buildings are destroyed by fire, they
must be restored by the merchants themselves.
(No specific provision was in the treaty to
cover this, presumably because it is a negative requiring no action.) Whereas the
said barbarian dragging in the precedent of
indemnification by the hongs, proposed a
clause for government indemnification.
Foreign goods having been unloaded and the
duties paid on them, the amount sold or
unsold is of no official concern. But the
said barbarian envoy had a provision that
if they were not sold after three years the
amount of the duties was to be returned.
(This is an ordinary commercial practice in
Western countries as a part of general
warehousing arrangements. Ch'i-ying and
other Chinese with whom Americans had to deal
down to 1860, apparently, failed to understand this practice. It was part of their
boast and pretext that they did not understand affairs of commerce which should be
dealt with at the ports and by the merchants
anyway.) The foreign hongs having been
abolished (Article XV), it is up to the
barbarian merchants themselves to carry on
trade with Chinese merchants. But the said
barbarian envoy had a clause requiring the
government to build warehouses to store their
goods for them. Only merchant ships are
permitted to go to the five ports to trade
and cannot go other places, whereas the said
barbarian had a provision that enemy states
and friendly states of the Celestial Court
be allowed to trade anywhere. (Article XXII
of the treaty makes full provision for the
trade of the United States to continue when

85

China is at war with any third state. This clause is in the most comprehensive terms. 'The vessels of the United States shall not the less continue to pursue their commerce in freedom and security, and to transport goods to and from the ports of the belligerent parties, full respect being paid to the neutrality of the flag of the United States: Provided that the said flag shall not protect vessels engaged in the transportation of officers or soldiers in the enemy's service; nor shall said flag be fraudulently used to enable the enemy's ships with their cargoes to enter the ports of China; but all such vessels so offending shall be subject to forfeiture and confiscation by the Chinese government.' It would appear either that Ch'i-ying failed to understand the import of this neutrality provision or that he made his rather vague statement on the assumption that the court would not understand its import.) Merchant vessels entering port and anchoring should be controlled by the consul (Article VI), but the said barbarian requested a clause providing that the Chinese government provide protection for all, and if a third government caused damage to them, China would avenge for those damaged. Now China has no means of restraining the private squabbles of foreign countries but the said barbarian envoy had a provision that if merchant vessels were captured by enemy forces, China would be called upon to help attack them. Foreign warships must anchor outside the ports, but the said barbarian envoy had a clause that as soon as a warship entered port it would exchange cannon fire (salutes) with the forts as a token of respect. (Article XXXII provides: 'Whenever ships of war of the United States, in cruising for the protection of the commerce of their country, shall arrive at any of the ports of China, the commanders of said ships and the superior local authorities of Government, shall hold intercourse together in terms of equality and courtesy, in token of the friendly relations of their respective nations. And the said ships of war shall enjoy all suitable facilities on the part of the Chinese Government in the purchase of provisions, procuring water, and making repairs if occasion require.' It would

86

appear that Ch'i-ying was trying to cover
up the positive concession granted to foreign
warships, whose right to enter Chinese ports
had always been challenged by Chinese officials,
by emphasizing the negative commission of any
mention of an exchange of salutes in the treaty.)
Foreign documents should be received by governors
general and governors along the coast for dis-
criminate disposition (Article XXXI), whereas
the said barbarian envoy asked for a clause for
the establishment in Peking of either a cabinet
or ministerial bureau to receive the despatches
of his country. (On this point Cushing had been
persistent. He said in a communication to
Ch'i-ying during the course of the negotiations:
'The government of the United States desires to
have a Minister at Peking. If this demand be
waived, it becomes indispensably necessary that
some other means be provided by which the government of the United States may make known its
wishes to that of China. The Secretary of State
of the United States will not transact the
business of the two nations with a mere Provincial Governor. Nor if he were willing to
do so, would that be satisfactory, because it
may well happen that the government of the
United States desires to invoke the inter-
position of the Imperial Government to correct
the gross errors or chastise the misconduct
of some Provincial Governor. And this is
quite as important to China as it is to
America; for if the United States should have
occasion to redress any wrong, and all access
to the court is closed up, so that no communication can be addressed to it, then the United
States has no remedy but by recourse to arms.
It was in this way that the late war with England
came to take place. If the English government
had possessed any means of directly addressing
the court, and thus bringing its views and wishes
to the knowledge of the Emperor, it would have
sought redress from the justice and magnanimity
of the Emperor, instead of bringing soldiers
into China. I have perfect confidence in the
good faith and firmness of Kekungpow (Ch'i
Kung-pao, i.e., Ch'i-ying, the Kung-pao, is the
term of address due him as holder of the
honorary title of Junior Guardian of the Heir
Apparent); but one of his successors may be a
bad man, and may conduct ill; and it is not

for the life of one generation, but for all
future time, that we are now arranging the
affairs of the two nations. I am sure the
Emperor will always do right; but I am equally
sure that Provincial Governors will sometimes
do wrong. My object, then in proposing that
there be provided some person or board at
Peking whom the Government of the United States
may address, is because it is one of the means
of preventing all occasion or possibility of a
breach of peace between China and the United
States. Such questions are not a provincial
affair, but a national one, because the peace
of the whole nation is involved. They must
of course come before the Court sooner or later;
and it is better that they should go to it
directly. And if there be any objection to the
Li Pu (Board of Rites), I propose the Nuy Ko
(Nei Ko, Grand Secretariat, commonly referred
to as the Cabinet or the General Council).
This was presented to Ch'i-ying on June 28,
1844.[50]) While the treaty is solely concerned
with amity and the prevention of controversy,
the said barbarian had a clause that should the
two countries take up arms, the merchants must
be allowed to withdraw to avoid injury. Some
were impracticable, some invited further evil
consequences. Besides these, those which were
trifling, far-fetched, grasping, or designing,
were by no means few. Your slave, along with
Huang En-t'ung and the other delegates repudiated one clause after another, not daring to
yield the slightest ground, arguing back and
forth, most of them more than ten times, and
the least of them, five or six times. When
the said barbarian envoy had exhausted his
arguments and run out of words, he agreed to it
as abridged.

As now fixed, the commercial regulations which
coincide with last year's new regulations amount
to eight out of ten. The clause providing that
merchant vessels, having paid duties and because
their cargo is not all sold, go to another port
to reopen sale, need not pay tonnage dues again
(second part of Article VI), the clause that
merchant vessels entering port without breaking
bulk and then wishing to go elsewhere, if they
leave port within two days, will not pay tonnage
dues (third paragraph of Article X), and the
clause that merchant vessels entering port,

paying all duties, and wishing to take goods
already unloaded to another port for sale,
will be exempt from repayment of duties
(Article XX), are all at variance with last
year's regulations, but the present situation
with trade at five ports is not the same as
the previous one restricted, to trade at the
one port of Canton. For barbarian merchants,
finding sales at one port unfavorable, to
tranship to another port is general brokerage
practice and does not call for undue rigidity
nor is it suitable when duties have already
been paid to collect them over again. So we
tried to make accommodation suitable to
commercial needs, at the same time diligently
trying to prevent evil consequences. (Cushing
pointed these clauses out as distinct and
practical gains in the American treaty over
the British treaties. They offset the British
commercial and warehousing base at Hong Kong.
Cushing wrote that 'new provision is made in
the amplest manner for the trade from port to
port in China.' Continuing he wrote: 'A ship
having touched at Canton has there paid tonage
duties and discharged a part of her cargo, may
proceed with the residue to any other port in
China without being subject to the payment of
tonnage duty a second time, and goods which have
been landed and paid duty at one of the ports of
China, may, at any time, be re-exported to any
other port of China, without being subject to
any further duty. This latter provision is
equivalent to a warehousing system for all the
coast of China.'[51])

To continue, the clause allowing them to lease
land in the treaty ports and build their own
churches and cemeteries (Article XVII also
covers houses and places of business), and the
clause about engaging Chinese scholars to
teach the vernacular, assist in procuring
writing materials, as well as to buy various
kinds of Chinese books (Article XVIII), your
slave at first refused to sanction. According
to the said barbarian envoy's reply, the
Portuguese at Macao and the English at Hong Kong
could both build churches for worship and obtain
land for cemeteries so that the living could
pray for blessings and the dead find burial;
that his nationals coming to China to trade had

not been numerous so he did not venture to
ask for a grant of land but if they were not
even allowed to lease land for building, they
would really be up against it; that their
engaging Chinese scholars and buying all kinds
of books was a practice of long standing and
that his request to incorporate it into the
treaty was to prevent official underlings'
having a pretext for causing trouble.

Reconsidering the matter of churches and
cemeteries, that is the barbarians leasing
land and building them themselves, it is one
that should not be stubbornly denied but the
restrictions had to be made clear; there must
be no compulsory leasing or coercion in
defiance of popular wishes. In case the gentry
are unwilling to grant a lease, the barbarians
can have no complaint. (Cushing cites the right
to build churches, cemeteries, and hospitals
in the five ports in his treaty as a gain over
the British treaties. As regards the second
item, he says: 'Provision is made for the employment by Americans of persons to teach the languages of the Empire, and the purchase of books
is legalized; it having been the custom here-
tofore for the Chinese Government to persecute
and oppress such of its subjects as either gave
instruction or sold books to foreigners in China;
which circumstance has been a great obstacle to
the study of the languages of China, and the
acquisition of the means of satisfactory intercourse with its Government.'52)

Now the various countries have been coming to
Canton to trade for more than two hundred years
and Chinese roughly conversant with learning,
such as linguists and writers, have communicated
back and forth. As the profession was profitable,
men were never wanting. (Article VIII provides
for the engaging of pilots, servants, compradors,
linguists, and writers.) When various countries
record local events, they use many Chinese
characters. There have been such books as
dictionaries and rhyming thesauri translated
into western writing, amply indicating that the
purchase of books has long since become common
and that no means have ever been found to pros-
ecute it. Thus there was no harm in according
his request.

Besides these, none of the articles, non-commercial but concerned with amity, is difficult to administer. The clause providing that merchants going unauthorized outside the five ports to carry on illicit trade, to smuggle, to transport opium or other contraband, shall be subject to arrest and punishment by Chinese local officials (Article XXXIII), was an insertion and the fact that the barbarian envoy agreed to it amply shows that these barbarians will conform to the laws of the Heavenly Court and not dare to act wilfully or perversely. (This is the exception to the general provision for extraterritoriality contained in Articles XXI and XXV. The real significance of the loss of sovereignty to China by the extension of extraterritoriality to all American, as well as European, nationals was either not understood by Ch'i-ying or was withheld in his memorial from fear of the censure of the imperial court. His comment on this single exception to the general rule, leaves the impression that Americans are to be subject to Chinese law and jurisdiction.)

His proposal that at the end of each year the consuls at the five ports report the number of vessels, kinds of goods, and prices to the governors general of the respective provinces for transmittal to the Board of Revenue for inspection (Article XXIII), also shows that the said barbarians are concerned with peaceful trade and unwilling to evade customs duties. Furthermore, the said barbarian envoy agreed to the customs schedule item for item, saying merely that foreign lead was a product of his country and the duty of four mace per picul, three times that on iron, must be regarded as excessive by comparison, and asked for a reduction. Your slave, Ch'i-ying, inasmuch as foreign lead is not a major commodity and his request was not unreasonable, therefore lopped off one mace, two candareens per picul, making it two mace, eight candareens. (Cf., Customs schedule, Imports, Class 13, Metals, Lead foreign, in pigs or manufactured, per 100 catties, 2 mace, 8 candareens.[53]) To this the said barbarian envoy acquiesced.[54]

Ch'i-ying was now in effect the foreign minister of China. Once the American treaty was concluded, he made preparations to meet the French mission which was already en route. This mission, headed by M. Lagrene, was even more pretentious and, due to the negligible proportions of French trade with China, even more puzzling to the Chinese. Lagrene was accompanied by his wife, two daughters, and a large suite, including the Sinologist M. Callery as interpreter. The mission reached Macao on August 13, 1844.[55] But even before the mission arrived, Ch'i-ying memorialized early in July (received at Peking on July 28), reviewing his experience with the Americans and applying that experience to the expected diplomatic tilt with the French. He said:

> I have thorougly investigated the circumstances of the various barbarian countries. As the interest of the United States was in trade, we could take advantage of this importunity in order to control and restrain her. Although there were several hitches, in the end she was gradually forced into our scheme. But France fundamentally does not regard trade as important. Her merchant ships coming to Kwangtung are not more than one or two a year. Her situation is very different from that of the English barbarians. The difficulty of handling them, compared to the American barbarians, is no less than twice as great. According to what I have heard, the said country and England are neighbors, only separated by a sea. The English barbarians formerly had them under their control. Later when they became strong and large, they rebelled and set up a state for themselves. They were repeatedly at war. Even when they ceased fighting and concluded peace, neither would accept inferiority to the other. The United States was also a dependency of the English barbarians. Because they were oppressed by the English barbarians, one of their countrymen, Washington, led the people in a war of resistance. The French barbarians sent troops to help them, but when the English barbarians made peace with them, the American barbarians were enabled to set up a nation. Therefore the French barbarians have the enmity of the English barbarians but the most friendly regard of the American barbarians. Thus, last year the English barbarians' defiance of authority had absolutely no connection with the French barbarians. . . . At this time the American barbarians had already made a request

to send an envoy to proceed to the capital,
but the French barbarians had not heard of
this. . . . At the time of my interview with
Cushing, he also stated that a French barbarian envoy named Lagrene would reach Kwangtung
not more than a month later.

I find that the French barbarians have never
had any rupture with China nor any great amount
of trade. If they have an envoy coming it
must be as before on the pretext of making an
alliance with China to attack the English barbarians, hoping for the glories of a superior
country, and in the expectation of Imperial
Favor. Probably on hearing that the American
barbarians have been denied an audience they
will not make a second (attempt) to go north,
but this is not certain. If Lagrene come to
China, no matter to what port he sails, means
must be devised carefully to conciliate and
curb him, then further complications will be
avoided. I shall wait for a thorough inquiry
into the situation and then memorialize fully
as occasions arise.[56]

The emperor commended Ch'i-ying for his skill
in handling Cushing, getting him to abandon his trip
to Peking and hand over his credentials. Although
apprehensive that Lagrene might proceed directly to
Tientsin and embarrass the court, it was hoped that
he would proceed to Canton, where Ch'i-ying could
dispose of him as he had Cushing.[57]

When the treaty negotiated by Cushing and
Ch'i-ying at Wang-hsia was received in Peking, it was
turned over to the Grand Council and the various
boards for examination and report. The spokesman for
the Council was Mu-chang-a, a member of the Kuo-chia
clan and Manchu Bordered Blue Bannerman. A chin-shih
of 1805, he was admitted to the Hanlin Academy, where
he continued his studies until 1809. He filled the
usual metropolitan and provincial offices, serving
repeatedly as lecturer on the Classics in the
imperial palace. In 1839 he memorialized on the
opium problem, had a share in directing hostilities
against the British, and prepared the defenses of
Tientsin against possible British attack. In 1842
and 1843, he supported Ch'i-ying in his appeasement
policy toward the English and urged upon the court
the adoption of his treaty and commercial regulations.
Now in 1844, as grand councillor and grand secretary,

Mu-chang-a still prevailed upon the court to continue a conciliatory policy toward the foreigners.
He continued in power until the death of the
Tao-kuang Emperor in 1850. Then the so-called
"war-party" came into power, determined to have no
truck with foreigners, and Mu-chang-a was identified
with Ch'i-ying in the conciliatory policy. He was
charged with selling his country for petty gain and
deprived of office, never to be employed again in
an official capacity. He was given the Fifth Grade
Button in 1853 for his meritorious subscription to
military supplies but died in 1856 without regaining
official status.[58]

On August 15, 1844, Mu-chang-a reported back to
the throne on the results of the deliberations of
the Grand Council and the various boards. Their
comments on the merits and defects of the treaty
should be compared with those of Ch'i-ying, cited
above, and those of Cushing to the State Department.[59]
The Board of Revenue notes that eleven of the fifteen articles concerned with commerce, coincide with
existing practice established by the Treaty of Nanking
and its supplements. The four making special arrangements to accommodate American port-to-port trade,
although something of an innovation, were still regarded as reasonable. Article X, covering the
requirement that ships' papers be turned over to the
consul within forty-eight hours, and Article XI, regarding the checking of the cargo with the bills of
lading, the Board noted that "the various customs
houses must examine assiduously and not allow the
carrying of misrepresented goods and resultant
smuggling, in the hope that there will be no injury
to customs or commerce."

The articles covering extraterritoriality and
protection of American nationals are commented on
vaguely without any indication that the loss of
Chinese sovereignty was appreciated. The exception
to consular jurisdiction, in Article XXXIII, is
specifically cited: "any of the said barbarians who
go unauthorized to other ports not open to trade and
and engage in illicit trade or smuggling, or carry
opium or other kinds of prohibited goods to China,
shall be subject to trial and punishment by the
Chinese local officials." The object of this group
of articles is recognized as "either to prohibit
extortion by rapacious underlings or prevent con-
troversies of people and barbarians, or rigorously

to guard against smuggling and illegal carrying of prohibited goods and should be effected as reported."

As to Articles XXVI and XXVIII, they agreed that "as long as the said barbarians are content to trade, the local officials should naturally on occasion afford protection. They should ask that hereafter barbarian ships, if plundered in territory under Chinese control, be allowed to submit reports to local officials to seize the plunder and the robbers and punish according to law. If plunder and robbers are not entirely recovered, there can not be indemnity for the stolen goods."

There was no objection to the provision in Article XVII for the leasing of lands for cemeteries, and any violation of foreign graves or molestation of foreign buildings was to be punished.

The various articles dealing with pilotage, registry, neutrality, shipwreck, correspondence, et cetera, they found "not in conflict at all with the port regulations previously established and should be carried out entirely as proposed."

But the article regarding the engaging of scholars to teach and the purchase of all kinds of books (Article XVIII) is essentially contrary to law. Besides, being very indefinite, it will lead to many evils. The said governor general and others, because the said barbarian asked many times, followed the precedent of supplying linguists and clerks and allowed them to engage teachers. Also the fact that the West has dictionaries, concordances, and various books, is evidence that they have been buying books. Temporarily obliged to acquiesce in order to conciliate the barbarian temper, naturally it is improper to make inconsidered changes and then cause the said barbarians to complain. We humbly think that the key to control of the outside is the opportuneness of holding in or giving leash; the method of governing internally is thoroughness of ob-servation. Now after the conclusion of the treaty, we should order the persons engaged by the said country to report their names, ages, families, and place of residence to the said local officials to keep on record, before they are allowed to go to the said barbarian establishments. As to books purchased, each book shop should keep a separate list. Titles, number of copies, and price of books sold, should be entered on the record at the time, and at the end of the year turned over in summary to the said local officials and presented to the governor general for examination, so that by examining the entries we can thoroughly discover miscreants and search out those from afar.

As to persons engaged (as teachers), those who wish to go need not be prevented; but if any make excuses for not going, (the foreigners) cannot require the local officials on their behalf to induce them to go. As to buying up books, those who wish to sell may supply them. If they raise their prices extortionately, (the foreigners) cannot involve the local officials, to buy them by force. This is in conformity with the treaty and can be reported to those in authority.

The Council and Boards also commented at some length on Article XVII covering the leasing of lands on which to construct houses and places of business, hospitals, churches, and cemeteries. Taking note of the special justification, advanced by Cushing for the insertion of this clause, namely, the different position of the American merchants who had no permanent base of operations such as Hong Kong or Macao, and Ch'i-ying's concern that the living be afforded the opportunity of seeking blessings and the dead of finding burial, the court felt that this article had been inserted as a result of high pressure methods and feared that when the foreigners had "bought and built much, they will seize more land." They noted, however, that the feelings of the Chinese inhabitants and the approval of local officials were to be taken into consideration in the selection and leasing of sites.

The drawing up of a treaty is comparatively strict and naturally there can be a compromise arrangement. We humbly consider in the building of churches, barbarian practice is well established, but the matter is untraditional. Notions readily raise doubts. Stupid people delight in the new and dislike the old and it will be hard to prevent

imitation. This should be discussed by the
said governor general with the various
governors to devise means of curbing it.
They cannot propogate or practice among the
people. Take pains to make the residents
of the seacoast understand that the barbarian language is not to be imitated and
barbarian rites are not to be practiced.
These points seem to be not without bearing
on customs and morals.

The matter of burials has now been agreed to.
On their part is ignorance of the virtue of
native burial; on our part, there is accord
with the policy of the burial of bodies.
From the point of view of Imperial magnanimity,
it is certainly not objectionable. But once
the sites have been determined, the boundaries
should be clearly defined and ever after
adhered to. After the various places have
been established, there cannot be further
encroachment on the plea of being cramped
for space. In this we should certainly, in
conformity with the treaty, make rigid prohibitions in advance.

The final comment is on the reduction of the
duty on foreign lead, imported by American traders
in some quantities. Cushing had asked for a reduction and Ch'i-ying had acquiesced to making the
rate two mace, eight candareens per picul.

The Board of Finance (Revenue) finds that
the tariff fixed last year has been agreed
to in toto by the said barbarians. As
foreign lead is not a large item, the matter
of reducing the duty should also be carried
out as agreed upon, and also the various
trading ports should be ordered to act
carefully in complete accord with the agreement, on receipt of an Edict authorizing
the recommendations.[60]

Ch'i-ying remained in Canton, after the conclusion of the Treaty of Wang-hsia, as imperial
commissioner for barbarian affairs and governor
general of Liang-kuang. As virtual foreign minister
for China, he continued to report to the throne on
on the movements of the English, French, and
American representatives. Late in August (memorial

97

received at Peking, September 17, 1844), he memorialized that Cushing had proposed a visit to Amoy and the other newly opened ports, but that the tao-t'ai, P'an Shih-ch'eng, had learned privately that he was planning to return to American immediately. John Francis Davis, British plenipotentiary, governor of Hong Kong, and superintendent of trade, also proposed to tour the five ports. Ch'i-ying felt that he had discovered a strong motivation of the Western states in their desire to emulate one another and to raise their own prestige by demonstrating their ability to gain favors from China.

> I find that England, the United States, and
> France do not accept inferiority one to another.
> They are constantly imitating each other in
> order to extol themselves. Thus as soon as
> the English barbarians had negotiated a treaty,
> the American barbarians immediately declared
> that if the great Emperor at any other time
> extended new favors to other states they should
> also be granted to the said barbarians without
> discrimination and insisted that it be included
> in the Supplementary Treaty. Even France, while
> her trade is actually not large, also recently
> had a cruiser proceed to Ningpo, Shanghai, and
> other places to interview officials. Although
> nominally this was to inspect the ports, still
> the purpose was to outdo the English barbarians.
> Now that the barbarian Cushing has asked to go
> to the four ports, the English barbarian Davis
> also requests likewise; the purpose to outshine
> is readily seen.
>
> I personally feel that as Foochow and the other
> places have been authorized to trade we can
> hardly prevent their going. Besides, since
> the various countries take the character of
> their treatment by the Heavenly Court as a
> measure of national prestige, a possible means
> of restraint and control is found right here.
> (Vermilion Comment: Hardly practicable!)
> Naturally (we) should treat them equally and
> not give rise to occasions for disgruntlement,
> encourage admiration and gratitude among them,
> and further strengthen their sincerity in
> turning toward civilization.

Ch'i-ying goes on to say that he has warned the littoral officials of the imminent arrival of Davis and the possible arrival of Cushing, should he decide to make his tour of the ports before returning to America.[61] In another memorial, received in Peking on the same date, Ch'i-ying reports the arrival of the French mission and that Cushing has abandoned the trip to the four ports and will depart for home, August 26.[62]

The rescript reflects the composure restored to the court as soon as the danger of renewed hostilities and of intrusion of the barbarian envoys into the Forbidden City was passed. So long as the foreigner could be kept at Canton, or even as far away as Shanghai, the court could afford to be magnanimous.

> Whether or not Cushing has returned to his country and what the trouble within his country is, immediately take care to learn discreetly, and clearly memorialize according to the facts. As to the outside barbarians striving to outdo one another, this is the usual condition. Now in handling barbarian affairs, granting them a treaty allowing them to trade in the various provinces has been an extraordinary favor. The said barbarians should only respectfully abide by the regulations, enjoy in common the blessings of tranquillity, and not wantonly hope for advantages outside the various provisions agreed upon. The nation in soothing and curbing outside barbarians regards all with the same charity and never shows the least partiality for one or another to give rise to disputes. If the said barbarians continue to make requests, the said governor general and others should take pains earnestly to explain and sternly to reject them. Let there not be the least taint of ambiguity to give rise to further complications.[63]

Still suspicious that Cushing might be planning to proceed to the ports or possibly to the north, Ch'i-ying took pains to learn on a trip to Macao that the American envoy had actually sailed for America. China could breathe easily as far as the United States was concerned. Peter Parker was left as charge d'affaires. He planned to visit the ports in Cushing's stead but, due to inclement whether, had postponed the trip and was residing quietly in the American factory at Canton.[64]

A month later, with Cushing gone and the Frenc
treaty out of the way, Ch'i-ying reviewed his
experiences and philosophized on barbarians in
general and American barbarians and Caleb Cushing
in particular. These thoughts are embodied in two
memorials, received in Peking, November 23, and
December 14, respectively. In the first, Ch'i-ying
said:

> Now, to recapitulate, after the conciliation c
> the English barbarians in the seventh month
> (August 6-September 5) of 1842,[65] the American
> and French barbarians in the summer and autumn
> of the present year followed on their heels.
> Within this period of three years, the bar-
> barian situation has changed in many respects.
> This is not manifested uniformly. The method
> used to tranquillize and control must also be
> changed. Certainly it lies in rectifying them
> through sincerity and still more essentially
> in controlling them with artifice. Some can
> be made to follow and cannot be made to under-
> stand. Sometimes by showing that there is no
> suspicion, refractoriness can be dispelled.
> Sometimes by considerate treatment, a sense of
> gratitude can be aroused. Sometimes by trusti
> a people broadmindedly and not being too criti
> of them, a situation can be saved. As the bar
> barians were born and bred in outer wilderness
> there is much in the institutes of the Heavenl
> Court that they do not fully understand, but a
> they always pretend to understand things, it i
> hard to explain reasonably. For instance, the
> Emperor's transmitted words are all passed on
> by the Grand Councillors, but the barbarians
> respect them as Vermilion endorsements. If
> shown not to be Imperial writings at all, then
> there would be no means of retaining their
> trust. This then is something that should not
> be made clear.

> When the barbarians eat together it is called
> a banquet. They always gather a large number
> together for a lavish feast and eat and drink
> together for pleasure. At Hu-men (Bocca Tigri
> and Macao on several occasions Your slave gave
> dinners for the barbarians and anywhere from
> ten-odd to twenty or thirty of their chiefs
> and leaders came. When he, on infrequent
> occasions, met them in a barbarian house or on

a barbarian ship they also formed a circle and sat in attendance and outdid themselves to present food and drink. He could not but eat and drink with them in order to bind their hearts.

Besides, barbarian custom extols women. Whenever there are honored guests they are sure to present the women. For instance, the American barbarian Parker and the French barbarian Lagrene both brought barbarian women with them. When your slave went to the barbarian houses to discuss matters, these barbarian women would suddenly appear to pay their respects. Your slave was composed and respectful but uncomfortable, while they were greatly honored. This is actually the custom of the various Western countries and cannot be determined by Chinese standards of propriety. If we condemn them hastily there will be no means of dispelling their stupid ignorance, and at the same time we would arouse their doubts. Furthermore, all the barbarians came in complete amity and we cannot but treat them with some cordiality.

When intercourse become more intimate there must be more precaution. Thus when I was negotiating article by article the treaties with the various countries, I always ordered the provincial commissioner Huang En-t'ung to make clear to the said barbarian envoys that a Chinese statesman in charge of the affairs with all countries never crosses the barrier or has personal intercourse. If ceremonial gifts are sent he can only firmly refuse them. For accepting them ambiguously, the laws of the Heavenly Dynasty are very strict. Not only is it contrary to the constitution, but it is also very difficult to evade the statutory regulations. The said envoys respected the instruction and obeyed. But when we met, if there were any small gifts, such as foreign wines or perfumes, the value of them was very slight, and as the intent was rather sincere it was improper to make a practice of rejecting them to their faces. Your slave gave them in return only personal accessories such as snuff bottles and pouches, to give the idea of returning more than was received. Furthermore, the four countries, Italy, England, the United States, and France asked for his picture. These were made and presented to all.

Although the various countries have rulers, their sex is not uniform and their tenure is not the same--far removed from (our) regulations. For instance, the English barbarians have a female sovereign, the American and French barbarians have male sovereigns. The English and French sovereigns are both hereditary, but the American barbarians' sovereign is popularly set up by the people for a four-year term, and after leaving office his rank is the same as that of a commoner. Nor are designations uniform. In general they plagiarize Chinese terms with a wanton display of boasting and ignorant presumption. This veneration for their own sovereigns is no concern of ours.

As to applying the terms of border dependencies to them, since they do not accept our calendar and do not receive Imperial investiture, they would by no means be willing to lower themselves to the status of Annam or Liu-ch'iu. These people outside the pale are in utter darkness in regard to designations and forms. If we use our documentary forms to determine authoritatively their rank, even if we wore out our tongues and parched our lips we could not avoid the smiling response of a deaf man. Not only would there be no comprehension but also friction would immediately appear. Certainly there would be no great advantage to the essential business of tranquillizing. Rather than quarrel with them over empty words with no real result, it is better to disregard a small matter to effect a large program.

The above observations are all based on thorough examination of the barbarian situation. A sure determination of the point which lies between triviality and gravity, delay and urgency, must provide a plan adapted to needs and permeating changes. Whether the situation be essentially trivial or immediately pressing, Your slave did not venture to make separate statements monotously to importune the Imperial ear. Now that barbarian affairs have been generally concluded, it behooves him to state them clearly in a supplementary memorial.

<u>Vermilion Comment</u>: This is the only way to do it. I have understood it entirely.[65]

The other memorial was written after Ch'i-ying had received acknowledgment of Cushing's credentials at the court and an imperial request for more information as to the style to be used in the reply. The court was willing to comply but realized that "to the said peoples living outside the pale (our) language is unintelligible. How should an Imperial Mandate issued by us be expressed in order to show the constitution of the Court?" Ch'i-ying was requested to draft an edict in suitable form and submit it for imperial approval and promulgation. He was also asked to explain "the cake of vermilion contained in the bronze box in which the credentials were forwarded." It is understandable that the court should fail to recognize the wax impression of the United States seal which was so different from the Chinese practice of stamping the seal on the paper in vermilion ink. Ch'i-ying replied:

Your slave finds that the location of the United States is in the Far West. Of all the countries, it is the most uncivilized and remote. Now they hope for the Imperial Favor which can be kept forever. We have both commended the sincerity of their love of justice and strengthened their determination to turn toward culture. The different races of the world are all grateful for Imperial bounty. It is only that the said country is in an isolated place outside the pale, solitary and ignorant. Not only in the forms of edicts and laws are they entirely unversed, but if the meaning be rather deep they would probably not even be able to comprehend. It would seem that we must follow a rather simple style. Our choice of words and use of expressions should in general show that the constitution of the Heavenly Court is to be respected.

Your slave has deliberated wholeheartedly and personally considers that in the present Imperial Mandate, the style employed should be simple and direct, the meaning used should be clear and obvious. There is no use in adhering to forms, but it is absolutely necessary to

103

maintain the constitution. This will be appropriate.

It is noted that the executive of the said country is called Po-li-ssu-t'ien-te, translated into Chinese it is president. Besides this this, he has no other designation. It would seem proper, therefore, to use this term to address him. When (the Mandate) is promulgated, it would seem proper to write it in Manchu. This would be more discreet. Besides, the people of the said country have occasionally been to Russia to trade and place the greatest value on Manchu script. This will further move them to accept it respectfully. I respectfully submit separate Manchu and Chinese drafts and present them for Imperial inspection. But I realize that my literary style is essentially commonplace and my translation (into Chinese) even more rough and deficient. As this is a proposal confidentially presented I did not dare entrust it to others. As it is entirely made up of everyday phrases which I have selected and translated myself, I really fear that it is not not without errors and omissions and my embarassment is extreme. Still I beg that it be authenticated to the Grand Councillors for examination and correction, and thereafter request an Edict to enforce it.

As to the formal Manchu calligraphy, I have not written in it for a long time. Consequently the material now presented is in the cursive style. I humbly ask that the Imperial Mandate issued to the said country also not employ the formal Manchu characters but be written in the cursive style. This is also suitable.

To continue, previously when I personally arranged the treaty with the barbarian envoy Cushing, we agreed difinitely that hereafter he must not request an audience nor could there be further demands. It would seem that there would be no further retraction.

As to the cake of vermilion contained in the bronze box of the said barbarian's credentials, it is a wax model of the seal of his country's sovereign, attached to the letter in order to show sincerity and respect, and has no other use.[66]

With the materials on both sides available, the negotiation of the Treaty of Wang-hsia appears not so much as a genuine tilt of diplomacy as an exhibition of shadow boxing. Throughout the negotiation, Cushing made use of the threat to go to Peking as a lever to secure and expedite the negotiation of a satisfactory commercial treaty, without any serious intention or necessity under his instructions to carry out the threat to go to Peking. As a matter of fact, he would have been somewhat embarrassed if his bluff had been called because the ships at his disposal would not have made much of a showing at the Pei-ho. On the other hand, Ch'i-ying used the threat of refusal to negotiate or of breaking off negotiations once started, or refusal to sign and seal the treaty after it was negotiated, to get Cushing to abandon his trip north and deliver his credentials at Macao. All the time Ch'i-ying was perfectly agreeable to the treaty itself and had accepted most-favored-nation treatment as a matter of policy before Cushing came to China. Under such circumstances, treaty negotiation could hardly fail. Each party was holding up a straw man, confident that it would be knocked down by the other, inasmuch as both were pre-agreed on the real issue of the negotiations.

Nevertheless, the negotiations show clearly the peak of a steadily growing foreign policy on the part of China, or at least of a group of officials in the Chinese court. Ch'i-ying, in the role of foreign minister, was gradually acquiring the experience and knowledge necessary for an intelligent handling of China's foreign policy. When she began to deal with the United States, China saw a cloud of foreigners, no bigger than a man's hand, gathering over a remote corner of her empire and only vaguely discerned that these foreigners were of different tribes or nations. The first policy that suggested itself was her version of divide and rule, to use barbarians to curb barbarians. It had often been demonstrated in Chinese history that the best way to escape from an attack of dogs was to throw a bone among them and start a distractive dog fight.

An advance was made in the Chinese understanding of the West, when under pressure of war, the court and a small group of gentry and officials at Canton accepted the fact of Western superiority in ships and armament and set out to learn their devilish ways.

The process was suddenly halted as far as the court was concerned with the termination of hostilities, but was to continue and increase at Canton and the other ports, until there was developed the familiar spectacle of the latter half of the nineteenth century--a materially advanced Chinese group on the periphery and an old-fashioned, self-conscious, but still arrogant and proud, aristocracy at the core of the Middle Kingdom.

The Ch'i-ying phase of this development, following the defeat of Chinese forces by the British navy, is in some ways a mere concealed acknowledgment of Western superiority in arms, but combines also elements of urbanity, shrewdness, and enlightened self-interest--qualities which if pursued should have given China a sound foreign policy in the course of the new few decades.

In the first place, Ch'i-ying was broadminded about commerce and was willing to recognize its increasing importance in the new money economy. He was frank enough to recognize the unwisdom of a blustering military policy, humble enought to appease his actual and potential enemies, and clever enough to present these un-Chinese ideas to the court in a form palatable but still strong enough to get done what he saw must be done. He does not take seriously the apologetic formula of the military men, such as I-shan, that the barbarians could be alternately restrained and led on to their own destruction. His view was that the barbarians were here to stay but that the situation could be handled to mutual advantage if China maintained her dignity and adjusted her commerce and economy. He, in effect, repudiated the prevalent Chinese idea that commerce was a provincial matter and saw, at least dimly, that the central government should regulate and develop the foreign trade now spread beyond the boundaries of one province. He shows considerable understanding of the significance of the extension of trade to five ports. He was quick to see that anything the foreigners wanted, such as trade or prestige, could be utilized as a lever against them. For instance, he anticipated a difficult time with the French because he did not understand wherein their interest lay.

Nevertheless, the Chinese documents do not reveal Ch'i-ying as a mature statesman in a nineteenth century sense. He might have been a modest, although not brilliant, one in the time of Machiavelli. He is guilty of failing to understand the significance of important measures, such as extraterritoriality and the conventional tariff. He is guilty of omission or deceit or both in his representations to his own sovereign. He maintained a rather false conception of the foreigners as rather childish people who wanted baubles to flaunt in front of their fellows, which was something of an obstacle to his recognition of their real aims.

And finally, and more or less incidentally, the Chinese documents reveal the traits of traditional Chinese scholastic thinking and writing. There are the rhetorical circumlocutions, the double, triple, and quadruple negatives, the paired and balanced sentences, the classical allusions, the historical analogies, and the threadbare proverbs and formulae. The Chinese love for semi-logical, numerical groupings is revealed in the break down of the Treaty of Wang-hsia into fifteen articles dealing with customs, nine clauses dealing with crimes and litigation, six of which are justifiable, three of which are obnoxious, and then of the individually objectionable clauses. There is also apparent in the analysis of the treaty, considerable confusion between the text and the explanations of Ch'i-ying and the transmitted arguments of Cushing.

On the other hand, the Chinese documents do not add much to the diplomatic lustre of Cushing. The Chinese reveal considerable respect for his cunning and persistence but on every issue important to them, they were able to maneuver him out of his position. On all the main points of the treaty, the Chinese negotiators were already prepared to concede. While on all the objectionable points, with the exception perhaps of the clause allowing the engaging of teachers and the purchase of books, they stood their ground and won their points. And as later developments will show, most of the provisions which Cushing regarded as constituting a diplomatic equivalent for Hong Kong, proved impracticable in the face of an indifferent local officialdom, a superior gentry, and a hostile and often violent populace. Perhaps, Cushing's greatest achievement was the inclusion of provisions to accommodate the peculiarly American port-to-port trade, as he said, constituting a substitute for an official warehousing system. And on this score, Ch'i-ying seemed to have thoroughly understood the issue and to have accepted it as an evidence of the changing and expanding nature of China's foreign commerce.

107

CHAPTER 5

EXTRATERRITORIALITY AND THE WABASH CASE

The right of Americans resident, or even tran-
sient, in Chinese territory to be tried by American
consular officers and under the laws of the United
States was incorporated in the first treaty concluded between China and the United States in 1844.[1]
Caleb Cushing, the American negotiator of this
treaty, gave this special privilege enjoyed by
American and other foreigners in China its first
formal and legal expression in the Treaty of Wang-
hsia.[2] Cushing also provided, in his report to the
secretary of state,[3] the first elaborate history
and rationalization of this legal fiction by which
Americans in China were regarded as being outside
the (extra) Chinese jurisdiction (territory). The
principle thus established was operative in China for
almost a hundred years[4] and came to be known as "extraterritoriality" often shortened for convenience to
"extrality."

The American treaty of 1844 became the type o
expression of extraterritoriality in China, and the
American envoy, Caleb Cushing, is recognized as the
author of the principle of extraterritoriality as an
exception to the customary practice of international
law among European and American states. Despite this
identification of the United States with the principle
of extraterritoriality in China, American contact
with Chinese legal procedure, prior to 1844, was
comparatively limited and by no means consistently
unfavorable to the Chinese. The British or, more
exactly, the English East India Company, had
numerous encounters with the Chinese law between

Reprinted from The American Journal of International
Law, XLV (1951), pp. 564-571.

1689 and 1838.[5] The Americans, coming into the trade late and with fewer ships and men involved, were involved in only three serious cases between 1784 and the conclusion of the Treaty of Wang-hsia in 1844.

The case of the American seaman, Francis Terranova, charged with killing a Chinese boat-woman at Whampoa and strangled at the order of a Chinese court, October 28, 1821,[6] is the one instance of an American being submitted to trial and punishment by a Chinese court and under Chinese law. The case received both English and American comment[7] and is generally recognized as being the principal American (negative) precedent for extraterritoriality. The second case also involved a homicide charge against an American national. An unspecified American was charged with killing one Sue Aman outside the American factory at Canton. This Sue Aman case occurred during Cushing's mission in China and was the immediate cause of his formulation of the principle of extraterritoriality and his drafting of the clauses in the Treaty of Wang-hsia.[8]

The third case in which Americans were involved is not a precedent for extraterritoriality because the Americans were the victims instead of the perpetrators of the homicide, and also because the case presented a favorable view of the fairness and efficiency of the Chinese courts. Chinese documents published by the Palace Museum in Peking[9] give a fuller account of the case than the previously available English and American documents. Examination of these documents and a re-examination of the American and British versions provide some interesting evidence that Americans were content with Chinese jurisdiction and opposed to the principle of extraterritoriality. This "servile" American point of view is openly expressed in trade journals of the period[10] and was often contemptuously noted by British traders and officials both in London and Canton.

The Wabash case is one of "ladrone pirates" in which piracy was accompanied by murder. United States Consul Wilcocks reported that the American ship Wabash, of Baltimore, Captain C. L. Gantt, was lying in Macao Roads "with a quantity of opium and seven thousand dollars in specie on board." On the night of May 26, 1817, while Captain Gantt was at Canton ascertaining the state of the market, a native boat, manned by fifteen Chinese, came alongside the Wabash. The ladrones boarded the ship and attacked the crew, "murdered the chief mate and one seaman, whose bodies they threw into the sea; wounded the second mate and two seamen; drove four of the crew overboard--two of whom were drowned, two swam to shore; plundered the ship of all the specie, thirty-five cases of opium, and many articles of less value, and then left her. The second mate died on the 28th at the hospital at Macao; the two wounded seamen have since recovered."[11]

Consul Wilcocks, through the hong merchants, addressed a memorial to the governor general at Canton demanding justice for the "outrage committed on a ship under the flag of the United States, while at anchor within the waters of this empire." In his report to the secretary of state, the consul added: "In enumerating the loss, I was careful not to mention the opium, as it was the prevailing opinion that the pirates had proceeded to a distant province, if not to Manila; in which case, very little hope was entertained of seizing them."[12]

Much to Consul Wilcocks' surprise and embarrassment, the Chinese authorities within a month captured the pirates and recovered "a considerable quantity of the opium." And, as the consul notes, "The latter circumstance occasioned not a little disgust" on the part of the governor general. Wilcocks took the position, however, that Captain Gantt had refused a pilot offered to bring him into the port, thus disproving any intention to bring in contraband goods. The governor general accepted this explanation and on June 13 invited Consul Wilcocks, with several other Americans, to witness the execution of five of the principal pirates. The execution took place, but Consul Wilcocks "for reasons it is not necessary to state . . . refused, but prevailed on two American gentlemen to attend."[13]

The governor general issued a proclamation on the case to Consul Wilcocks, via the customs superintendent (hoppo) and the hong merchants, in which he said:

> Piratical banditti plundering a foreign
> ship and murdering the mercantile sea-
> men is the highest possible degree of

cruelty and wickedness. The said foreign
ships, having crossed the seas for commercial purposes to be murdered by pirates,
is an extremely lamentable case.[14]

Later, the first official notice by China of
American participation in the opium trade was made
by the governor general. He notified Consul Wilcocks
that "foreign opium, the dirt used in smoking, has
long been prohibited by an order received; it is
not allowed to come to Canton," and requested the
consul "to write a letter immediately back to your
country and tell these things to your honorable
country's president."[15] The notification was
duly made and John Quincy Adams, as secretary of
state, informed Consul Wilcocks that the prohibition
had been duly published in the United States.[16]

The Chinese documents on the Wabash add a good
deal of illuminating detail as to the techniques
of Chinese criminal procedure, the character of
Chinese officials and of the criminals involved, and
the opinion held by China of the United States. As
the earliest Chinese official documents dealing
with our country, these two memorials and one
imperial edict of 1817, merit some attention by
American historians.

The Chinese account of the pirating of the
Wabash is found in a memorial from the governor
general of Liang-kuang, Chiang Yu-hsien, dated
July 19, 1817.[17] Chiang Yu-hsien (1766-1830) was
a Chinese, native of Liao-tung, a peninsula on the
southern coast of Manchuria, who had become a
bannerman in the Manchu military organization. A
degree man in the Chinese civil service examination
system, he had received his chin-shih (doctor's)
degree in 1784 and served in various offices. In
1816, the year before the Wabash case, he had memorialized on the reception of the British mission headed
by Lord Amherst.[18] There is no other indication of
interest in foreign affairs.

The memorial first makes clear that the piracy
took place near the hsien (county) border, so the
officials of two counties were involved, as well as
the prefect of Canton, in whose jurisdiction both
the hsien lay. Upon being notified of the crime,
the governor general made all these officials, as
well as the coastal garrisons and sea patrols,

responsible for the capture of the pirates. Heavy rewards were offered for their capture. As a result of these vigorous steps, fourteen of the fifteen pirates were captured, and these are all listed by name. The corpses of two of the murdered Americans were recovered and identified, but the bodies of the three who were thrown overboard and drowned were not recovered. The five Americans are also listed by name, but as the English accounts do not give their names, it is possible to reconstruct the English names from the Chinese only tentatively. Of the loot, a total of 838 dollars in treasure was recovered and sixteen cases of opium. This was taken to Canton, identified by Captain Gantt and the "treasure" returned to him.

Chiang Yu-hsien identifies the pirates as Tanka (tan-chia or tan-min) or "boat people." The Tanka were outcasts of Canton, and were forced to live in their boats, constituting one of the four minority groups[19] barred from the official examinations and limited to certain menial occupations.[20] As the Tanka did not have "house numbers" and were not included in official registers, it was more difficult to apprehend them and impossible to enforce the usual Chinese responsibility on their families or villages.[21] The pirate leader, Li Feng-kuang, "knew barbarian language thoroughly" and had worked for many years lightering barbarian goods on the Macao waterfront.

According to the memorial, neither Li Feng-kuang nor his fourteen accomplices were professional pirates or hardened criminals and the attack on the Wabash was an impromptu affair. Li Feng-kuang recognized the opium spread out on the deck and proposed to his Tanka friends who were fishing in the vicinity that they blackmail the captain by posing as revenuers. When the Tankas came alongside, Li Feng-kuang "shouted to the barbarians (in English)[22] that they were carrying prohibited opium and demanded hush money." The mate, called "Harry" in the Chinese account, refused and started to argue. Li Feng-kuang, who was already aboard the Wabash, "saw that the hold was stacked full of wooden chests, surmised that they contained silver," and decided to give up the pose of revenuer and become a pirate. He called to the others to come aboard and seize the chests. The American mate and the seamen "took up foreign swords to resist the seizure."

There follows a blow-by-blow account of the fight, describing just how and where each American was wounded and thrown into the sea. The Chinese had only bamboo poles, but they took the swords from the Americans and used them effectively. When the fight was over the Chinese victors took to their boats and fled to a sandbank "where they opened the chests and found that sixteen contained opium and two, silver, amounting to 5000 dollars. They divided up the silver but as the opium could not be brought into port, they dumped it and the two empty silver chests on the beach," where they were later recovered by the officials. The pirates then "rowed their own boats to an unfrequented cove, came ashore, and scattered."[23]

The governor general accepted the argument of Consul Wilcocks, which was explained by the linguist, that Captain Gantt had no intention of entering port with the opium. The linguist reported that Gantt "had told him orally that it was his first trip to Canton to trade and he did not know that opium was prohibited. Just before he got into port he heard that it was illegal so he did not venture inside. Moreover, he said that the overseas Chinese (pien kuei-tzu) are fond of smoking opium and he could sell it elsewhere."[24] This made sense to the Chinese officials and the governor general was satisfied that there was no deception involved.

The penalties imposed on the fourteen culprits are carefully discussed and assigned, varying from immediate decapitation for the five found guilty of murder to banishment "4000 li to the frontier and be tattooed according to law."

The guilt of Captain Gantt for bringing opium to China was also considered. He was called "ignorant and rash" but determined not guilty. The governor general decided that the recovered opium could not be returned to him but should be taken to the gate of the barbarian factories and burned, which was done. The American's "treasure," however, "which has been recovered will be restored and that not recovered must, according to law, be made good." This decision included repayment for the opium which was lost and that which was recovered and destroyed. Nevertheless, Captain Gantt was advised to return to America and admonished never to return to China.

Finally, the governor general recommended all the prefectural and district officials who participated in capturing the pirates and recovering the loot for imperial recognition and reward. The pirate chief's deposition and the translation of Captain Gantt's statements were forwarded to Peking with the memorial.

In a supplementary memorial under the same date,[25] Governor General Chiang Yu-hsien, apparently anticipating that his decision to clear Captain Gantt of all smuggling charges would be challenged by the court at Peking, presented further evidence of his innocence. First, the Canton Customs House register had been examined and Gantt's name did not occur. "Thus his statement that it was his first trip to Canton and that he was not cognizant of the law is indisputable." Second, the Americans were the Number Two trading people at Canton (the English were Number One) and had always been respectful and compliant. Third, the United States was in a special category because of the peculiar nature of its government, its peculiar institution of the electoral college, and its laissez-faire policy regarding trade:

> These barbarians have no sovereign (chu) and have only a head man (t'ou-jen); each tribe selects several persons who draw lots and serve in rotation for four years each. In matters of trade, each individual is allowed to put up capital and do business without any control or commission from their head man.

Fourth, Li Feng-kuang had no authority to arrest Captain Gantt in the first place and had then turned pirate and committed murder. Consequently, the discovery of the opium was accidental and Captain Gantt was guilty of no crime. The governor general made clear, however, that "if the said barbarian had dared to bring his opium into port and officials had seized it and inflicted casualties, there would have been no redress and besides the said barbarian would have been punished for violating the prohibition." The fact that Gantt's ship did carry opium was justification for sending him away and warning him never to return. The governor general was happy to state that Captain Gantt had now left Canton for home.

114

The emperor expressed his approval of the punishment of the pirates by a vermilion comment (i.e., a personally scribbled note in the emperor's own hand) in the text and endorsed the original memorial with a routine commitment to the Board of Punishments for appropriate action.[26]

The supplementary memorial, however, went too far in catering to foreigners and came too close to nullifying the imperial prohibition of opium. The emperor presumably expressed his disapproval orally to the grand councillors, who presented the memorial in audience, and endorsed the supplement with an order to "draft a separate edict."

The imperial edict, dated August 10, 1817, is addressed to Governor General Chiang Yu-hsien.[27] It is a blast in no uncertain terms charging that Captain Gantt should have been punished for carrying opium, that indemnification for the opium was an error, and insisting that the Americans at Canton be specifically notified that hereafter the opium prohibition would be strictly enforced. The punishment of the Chinese culprits, it was clearly restated, was entirely proper. In conformity with this edict, the specific notice to the Americans of the imperial prohibition of opium smuggling, noted above, was sent through the Hong merchants to Consul Wilcocks, September 23, 1817.

Besides the obvious relevance of this Wabash case to the opium question, there are a number of points which bear on the question of extraterritoriality, or more specifically, the competence of China's police and judicial system. First, it is clear that the Americans found the Chinese officials prompt and vigorous in the capture and punishment of the culprits, beyond their reasonable expectation; second, the Americans found the local officials lenient toward their own questionable conduct, certainly with no anti-foreign tendency. Third, Chinese justice meted out to Chinese was stern but discriminating. There is no indication of blanket charges and wholesale execution. Fourth, the Chinese officials did not insist on responsibility of family and village in this case involving boat people or Tankas, but dealt with their guilt on an individual basis. It does not necessarily follow, but might be argued, that the Chinese might see the rationale of relieving other groups, e.g., Americans

115

and British, from group responsibility. Fifth, and finally, the Chinese judicial practices, although not specifically described in these memorials, show both differences from, and similarities with, Western practices: (1) magistrate-type trial instead of jury trial; (2) extensive use of signed depositions by both accusers and accused and lesser use of witnesses; (3) emphasis upon signed confession; (4) elaborate use of material evidence, such as the lethal weapon used in the crime and the captured loot of the robbers; (5) careful reporting of criminal cases to Peking, personal scrutiny of these reports by the emperor, and review of the acts of the provincial officials by the Grand Council and appropriate boards in Peking.

Although all of these documents were not available to contemporary Americans, who could not be expected to regard the question objectively anyway, there is considerable evidence that American traders were not only "respectful and obedient" but regarded any insistence on extraterritorial and other special rights in China as high-handed and unjustified. It is only necessary to peruse contemporary trade journals in the United States to bear this out.[28] Americans were eventually convinced of the necessity of extraterritoriality, but there was a good deal of precedent against it, and many American traders and educators came to regard it as a mixed blessing.

CHAPTER 6
THE CHARACTER OF AMERICAN TRADE WITH CHINA,
1844-1860

Terminus had passed away, with all the deities
of the ancient Pantheon, but his sceptre
remains. Commerce is the God of boundries,
and no man living can foretell his ultimate
decree.[1]

The Treaty of Wang-hsia, the first treaty between
the United States and China, was signed July 3, 1844
by Caleb Cushing for the United States and Ch'i-ying
for China. It was essentially a commercial treaty.
In so far as there was any policy expressed in it, that
policy was shaped by the sixty years of active trade
carried on at Canton by captains and supercargoes out
of Boston, Salem, and New York. The opening of China
in 1844 was hailed as the discovery of a new continent,
ready peopled with two million people clamoring for
American goods. The trade journals were confident that
America was destined to dominate the trade in the
Indian and China seas, particularly after the antic-
pated occupation of the Pacific Coast, Oregon and
California, of the Sandwich Islands, and the com-
pletion of a transcontinental railroad. "For the last
three centuries the civilized world has been rolling
westward; and the Americans of the present age will
complete the circle, and open a western steam route
to the East."[2]

The general character of the period from 1844-1860
was one of tradition, a period of uncertainty between
the increase of foreign trade which followed the War

Earl Swisher, "The Character of American Trade With
China, 1844-1860," University of Colorado Studies,
Series C (Studies in Social Studies), I, No. 2 (1941),
pp. 165-180. Reprinted with permission from the
University of Colorado.

of 1812, the periods of buoyance and decline that succeeded one another up to about 1846, and the almost complete absorption of the country in internal developments and problems after the Civil War. At the same time it was a period of expansion, despite the tendency already apparent for capital to go into manufacturing rather than commerce.[3] The factors in this increase have to do with three commodities, all of which are traceable in the course of the trade with China; namely, tea, cotton manufactures, and California gold.[4]

In 1844 there were twenty-seven American ships trading to China with a tonnage of 11,262. The volume of the trade did not vary greatly until 1850, when the number of ships jumped to forty-one and the tonnage to 21,969. The next year it nearly doubled again, and maintained itself between 81 and 100 ships until 1855 when it reached the high point of the period: 111 vessel with a tonnage of 101,660. From that year until 1860 the totals were irregular: 98 in 1856, 58 in 1857, 66 in 1858, up to 100 again in 1859, and then a slump to 82 ships with a tonnage of 78,370 in 1860.[5]

The period presents a constant struggle on the part of American traders to find an outward cargo which would be marketable in China. The first American ship to reach Canton in 1784 had been loaded with Yankee ginseng and this herb retained a place in the trade throughout the period. The amount varied widely from year to year, but averaged about 200,000 pounds, with a value of some $100,000. The consumption of this tonic was, however, limited and practically static. A large shipment immediately lowered the price. For instance in 1849, there were 584,021 pounds of ginseng sent to China which brought $182,966. In 1856, the amount was only 350,000 pounds but the value, $175,705, was almost equal. The lowest year was 1854, when only 37,491 pounds of ginseng were sent. There is no noticeable development in the trade. Ginseng continued a valuable item in American cargoes but could never serve as an equivalent for Chinese tea.

The fur trade which had been valuable earlier in the century, lingered on into this period but the amoung was not large, from $3,445 in the low year to $58,201 in the highest year to 1853. After that the amounts were neglibile to 1858, when furs dropped out of the Chinese trade altogether.

There was some trade in tobacco during the period but it was evidently a poor substitute for opium. The amounts sent to China were negligible for the most of the period up to the last year, when the amount suddenly jumped from 135,153 pounds in 1859 to 664,280 pounds in 1860. The introduction of tobacco was, however, a slow and speculative process, and never succeeded until modern high-powered salesmanship and advertising were employed in China.

The principal effort on the part of the American traders, particularly those trading out of New England, was to introduce both raw cotton and cotton piece goods into China. The difficulties of this enterprise can be appreciated when one recalls that cotton wool was a staple export of India and that Chinese nankeens, stout cotton goods, had been famous before the New England mills were built. The United States had used Chinese nankeens worth a million dollars as late as 1820.[7] Cottons, both white and printed, were sent to China in varying quantities, and the agents of the New England houses were often hard put to it to dispose of them. Persistence, however, had some results, and eventually considerable amounts were consumed. White goods, sheetings, maintained themselves bravely through the first decade and reached a high in 1852 and 1853. By 1860, however, they had declined to the small figure of $201,324. Printed goods showed marked increases in the last decade reaching a high of $591,185 in 1860. In 1855 a small quantity of duck was introduced and by 1860 had reached the sizeable figure of $61,098, seeming destined to drive the picturesque matting sails from the Chinese rivers and seas.

The total export to China increased from $1,110,023 in 1844 to $7,170,781 in 1860 or an increase of more than six fold. In the meantime the total export trade of the United States had increased only a little more than three fold. In 1860, however, the China trade was less than 2 per cent of the total export trade.

As regards imports from China, there was no such floundering around for cargoes. The staple was tea for which there was a steady and in-creasing demand in America and of which there was a dependable supply in China. In 1844 there were 15,353,518 pounds of tea imported, just double the amount brought in the year of the Cushing treaty.[8]

In silks the figures are very scrappy but it is evident that Chinese silks had almost disappeared from the American market by 1848, and at about the same time raw silk began to be imported in small but increasing amounts. Pongees, or coarse silks, seem to have maintained a small demand throughout the period. These figures are partly accounted for by changes in feminine fashions and partly by the fact that the weaving of silk was being undertaken in America, although the industry was still in its infancy. A very considerable increase in silk goods imported from England indicates either that they were coming to the United States indirectly or that the raw silk was being manufactured in England.

There was a small trade in camphor, largely from the island of Formosa, which was then Chinese territory. The rest of the imports consited of "chow chow" or miscellaneous Chinese notions such as fire crackers, matting, wicker furniture, porcelain, shawls and other embroidered goods, cassia, and many other things which became familiar articles in New England homes.

The total imports from China increased from $4,931,255 in 1844 to $13,566,587 in 1860 or nearly three fold during the sixteen years. This was a little less than the rate of the increase in the total imports to the United States. The China imports comprised only about one-twenty-eighth of the total imports in 1860.

But aside from the general increase in Sino-American trade, the whole commercial relationship began a new phase in 1844. The monopoly system under the so-called hong merchants was abolished, and competitive trade with independent Chinese merchants was inaugurated. Canton ceased to be the staple port and was immediately rivaled and soon outstripped by Shanghai. Customs and tonnage dues became fixed by law rather than by the whims of the customs superintendent (hoppo) and the linguist, and the old system of gifts and bribes became unnecessary. To the merchants of the day, however, these changes were anticipated with mixed feelings. Particularly the American merchants seemed to have enjoyed the hazard and haggle of pre-treaty days-- a system or lack of system which had become increasingly galling and finally intolerable to their

English cousins. The American merchant, then, was dubious about the consequences if the old system was to be abolished. The home offices of the firms, however, accustomed to a more conventional way of doing business, anticipated happy results from the new trade regulations and tariff schedules.

William Appleton of Boston wrote to his agents in Canton in December, 1842:

> By the Overland Mail we learn that a Peace had been concluded between the English and Chinese by which some of the northern ports are to be opened to foreign trade. We hope to hear from you what effect this is likely to have on trade to Canton; we think it must lead to an improved demand for cotton goods, and shall be disappointed if we do not receive faborable sales of the quantity sent out on the Mary Ellen.[9]

Two years later Appleton wrote to Dr. Parker in Canton that Cushing had returned with the new treaty and that he was confident that it would "render the trade with China hereafter more secure against interruptions from misunderstandings with the local authority."[10]

Old China Hands were more cautious. Augustine Heard wrote in April, 1843:

> Foreigners will suffer severe losses if, on account of the opened northern ports, they pour in upon China a very great quantity of western products; for though the consumption of them must, in time, be greatly increased, the change cannot be instantaneious. New habits of business will have to be introduced, at the north, and the people there will require time, both to turn their capital into the channels of trade and to become acquainted with foreigners.[11]

The Americans in China were particularly doubtful about the wisdom of abolishing the hong system and the security it afforded. They feared that it would be difficult to collect debts if the Chinese merchants were not collectively responsible.[12] The credit system would be destroyed. They foresaw that whatever arrangements were made

121

to regularize duties, the local mandarins would manage to squeeze buyers in some new way and imports would be burdened as much as before. They did hope, however, that port charges would be effectively reduced.[13]

The advantages of the hong system were more apparent to the independent American firms than to the English traders who acted as a unit and could at any time bring pressure on the Chinese through the British navy. For instance in December, 1842, a riot occurred in Canton causing considerable damage to the American factory. Commodore Kearney was unable or unwilling (the merchants charged him with lack of vigor in pushing their claims) to get a settlement from the local authorities.[14] The merchants themselves, however, were able to hold the hongs responsible for the losses, leaving them to settle with the officials as best they could. The American claims were paid in full in April, 1843.[15]

They realized that the real difficulty was in dealing with the people, whose temper, in Canton, was not improving. "The people of Canton have committed no new acts of violence," an American wrote in 1843, "but they have threatened to burn down the Factory in which (the English) negotiations are going on. They are by no means contented and though tranquility may continue, it may, on the other hand, be interrupted by the most trifling accident."[16]

Trade was at a standstill while the English and Chinese were negotiating the supplementary treaty at Canton in 1843, but when the new regulations went into effect, business was resumed.[17] In January, 1844, Augustine Heard sold 2500 bales of American cotton and reported that the Chinese prejudice against American staples was being broken down and that a much larger quantity could be sent out the next year.[18] An agent sent up the coast found that there was a good demand for American drills. It was anticipated that Cushing would appoint consuls at the new ports and that this would stimulate trade. "Our raw cotton is not yet liked at the north but it is certainly coming more in favor here; and will eventually supersede the Bombay if prices in America continue low."[19]

Trade was begun in a tentative fashion in the
northern ports in 1844. There was some difficulty
at first because the local mandarins were not
informed of the new trade regulations which had been
agreed to at Canton. Trade in the northern ports
was also delayed because the Canton officials
were loathe to give up a lucrative monopoly which
they have enjoyed so long.[20] Shanghai was very
early recognized as the most valuable of the four
newly opened ports. It was close to the great
emporium of Soochow, commanded the Yangtze valley
and the terminus of the Grand Canal, and was in
easy connection with the finest silk and green
tea areas of China.[21]

At the beginning of 1845, Russell and Company,
the largest American firm in China during this
period, made a summary of the China trade which
gives a comprehensive picture.[22] To them it
appeared that the new system inaugurated by
treaties with England, the United States, and
France had caused a great increase in importation
into China and apparently a wider use of foreign
articles. The export of tea, silk, and silk piece
goods showed little if any increase. The result
was a balance unfavorable to China covered by a
materially increased exportation of silver. It
appeared very doubtful how long the Chinese could
stand this drain, and they felt sure that eventually it would limit the demand for foreign goods.

The opening of China to foreign trade appears
to have been a great boon to the opium trade which
had been steadily increasing since 1830. The consumption of the drug in the two years and a half
prior to 1845 had been at the rate of 35,000
chests a year. A chest contained 133 1/3 pounds
(one picul) and the price, during this period,
averaged $700 per chest. Most of the opium came
from India although Turkey opium was again coming
into use. Most of the American firms undoubtedly
dealt in it to some extent, and Russell and Company
on a rather large scale, although entirely on
commission from British firms. Olyphant and
Company, the one firm that refused to trade in
opium, earned the name of "Zion's Corner." It was
reported that eight or ten vessels owned by
Americans and operated under the American flag were
engaged in the contraband trade in 1849.[23]
Nevertheless it is clear that the bulk of the trade

and an even larger percent of the profits went to the British. Most of the opium was produced on plantations owned by the East India Company, and was taxed heavily by the Empire on exportation.[24] The American share seems to have been largely distributing the opium up and down the coast in small, fast opium clippers.

The effect of opium on American interest is thus described at this time:

> If the opium trade could be abolished there is but little doubt but that goods would be sold to an extent equal the amount now paid for that article, and that those goods would be of American rather than British growth. By such a result, the Americans account would be more nearly balanced in the direct trade with China, and as a consequence the amounts due the United States in London would come hither in specie, instead of as now being appropriated to the liquidation of the bills running upon London from China.[25]

Opium, like bootleg liquor, had the virtue of being salable in ever increasing amounts in China despite depressions, civil wars, anti-foreign sentiments, or governmental opposition. It always commanded cash or could in the interior be readily bartered for exportable goods. Through a comprehensive system of "protection", unnecessary to explain to any American who can recall the prohibition era, the chances of capture and punishment were practically nil. On the other hand the introduction of any legitimate foreign product into China was a slow and laborious process. A demand had to be created. The product had to be carefully adapted to Chinese needs and an attractive chop or trade mark devised. And when these requirements were fulfilled, every disturbance of threat of violence within China or exerted from the outside, immediately stopped the importation.

Russell and Company reported that the consumption of raw cotton had increased somewhat under the new system but still out of a total import of 277,474 bales only 630 were American. Of manufactured cotton, the American shipments had been heavy but the market was not well sustained. The

Chinese still preferred British cotton yarns to American. There was some trade in lead, copper, quicksilver, and ginseng but only in limited quantities.

Based on the records of goods paying duty, American imports to Canton during 1845 amounted to $2,478,048, just about one-fourth the English imports, but more than equal to all the imports of other European states put together.[26]

The fears of the American merchants of the new system was soon justified. Early in 1845 Appleton and Company in Boston complained that a shipment of camphor from Canton was adulterated with a generous admixture of sand.[27] In 1848 a shipment of tea from Sequa, a former hong merchant, was found to be fraudulently mixed and the American buyer in Canton complained: "we are so much in the power of the Chinese that it is an impossibility to prevent it if they are so inclined."[28]

In Canton, with the abolition of the hong system new and irresponsible buyers offered better prices to the foreigners, but sales had to take into account a large element of risk. This led to charges of mishandling and angry defenses passed the American houses and the Canton commission agents.[29]

Trade soon began to shift from Canton, where the hongs had established a reputation for dependability and where debts were secured by joint responsibility, to Shanghai where new merchants were starting from scratch. Americans were convinced that Shanghai was destined to become a great port and needed "only encouragement, or rather indifference from the local authorities to enable it to prosper."[30] Russell and Company established a branch house there in April, 1846.[31] Augustine Heard sent an agent up the coast in July and announced to his clients that he would do business both at Canton and Shanghai thereafter.[32]

The crash came early in February, 1846, when one of the Shanghai Chinese houses heavily indebted to foreign firms failed. The high prices which had attracted American merchants to Shanghai were associated with bad debts.[33] During the spring two more large Chinese firms failed. All three of these firms were represented by Cantonese who were outside the old respectability of the hong system and embarked on large deals without adequate capital.[34] Trade was reduced to barter, or cash (or opium, which was as good as cash), as no credit was available.[35] The relapse, however, was only temporary and Shanghai trade steadily advanced.

The teas bought in Shanghai were cheaper and caused heavy losses on cargoes bought in Canton. Tea which formerly came to Canton was diverted from the inland to Shanghai, where trade was brisk, while the scarcity in Canton raised the prices demanded there.[36] When Appleton sent out an agent in 1848 to purchase teas in China, he went first to Canton but almost immediately transferred to Shanghai.[37] He was convinced that, although buying required more judgment there, the natural location fitted it for the major entrepot.[38] The sharp turn came in 1848-1849.[39]

By 1851, Shanghai was definitely established as the center of American trade. Canton began to decline, for where the tea trade was, there was the heart of the China trade, also. "This was formerly the most busy season of the year in Canton," wrote Richard P. Dana, "but now there is very little doing. Two large ships have sailed hence during the month, the North Carolina and Matilda, the former being almost entirely filled with chow chow goods. The fine clipper Gazelle is loading up in the course of ten days. Her cargo will comprize a considerable portion of chow chow goods."[40] Difficulties in Canton between the natives and the English became mere local incidents which did not interfere with the steady flow of trade.[41]

In 1853 the harbor master at Shanghai reported that for the preceding year American tonnage exceeded that of any other nation. The number of British vessels was 102 with a tonnage of 32,700. There were only 71 American vessels but their tonnage amounted to 40,365. The remainder of the trade of Shanghai consisted of 14 vessels with a tonnage of 2835, divided among the French, Danish, Hamburgers, Spanish, Hawaiians, and Dutch. Even in tea, the American trade almost equalled the British for that year.[42] This competition is

reflected in the complaint of Russell and Company:
"The Challenge is bound for London and is opposed
by the local Insurance offices here, on the pretext that her spars are not in good order, although the real motive is said to be the size
and speed of the ship. The obstacles thrown in
the way of American ships bound to Europe only go
to show the necessity of an American Insurance
Office fully capable of protecting American ships
from the growing jealousy of British capital and
ship owners."[43]

The American ships were, in fact, handicapped
by their large size, averaging 710 tons. Many of
them could not enter the smaller ports and rivers
and were excluded from coasting trade. The English
ships averaged only 310 tons. The total English
shipping still exceeded the American in 1859, when
the former had 1391 ships in the China trade with
a tonnage of 431,308, while the United States had
457 ships with an aggregate of 322,946 tons. The
total of foreign ships in China was 4013 amounting
to 1,247,656 tons.[44]

The British merchants always had the advantage
of opium. "They send the Drug into the country,"
complained Captain Cole, speaking of the practices
of Jardine and Company, "and make contracts for new
Teas paying for them in this article. Opium in the
country is considered quite equal to cash . . . .
Their recources (sic) and influence are great
indeed. Steamers and sailing clippers with their
house flag predominate on the coast and they are
certainly supposed to have great advantage in
tea purchases."[45]

The trade of the bustling new port, growing up
without the traditions of monopoly and restraint,
was totally different from the "steady old custom"
of Canton. The Chinese traders who controlled teas
and silks were, on the whole, the superiors of the
Western traders. "It is acknowledged by all that
the Chinamen have it all their own way in
Shanghai."[46] It was hoped that if the Yangtze were
opened to trade, the foreigners could deal directly
with the tea farmers and get away from this
"Algerian Club of Tea Sellers in Shanghai who have
grown so immensely rich and powerful that if anyone
of their associates should make a sale without con-
sulting the Board certain death would be his

portion. When we can brake (sic) up this system of
making tea purchases, then we shall see some sport
in the tea markets."[47]

The persistent efforts of the American merchants to establish American goods in the China
market thus constitute the most interesting and
significant aspect of this period. As a result
China began to assume the position of a market
rather than solely as a source of desirable cargo
that could not be procured elsewhere. The advantage
the English had in the ever-wanted opium was
gradually overcome by the patient development of a
demand in China for American coal, cotton, piece
goods and other manufactures.

The Chinese, long accustomed to the India
staple, were prejudiced against American raw cotton
but the American exporters were confident that in
time their staple would come to enjoy the same preference in China that it did in Europe.[48] It was
loaded at New Orleans and was useful in ballasting
the ship for the outward voyage and if it would
sell in China for cost plus freight, it was worth
while to the trade. Even if it had to be disposed
of below cost, there was always the hope of building
up a trade that would become profitable.[49] By
1845 American cotton was being sold in Canton at as
good rates as the Madras and Bombay staples,[50] and
it was gradually introduced into the northern ports.

The introduction of manufactured cotton goods
was even more vital, particularly to New England
houses. The cargo of the Mary Ellen sent out by
Appleton in 1841 gives an idea of the trade. She
carried 256 bales of cotton sheeting, 600 bales of
cotton drillings, 4500 pigs of lead, and 26,000
Mexican dollars. The cargo was consigned to
Augustine Heard with instructions to dispose of it
quickly, even without a profit, because more
cottons would follow, and the price would be de-
pressed if they were allowed to accumulate. The
return cargo was, of course, tea.[51]

In 1844 a large shipment of cotton flannels
was sent out, hoping the Chinese could be induced
to use them, particularly in the northern ports.[52]
They were new to the trade, however, and considerable difficulty was experienced in getting rid
of them. Every devise was used to get American

cottons to the people. "We purpose to land about two thirds of the parcel in Canton," wrote Russell and Company of the cargo of the Loo-Choo in 1844, "to place a few with our agents at Macao and Hong Kong for sale; to send small parcels to the Eastern Ports, and also to make trial of them in our opium vessels on the coast, for sale to the floating population they meet with--besides making trial of a portion at Manila."

A sample cargo in 1847 indicates an important change in the nature of the trade since 1840. The ship was laden with pig lead and cottons, the latter rather more diversified than formerly, but instead of the Mexican dollars of former years was supplied with bills in London for 15,000 pounds sterling.[53]

The Mexican war sent a ripple through the China trade because of the possibility of England's becoming involved in it.[54] The American trade was so tied up with London, particularly with Baring Brothers, that any interruption of communication would have been disastrous.[55] There was also the possibility of Congress putting a tax on tea, which had been on the free list since 1832, to pay for expenses of the Mexican campaign.[56]

The Taiping Rebellion in China and its excrescences were a much more serious deterrent to the establishment of new markets. Richard P. Dana wrote in 1852:

> The political disturbances in the neighboring provinces have again broken out and nearly ruined the market for imports, as the dealers are afraid to send any goods into the country and hence do not purchase.
>
> Had it not been for this, the Canton market should easily have taken a few cargoes of American cottons at fair prices. We shall probably be obliged to send these goods to Shanghai. That market has taken off an astounding quantity of these goods this season and still appears to have a vigorous appetite.[57]

The next year, when the Rebellion had still further paralyzed the trade, Dana wrote: "I fancy that the 'Drill Dragon' will say 'no can' when they offer him high with Yankee cloth, and will keep his jaws closed tight so that we shall not be able to stick in a piece of Drills edgeways."[58]

The New England merchants were ready to adapt their product to suit the Chinese market. Captain Cole noticed that the junks at Foochow were beginning to use cloth sails and recommended the sending out of a heavier drill that would fill this need. He suggested that an attractive chop with a dragon or a peacock, in two colors, if possible, be used to make the product sell.[59] Samuel Hooper went to some pains to get up a junk chop for his drills sent to the China market.[60]

A curious evidence of the groping for products to send to China was the sending of a keg of cobalt with the explanation, "It is produced from a mine in the western part of our country and was sent to us with the request that we would send it to China to ascertain its value there and the extent to which it might be sold there." It was presumed that it could be used for "painting azure blue on porcelain and glazed copper vessels."[61]

When small coasting steamers began to be used in China, there developed a market for coal, which formed a good ballast for the outward voyage. A small lot was sent out on the _Egeria_ in 1858.[62] "The Chinese are beginning to like our anthracite better than their own," wrote Captain Cole, "and even if the country around Nankin should be cleared by the Imperialists and the communications with coal districts be open it always has commanded 8 taels here in Shanghai. But if the great Yangtse Kang is opened to steam navigation, which it must certainly be within a short time, vast quantities of our coal would be wanted."[63]

California figured in the China trade on several scores; the extension of the proposed transcontinental railroad by means of a steam route across the Pacific, the gold dust sent to China, and the Chinese laborers sent to the "Golden Mountain" to supply the manifold needs of a new and expanding community.

Before the discovery of gold, Thomas Butler King, chairman of the committee on naval affairs reported to the House on a "Steam mail-packet route to China" and rail communication from the Mississippi to the Pacific. Shanghai was to be the goal; the route was to follow the great northern circle via the Aleutian Islands.[64] There was no reason why manifest distiny should stop at California.

> There is a god in History, and the finger of an Almighty providence is evident in many events which have marked the last three years' march of America. More than human wisdom has thrown wide that western portal of our land, and welcomed over its threshold the natives of a nation old as tradition, and until now, as immobile as their own stone-eyed Boodh. When China, the hoary type of antiquity, embraced America, the young bride of futurity, we may be sure that it was prophetic of more than mere gold-digging for both.[65]

In that orotund age it was clearly the duty and destiny of America to have commercial intercourse with all the world. No eastern despot had the power to alienate our natural right to trade with his subjects.

The proposal was repeated with more specific details in 1853. A line of six steamers, subsidized by Congress was to make fortnightly trips from California to China, touching at the Sandwich Islands and Japan "so soon as communications are opened with that Empire." The plan was set forth as the only means of meeting and overcoming England's overwhelming preponderance of trade.[66] A report was made to the House of Representatives which declared that the effect of the scheme would be "to revolutionize in our favor the commerce of the world, and more rapidly advance our greatness, wealth, and power than any event which has occurred since the adoption of the Constitution." R. P. Forbes, long with Russell and Company at Canton, regarded some of the claims as extravagant, and deflated some of the sentimental altruism tacked on the project, but approved the plan itself. With a shrewd eye trained by long experience in the East he observed: "Some delay in the progress of China must result from the present unsettled state of the country, but when the rebels have done quarrelling with the Imperialists and with each other, the progress will begin."[67]

The enthusiasts for this expansive policy in China would not have the United States copy England "in winning triumphs with the sword" nor pursue the "strategic and jesuitical policy of Russia" but would have our merchants peacefully penetrate the Asiatic countries and concentrate on the Pacific rather than the Atlantic, and to be ready "with something more of original enterprise, to profit by the opening which the Chinese revolution may produce, and advance more boldy with our wares and fabrics into a quarter of the globe to which we have been too long comparative strangers."[68]

The hand of God was ever working new marvels. "The gates of China, hermetically sealed for thousands of years, are opened by no mere mortal hand," wrote Dr. Scott of New Orleans,

> but not before the same hand had peopled
> the solitudes of the great southern
> ocean, and cities and nations with the
> language and commerce, the literature,
> the religion and the institutions of
> liberty had arisen to meet the salutations
> of the celestial empire with responsive
> salaams. Suddenly a new nation, as it were,
> had sprung up on the opposite shore of the
> ocean that washes Chinese territory; and
> thither by Providence, are gathered the
> surplus hosts of the world.[69]

The zeal was so great that it was even proposed to cultivate poppies in California to provide opium for the China trace. This scheme had the double advantage of enriching Americans and at the same time enabling them to compete with England and deprive her of the profitable opium traffic, "and God knows if the British could go on misruling India as they do, without these millions." The writer observes complacently that California opium "very likely would create a commercial revolution in the east, the sequel of which can be but good to the United States' trade and industry and mischievous to the proud rulers of the east."[70]

The news of the discovery of gold in California reached China early in 1849. "The Chinese are perhaps the only people who do not realize the excitement growing out of the late discovery," wrote Russell and Company. "Some 8 or 10 vessels have however sailed from here taking away our redundant and unemployed foreign population with perhaps some advantage to those who remain." The first ship to bring the news brought also three hundred dollars worth of gold dust and it was predicted that China would be a good market for the metal, after the constant drain of specie for many years.[71]

The demand for vessels for California diverted direct trade from the United States, but many of them resumed the old indirect route which had been familiar in fur trade days.[72] Gold dust, although it did not replace credit on London, became a regular part of the funds with which American ships purchased return cargoes. The Oxnard[73] carried $23,554 in gold dust to Canton in 1850.[74] The Cygnet, the same year, carried $10,000 in gold dust and $6930.25 in coin.[75]

The Chinese did not long remain indifferent to the lure of El Dorado. In Canton terminology, California became "Golden Mountain"[76] and the demand for passage gave employment to American vessels. Richard P. Dana wrote that the Witchcraft and the "fine clipper Challenge" were carrying Chinese passengers to California. The latter's capacity, according to governmental regulations, being 600. The fare was $50 each. He wrote in March 1852, that since January some thirty ships had left for California and twenty-five others were under dispatch. The number of Cantonese emigrants that year would amount to 16,000.[77]

The emigration was kept up by favorable reports from those already in the land of gold, and gave considerable impetus to the trade. "The Swordfish clipper is just in from California and reports that the Celestial, Flying Fish and Golden Gate were to follow immediately. The Game Cock is daily expected from Bombay. This ship as well as the Surprize from England are making long passages for such clippers."[78]

These years from 1844-1860 were years of expansion for American trade with China. Most of the diplomatic problems of the period are traceable in the trade and in so far as a policy was formulated during the period, that policy grew out of the experience of the American traders. The most conspicuous and consistent factor is the development of the trade in New England Cottons. The houses in Canton and Shanghai came to see more and more clearly that their best interests were served when China was least disturbed, either internally or by pressure from the outside. This was not merely the traditional interest of the businessman in the status quo, but was due to the nature of the American stake. English trade with its solid base in the opium traffic and its headquarters at Hong Kong was far less dependent on the good will of the people in general. The Americans had to get the Chinese to like their goods, and even to like their merchants and prefer them to the English traders. The Americans had far less to gain and far more to fear from high-handed methods against China.

The situation, in which competition with the English was becoming stronger, was complicated by the dependence of the American trade on London credit. This was partially overcome by the increased export of American manufactured goods and was temporarily checked by the export of gold dust, but nevertheless remained very real and large throughout the period.

The California factor was important during this period but did not remain significant long after 1860. The reaction against Chinese immigration soon set in and western United States was soon far more absorbed in development and in the exploitation of natural resources than in commercial expansion. Although the China trade continued to increase, its relative importance steadily declined.

CHAPTER 7
ATTITUDES OF CHINESE OFFICIALS TOWARD
THE UNITED STATES, 1841-1861

The enigma of Chinese psychology and of the
mental attitudes of Chinese toward Europeans and
Americans has long intrigued Westerners. Every
tourist and businessman in China has wondered in
his occasional reflective moments, what the rickshaw
coolie or the domestic servant "really thinks" of
him. Diplomats have been at a loss to understand the
point of view of their Chinese and Manchu colleagues
and, failing of any solution, have either attributed
to them their own feelings or attitudes or have
dismissed them as "inscrutable Orientals." Nevertheless, an understanding of Sino-Western relations on
any level must discover some basic Chinese point of
view on which to function.

Superficial and somewhat farcical explanations
of China's attitude toward the West have long been
current in Western literature. Perhaps the best
known is derived from the "mandates" and letters of
the emperor of the Ch'ien-lung period to George III
of England on the occasion of Earl Macartney's
mission to China in 1793.

The preamble to one of these "mandates" is often
cited to show the haughty presumptuousness and super-
cilious condescension of the Chinese Emperor toward

Chapter 3: "Attitudes of Chinese Officials Toward
the United States, 1841-1861," in Earl Swisher,
China's Management of the American Barbarians
(Association for Asian Studies Monograph No. 2,
1953), 39-54.

the upstart king of a small and distant isle. The text is familiar:[1]

> You, O King, live beyond the confines of many seas, nevertheless, impelled by your humble desire to partake of the benefits of civilization, you have dispatched a mission respectfully bearing your memorial. Your Envoy has crossed the seas and paid his respects at my Court on my birthday. To show your devotion, you have also sent offerings of your country's produce.

Somewhat less familiar is the letter of the Tao-kuang emperor addressed to President Tyler on the occasion of Caleb Cushing's mission to China in 1843-1844. The letter is much shorter and therefore less condescending than the earlier one to George III. The Emperor "hopes the President is well," commends Cushing for the long distance he has traversed to come to China, and is considerably relieved that the American envoy has agreed to negotiate at Canton with Ch'i-ying (Kiying). "We could not bear to order him to submit to the hardships of further travel (and thus) he was prevented from coming to Peking and being received in audience."[2]

Numerous similar examples of Chinese official attitudes toward the West, during the period before 1861, could be cited. These are interesting and important but they all bear the stamp of diplomatic language. Condescending as these Chinese documents appear to the nationalistically minded Westerner of the nineteenth century, they were still couched in the polite forms reserved for strangers from afar and guests of the empire. To the Chinese officials of the day, these imperial mandates appeared magnanimous and probably better than the foreigners deserved.[3] Formal letters from the emperor to king or president can hardly represent fully the attitudes of Chinese officialdom toward the West.

As a small contribution to the larger topic of China's reaction to the Western impact, the present chapter presents certain attitudes toward European states, but concentrates on the attitudes of Chinese officials toward one Western state, namely the United States, over a limited period, 1841-1861. The materials used differ in type from those cited above in that they are limited to opinions and evaluations current within the Chinese official family circle. The materials used herein are exclusively those in

circulation between province and court, between
governor general and emperor, or between provincial
official and Grand Council in Peking. They represent
quite a different category from the formal exchange
between states, even those between kings of lowly
"tributary" states and the Son of Heaven.

The purpose of this chapter is to present some
two hundred examples of Chinese official expressions
of attitudes toward Western states and individuals.
These examples have been culled from several thousands
which occur in the one hundred and sixty chuan or
chapters of Chinese documents covering her foreign
relations of this period (1841-1861), all of which
have been examined with some care. The examples
cited range from the meaningless cliche to shrewd
observations gleaned from first-hand experience
in dealing with Europeans and Americans. An attempt
has been made to classify these opinions according
to type and subject matter and also to show some
early evolutionary tendency in the direction of the
formulation of a Chinese foreign policy.

Before passing judgment on the Chinese officials
and statesmen of this period, it should be borne in
mind that very few of them had any extensive contact
with foreigners. As stated earlier, the trading
contact at Canton was restricted to the hong merchant
and the hoppo (customs commissioner) and it was but
rarely that the local magistrate, the governor, or
the governor general, even at Canton, had any personal
relations with foreigners. After 1842, the contacts
between Western commissioners and local officials became more common but the relationship was still
outside the bounds of routine officialdom and no
specialized department of foreign affairs existed.

During this period, Chinese officials were faced
with a baffling and unwanted situation and were
forced to deal with it as best they could. The first
tendency, naturally, was to force the new wine into
old casks. When this did not succeed, a few Chinese
officials began to experiment with new casks which
could contain the strong and corrosive element
introduced from the West. This procedure required a
kind of experimentation and curiosity for which the
tradition-bound Confucian official was ill suited.

The clues to a new foreign policy for China came
from outside the official circle. Hong merchants in
Canton and newly rich gentry in Shanghai were probably

the first to recognize the possibilities of dealing
advantageously with foreigners, but their ideas
gradually permeated the lower ranks of officialdom.
Before the end of the period, however, the beginnings
of a new realism are apparent in the opinions of a
few top-ranking Chinese officials. By the end of the
Hsien-feng period, it is possible to detect a new
kind of statesmanship in the ranks of Chinese officialdom.

At the outset, the reader must be reminded again
that the Chinese government, down to the enforced
establishment in 1861 of a foreign office, at first
called the Tsungli Yamen, dealt with European
countries and the United States in a special category
called "barbarian affairs" (i-wu). This category
was distinguished from China's relations and correspondence with Mongolia and other Asiatic states,
including Russia, through the Court of Dependencies
(Li Fan Yuan),[4] and with numerous tributary states,
through the Board of Rites (Li Pu).[5] This special
category is attested in various official sources.
For example, the collection of documents which is
the basis for the major portion of this book is
called "The Management of Barbarian Affairs from
Beginning to End" (Ch'ou Pan I Wu Shih Mo). As
another example, when the British forces captured
Canton in 1857-1858, they found in the governor
general's yamen a file of British, American, and
French treaties and correspondence labeled the
"Management of Barbarian Affairs Yellow Chest" (Pan
Li Wu Huang Hsiang).[6] Again, when the British and
French looted and burned the Summer Palace near
Peking in 1860, they destroyed one copy of the
foreign office file labeled "Records of the Four
Barbarians" (Ssu I Ko Tang).[7] The Grand Secretariat,
in an official edict as late as 1858, referred to
Yeh Ming-ch'en at Canton as "Imperial Commissioner
in-charge-of Barbarian Affairs" (Ch'in-ch'ai ta-ch'en,
pan-li i-wu).[8] Thus the official use of the term
"barbarian affairs" is well established.

Not only was the term "barbarian affairs" used
officially throughout the period to 1861, but it
clearly carried overtones of contempt for foreigners
and this attitude was, on occasion, utilized to
arouse the populace against Westerners in China.
When Lo Tun-yen was engaged in recruiting local
militia in Kwangtung in 1858, he wrote:[9]

As to Your official's previous statements
regarding the cutting of a great seal to furnish

a recruiting caption, because popular indignation against barbarians was great, ever since the barbarians entered the city the local officials have forbidden any use of the term 'barbarian affairs,' even going to the length of referring in writings and public documents to 'barbarian affairs' as 'ocean affairs' and as the 'affairs of foreign countries,' not daring to revile them with the term 'barbarian.' Your officials, after repeated deliberation, insisted on the cutting on the seal of the inscription 'Management of Barbarian Affairs' to enable us to arouse popular feeling.

Another Chinese official, Ho Kuei-ch'ing, governor of Liang-chiang in 1858, made a clear statement of terminology:[10]

Those barbarians who trade back and forth are called barbarian merchants; those who superintend the trading affairs of the various ports and take the surplus for their country's use, were first called public envoys. Now they presumptuously call themselves ministers, while we regard them as 'barbarian chiefs'.

At the same time that Chinese officialdom used this derogatory terminology to apply to foreigners, it frowned upon American presumptuousness in using the imperial pronoun Chen for the President of the United States,[11] was scornful of the use of an equalitarian expression like "Chinese and foreigners are one family,"[12] and was indignant when the British (1858) "did not allow the use of the two words 'foreign devil' (fan-kuei), and when proclamations of the Imperial Commissioners of 'Great Britain' (Ta-ying-kuo) and 'Great France' (Ta-fa-kuo) were put up everywhere in Canton."[13]

There is thus no question that the term "barbarian" was commonly and officially used in nineteenth century China. Nor is its use new in Chinese literature. The term i is used in classical Chinese to denote "rude and barbarous tribes," especially "those on the east of China, of whom there were nine tribes."[14] These tribes, said Confucius, "even with their princes were still not equal to China with her anarchy."[15] Mencius said, "I have heard of men using the doctrines of our great land to change barbarians, but I have never yet heard of any being changed by barbarians."[16]

These barbarian tribes surrounding the Middle Kingdom are represented throughout the classics as peoples unschooled in the writings and philosophies of China, but eager to be "transformed by the virtue" of China. "When (T'ang) pursued his work (of civilization) in the east, the rude tribes of the west murmured. . . Their cry was--why does he make us last?"[17] In the Book of History (Shu Ching), the term i is modified by various place names, such as the Huai-i, Lai-i, Ho-i, and K'un-i, as well as the "island barbarians" and the "southern barbarians," just as in the Manchu dynasty it was qualified as the "English barbarians," the "French barbarians," and the "American barbarians."

The colloquial equivalent of the classical "barbarian" is "foreign devil," and in some districts "foreign dog."[18] The British bitterly resented the use of i or "barbarian" applied to them, and consistently refused official communications in which the term was used.[19] As soon as they were in a position to dictate to the Chinese, as in Canton in 1858, they sternly forbade the use of "opprobrious language," either spoken or written.[20] Americans were less sensitive about what the Chinese called them and the most distinguished American sinologist of the nineteenth century, S. Wells Williams, maintained that while "foreign devil" was disrespectful, i or barbarian merely meant that the person so designated could not read Chinese. He said that "used as a general term, without opprobrious addition, I is as well adapted as any other to denote all foreigners."[21]

Having established the fact of general official use of the term i or barbarian, our main interest is to ascertain how it was used in official papers and what it connoted. The Chinese documents dealing with foreign countries, prior to 1861, consist on the one hand mainly of memorials from the governors general, governors, other provincial officials, occasional censors, and imperial princes, all addressed to the court of Peking, and, on the other hand, of edicts, issued in the name of the emperor by the Grand Council and the Grand Secretariat. These documents circulated only within the circle of Chinese officialdom and so are completely unguarded. They are entirely free from polite phrases or diplomatic embroidery.

Many of the characterizations of Britons, Frenchmen, and Americans as "barbarians" appear to

140

be conventional and, as official <u>cliches</u>, occur over and over in the texts with apparently little meaning. One of the most persistent official expressions is that "Barbarians are by nature inscrutable,"[22] which neatly counters Bret Harte and Kipling. Other common expressions are: "Barbarians are inherently cunning and malicious";[23] "Barbarians are by nature impatient and without understanding of values";[24] "Inconstancy is a fundamental trait of barbarians."[25] Barbarians were also insatiable,[26] avaricious,[27] and they "cunningly devised many plans."[28] Some of the expressions used are more derogatory. "Although barbarians have the feelings of dogs and sheep, they still have regard for their own interests."[29] "Their dog-sheep nature is fundamentally hard to subdue."[30]

Beyond these generalizations were observations which appear to be first hand, and to represent actual evaluations of "barbarian" character as distinguished from Chinese and Manchu traits. For instance, such statements as "It is the nature of barbarians to be impatient,"[31] and "Barbarians think only of profit,"[32] are easily identifiable. The harassed Chinese official on the frontier also saw an element of weakness in the Western temperament: "Barbarians are most resentful of annoyances and if these accumulate perhaps eventually they will be discouraged."[33] On the other hand the barbarians were "fickle and inconstant, perverse in feelings and words, not by any means to be managed by mere words."[34] Reasoning with them was futile because they "respected strength and ridiculed weakness."[35]

Repeated contact with Western fleets and landing forces convinced the Chinese officials that "barbarian nature is inscrutable and our defense must be rigorous,"[36] but they reassured themselves that while barbarians ". . .are naturally arrogant and anxious to excel, craftly and greedy for gain, . . .once badly beaten, they will refrain from opposition."[37] Military force was the only argument they could understand because they were "suspicious and liked action."[38] The combination of the subjective and traditional Chinese official attitude with an enforced realism is well expressed in the statement, "Although these barbarians have all the characteristics of human beings, they are unusually cruel and cunning and depend on the strength of their ships and the superiority of their cannon."[39] The Chinese officials were no longer dealing in generalities, but were giving expression to the hard fact of Western material strength.

Adding to the consternation of the Chinese official was the discovery that there were different kinds of barbarians. When a British ship was wrecked on Formosa in 1842, the local official reported "that the eighteen white barbarians captured include the leader . . .and two accomplices, who are all red barbarians. Besides, there are four persons . . .(who are) also red barbarians. Because their hair is slightly yellow, they are called red barbarians. Along with the eleven white barbarians, they are all natives of the English mother country . . .In addition, there are thirty black barbarians, all natives of Bombay." The Formosan official professed horror at the violent attitude of the British and reminded the emperor that "these island barbarians from ancient times onward have known only love of gain and fundamentally are not different from dogs and sheep."[40]

Another early memorialist lapsed into the colloquial in distinguishing the different kinds of barbarians: "White Devils are fond of women, Red Devils are fond of money, Black Devils are fond of wine."[41] According to still current Cantonese terminology, these three categories would refer to Portuguese, British (or Dutch), and Sikhs (or Parsees) respectively. Even as late as 1859, Prince Seng-ko-lin-ch'in was confused by S. Wells Williams' refusal to acknowledge as an American a captured Canadian soldier, and was not particularly helped by Williams' explanation "that the soldiers of the three countries are interchangeable, that America contained Englishmen and Frenchmen, and when there was fighting, the flag was the only criterion."[42]

By the middle of the century, however, the principal Western countries represented in China were well known and the Chinese official began to make comparisons. "While all barbarians are insatiably avaricious by nature, Russian barbarians are inscrutable and French barbarians are crafty."[43] "The barbarians' attitude is not uniform. The English and French defy reason and, while the Russians and Americans are affable, they too want to satisfy their demands, so there is no distinction between them . . . Thus, while Russia and America realize English and French tyranny and presumptuousness, they do not prevent it; on the contrary they both condone their acts, sitting by to get the fisherman's share."[44]

The allusion is to the Chinese fable of a kingfisher that seized a clam, which in turn closed on
the kingfisher's bill. Neither was willing to let
go until a fisherman came along and took them both.
According to another observation, "the English barbarians' craftiness is manifold, their proud tyranny
is uncontrollable; Americans do nothing but follow
their direction."[45]

   The British, of course, were the prototype of all
barbarians. The Chinese found them "overbearing and
tyrannical,"[46] "unusually cunning,"[47] "by nature and
appearance treacherous and unusually faithless,"[48]
"devoted to trade."[49] and "fundamentally not different
from dogs and sheep."[50]   Besides these generalizations,
there was an occasional specific example of the Englishman's actions in China, such as the report from
Canton during British-French occupation, 1858, of
" . . .having their chair bearers . . .wear red but-
tons and peacock feathers [Chinese official insignia],
intentionally insulting China, which was even more
obnoxious. We hear that this is all Harry Parkes'
doing."[51] Which, we might add, it was.[52]

   The French were identified in the Chinese mind
with mercenary soldiers and Catholicism. When
de Bourboulon came to China in 1854, his position
was analyzed as follows: "Although the French barbarians' trade is not large, their military strength
is very great. Whenever the other barbarians need
soldiers they all make sure their strength. Their
nationals in China are engaged only in the propagation
of Catholicism and they have long since asked permission to establish a Catholic Church in the capital, to
preach in the North, and to travel throughout the
interior."[53] The Chinese were convinced that the
other Western countries were absolutely dependent
on France for troops: "So these barbarians, using
this to their own advantage, sit back and get rich
like so many merchants."[54] It was the good fortune
of the Canton Imperial Commissioner Yeh Ming-ch'en
to discover why French trade with China was slight.
"In the one item of tea, the barbarian traders of
this country [France] do not trade much with our
Chinese merchants. After persistent inquiry it has
been learned that this country's everyday hot drink
is called coffee, which is produced in barbarian
lands. This takes the place of Chinese tea, while
England and America cannot get along without Chinese
tea."[55]

Russia comes into the picture only at the very end of the period and Chinese officials were generally distrustful of her. Even when, in 1860, Russia offered to train and equip a modern Chinese army, Prince Kung shied off. "As these barbarians are naturally crafty with rich promises and honeyed words, Your officials could hardly be sure they were not harboring other purposes."[56]

The United States presented a confusing and conflicting problem to the Chinese officials. They were inclined to think that Americans "compared with the Russian barbarians are trustworthy and their speech reasonable, but they are very suspicious and obstinate."[57] They were, hopefully, thought to "resent the English barbarians and revere China."[58] Geographically, the United States was regarded as being even further to the west than Europe, just as we regarded China as the "Far East." Pacific Ocean consciousness was very late in developing and there was no Commodore Perry to explain to China, as he did to Japan, that both Japan and China were just "off the coast of California." The Chinese had a hazy picture of the United States as "an isolated place outside the pale, solitary and ignorant."[59] One can imagine Peter Parker trying diligently to get across a picture of the New England trade, of the great open spaces, and of the hardy virtues of the frontiersman, but all China understood was that America was "maritime, uncultivated, and primitive."[60]

When Caleb Cushing arrived to negotiate the first treaty in 1844, his bearing and language were regarded as respectful and obedient, and he was given credit for sincerity in conforming with Chinese customs and admiring Chinese principles, but the court was concerned about a medium of communication. To the Americans, "living outside the pale, (our) language is unintelligible." How, in Heaven's name, could a letter be addressed to them? Ch'i-ying replied:[61]

> Your slave begs to note that the location of the United States is in the far West. Of all the countries it is the most uncivilized and remote. Now they hope for the Imperial Favor of granting a special Imperial Mandate which can be kept forever. We have both commended the sincerity of their love of justice and strengthened their determination of turning toward culture. The different races of the

world are all grateful for Imperial charity.
It is only that the said country is in an
isolated place outside the pale, solitary and
ignorant. Not only in the forms of edicts
and laws are they entirely unversed, but if
the meaning be rather deep, they would probably
not even be able to comprehend. It would seem
that we must be somewhat simple and use words
that will express our meaning.

Ch'i-ying goes on to recommend a Manchu text,
although he himself (a Manchu closely related to the
imperial family) was unable to write the formal
Manchu scirpt required in official correspondence,
because "the people of the said country have occasionally been to Russia and place the greatest value
on Manchu letters."[62] Incidentally, Caleb Cushing,
in preparation for his diplomatic mission to China,
had studied Manchu in preference to Chinese.

After the Treaty of Wang-hsia was signed,
Ch'i-ying, possibly from materials furnished him
by Cushing, presented the court a thumbnail sketch
of American history:[63]

. . .America was originally a large continent
in the extreme west, as different from China
as night from day, a vast country with a sparse
population. Before the Ming (1368-1644), no one
knew the country. . .Although she established
her country not more than a few decades ago,
her territory is broad, her people diligent, and
her products abundant. Hence of all the barbarians of the west, which along with England
and France are regarded as great powers, only
the United States is noteworthy, while Holland
and Spain, although established previously, on
the contrary do not come up to the recent status
of the said country.

Ch'i-ying felt that the United States should be
rewarded for her peaceful and respectful attitude,
but could hardly be allowed to go to Peking as "the
said country has never come to court or paid tribute.
With the laws of the Heavenly Dynasty they are not
fully acquainted."[64]

The United States was regarded as a particularly
difficult problem. From time to time Chinese officials
saw the advantage of favoring her with an imperial
audience as a means of getting American support against

145

England and France, but they could never see just how it could be facilitated. The Americans were friendly, but they seemed to have no sense of dignity or understanding of ceremony. I-liang, governor general of Liang-chiang in 1853, expressed this contradiction:[65]

It is noted that the outside dependencies conquered by our Dynasty all have annual presentations, and the liege officials of the various countries paying tribute, after they arrive at the capital, must first practice the ritual of bowing and kneeling. Thereafter they are ordered to be presented according to rank. Besides never having been in the class admitted to audience, the United States ordinarily has no official costumes, and still they claim equal rank for themselves and ignorantly puff themselves up. They are not worthy of consideration. How can we treat them like the various dependent states and cause the development of other difficulties? Yet it is impolitic to treat them with unusual courtesy and cause the gradual budding of covetous desires.

The problem of dealing with the United States was made more difficult by her lack of sinologists. Ch'i-ying complained in 1844:[66]

. . .The Americans' difficulty of understanding is much greater than the English barbarians' because the English barbarians had Morrison and others. Although they were artful and cunning they were somewhat conversant with Chinese written and spoken language and when there was business one could discuss it with them. The American barbarians have only Parker and Bridgman who do not know many Chinese characters. They are versed only in the Cantonese local dialect, with the result that it is hard to understand each other's point of view, and a great deal of energy is consumed.

The Chinese officials gradually became convinced that they could expect nothing but good intentions from the United States and that no assistance, either against the British or against the Taipings, was forthcoming. Even the most hopeful complained "that the Americans ordinarily speak respectfully but are taking advantage of the present situation to make demands; while they speak of 'helping to put down rebellion,' absolutely no faith can be placed in them."[67]

The personalities of individual Americans made no great impression upon Chinese officialdom during this period, probably because of the language difficulty. A gifted linguist like the English Sir Harry Parkes made a much greater impression, adverse though it was, upon them. It was observed that the American "Chief McLane's language and actions, compared to the English chief, Bowring, were fairly respectful and obedient," but "his attitude was still inscrutable."[68] He did receive, however, one of the few specific credits conceded by Chinese officials to foreigners during this period. Ho Kuei-ch'ing said that "it was the American Chief McLane who decided that as the Hung [i.e., the Taiping] rebels had none of the five relationships wu-lun or moral obligations nor even a criminal law they were not worth consideration, and so he shifted American policy in our direction."[69] Humphrey Marshall is given the dubious honor of weakening the white man's solidarity in China. One official observed "that of the various countries trading at Shanghai, only Consul Alcock and Vice Consul Thomas Wade are most crafty. Last year American Commissioner Marshall told Wu Chien-chang confidentially that their attitude was inscrutable."[70]

The only American commissioner, to 1861, who knew any Chinese was Dr. Peter Parker, and he, like Sir Harry Parkes, was singled out by the Chinese officials for attack. They said that "his mentality was inscrutable,"[71] and offered an elaborate explanation for his warped mind:[72]

. . .After the American envoy, McLane, went home, last winter Parker replaced him and came to Canton. This chief was originally an American physician, had been in Canton for twenty years, and was generally regarded as crafty. In 1854, when the Cantonese rebels were making trouble, this chief had secret relations with various rebel leaders and besides he boasted to various barbarian merchants that the rebels were sure to succeed. Then when the government troops reduced the rebels to complete submission, the chief lost so much face that in the summer of last year he went home of his own accord. Unexpectedly, after McLane went home due to illness, the king of that country, as he [Parker] had been in

147

Canton for many years, sent him back to Canton to take over the duties as envoy. Chief Parker still cherished resentment in his heart and was determined to find other expressions for his personal views and to silence people's ridicule.

It was one thing for the Chinese official to identify and attempt to understand the barbarian on the border; it was another thing to know how to handle him. One basic principle was that "the laws of the Heavenly Court being established cannot suffer the least change."[73] The barbarian must be dealt with within the frame of the Chinese constitution. The emperor "regards Chinese and outsiders with the same benevolence; those who obey, he soothes; those who rebel, he chastises."[74] When the Americans sought the advantages that Britain had gained in 1842-1843, this traditional formula was applied. "Naturally (we) should treat them equally and not give rise to occasions for disappointment, encouraging admiration and gratitude in them, and further strengthen their sincerity in turning toward civilization."[75]

Another classical principle, and the one most often cited and hopefully clung to throughout the nineteenth century, was to "use barbarians to curb barbarians."[76] This might be applied negatively, to prevent the powers from getting together: "Divide and rule";[77] or positively: "Play them off and encourage them until they destroy one another."[78] It was reasoned that "as dogs and sheep are naturally inconstant, it should not be hard to separate them and, by using barbarians to curb barbarians, to sow mutual disaffection and gradually weaken them."[79]

It was regarded as hopeless to apply to Europeans and Americans even the forms used in dealing with Annam or Liu-ch'iu. "These people outside the pale, in regard to the designations and forms are in utter darkness. If we use our documentary forms to determine authoritatively their rank, even if we wore out our tongues and parched our lips we could not avoid the smiling response of a deaf man."[80] Consequently it was better to rule barbarians with misrule and not try to rationalize. Ch'i-ying expressed this point in 1844, in reporting his negotiations with Cushing:[81]

As the barbarians were born and bred in outer wilderness, there is much in the institutes of the Heavenly Court that they do not understand but as they always pretend to understand, it is

148

hard to explain reasonably. For instance, the
Emperor's transmitted words are all passed on by
the Grand Councillors but the barbarians regard
them as <u>Vermilion Endorsements</u>. If shown not to
be <u>Imperial writings at all,</u> then there would be
no means of maintaining their trust. This, then,
is something that should not be made clear.

In spite of the discouraging and thankless task
of trying to deal rationally with Englishmen, Frenchmen, and Americans, the Chinese official's deep-rooted
faith in human nature never quite failed him.
"Although they are wolf cubs with wild natures and
we dare not trust that they will not turn on us, still
sincerity can accomplish wonders and it would seem
that we should be able to bring them under our sway."[82]
The means, however, would have to be on a fairly low
level because "after all, the natures of scorpions
and wolves can never be treated with human reason."[83]

With more personal contacts established between
Chinese officials and foreigners in the ports, a more
realistic attitude toward foreign relations gradually
developed. Before the end of the period (1861), a
Shanghai official memorialized that the only method
of handling barbarians was that suggested by the
emperor, namely: "Holding firmly to the treaties, to
exemplify them with good faith, humble them with
reason, and mollify them with favor--these three,
and besides them there is no good plan."[84] When more
and greater concessions were wrung from China, officials rationalized this as a policy of "giving leash
as a means of control."[85] Some argued that "the method
of controlling barbarians consists entirely in conforming to their nature and taming them,"[86] although
the emperor and the court were inclined to take a
dim view of this. Ultimately, the heretical view
came to be expressed that China must "use their
methods and adapt them to her own uses."[87] Chinese
officials were beginning to realize that the West
might have something of value to China and that the
darkness outside the pale might not be as dense as
they had imagined. One high court official urged
that Wei Yuan's <u>Hai Kuo T'u Chih</u>, an atlas of Western
countries based on foreign sources, be made available
to all government officials in order to bring about
a better understanding of the world outside of China.
"Now today," argued this proto-reformer, "the
countries beyond the seas are daily striving for
mastery. Although as man sees things, there are
differences between China and the outside, as Heaven

149

sees them there may be no difference between them. The Book of History says, 'Great Heaven has no affections; It helps only the virtuous.'"[88]

A Shanghai official expressed the same revolutionary idea in more practical terms and even suggested that China herself might be at fault: "When we negotiate with these barbarians it is essential to have someone thoroughly familiar with the barbarian temperament in the hope that in the exchange of civilities, everything will be in order. Besides, the wording of our state papers is full of meaningless conventions. It is always from these trivialities that calamities develop. So we should consider everything carefully."[89]

Freed from the conventions and prejudices of Canton, Shanghai officials became convinced that it was not impossible to get along with foreigners and actually boasted that they had found the secret: "Shanghai's management of barbarians has consisted of taming them by catering to their moods. If the barbarian mood was avaricious, we feigned indifference to money; if the barbarian mood was proud, we treated them with deference; if the barbarian mood was crafty but had a false front of sincerity, then we showed trust in them. Therefore, for more than ten years there has been mutual accord, and no trouble. There was not a barbarian merchant who did not enjoy carrying on his business, so this became the point of concentration for barbarians."[90] Spoken like a true member of the Chamber of Commerce, but what a far cry from Yeh Ming-ch'en!

The proud Chinese were not humbled, but a few of them did begin to realize, somewhat bitterly, that the tables had been turned on them. "These barbarians for twenty years have contemptuously regarded us Chinese as being without leadership";[91] "their belittling of China is a matter of long standing."[92] They complained that the British "regarded the gentry as yamen runners and took good people for outlaws,"[93] and quoted an English journal published in China to the effect that "Chinese are hard to reason with and it is only by inspiring them with fear that we can gain our ends."[94]

By 1861, with the establishment of the Tsungli Yamen in Peking, Chinese officials had gone a long way from the childish concepts of red, white, and black barbarians. Western ships, steam engines, and cannon were not only admired but were being imitated in China. The Maritime Customs Service, set up under foreign inspectorship at Shanghai, was being extended to other ports at the request of Chinese officials.

The link between this early period and the later period of reforms and westernization was, perhaps, Tseng Kuo-fan. As early as 1861, he had abandoned the Chinese-barbarian concept of the world and was discussing intelligently the "Atlantic countries, England, France and America,"[95] as compared with Pacific countries like China and Japan.

Unfortunately, however, Tseng had illusions about the United States which were not borne out by the facts. "Americans," he wrote, "are of pure-minded and honest disposition and have long been recognized as respectful and complaint toward China."[96] He went on to cite instances of proffered American aid to China from 1839 to 1860, showing that they had consistently tried to pursue a policy of separate from the English and French. Without knowing that the United States was already committed to the "cooperative" policy" toward China, Tseng Kuo-fan went on to conjecture: "Probably by secretly blocking the Russian barbarians' overtures to China and preventing them from winning over the Americans' sympathies, the Americans could be made to realize that China is not the least suspicious of them, and might even be induced to turn around completely and draw nearer to us--one cannot tell."[97]

CHAPTER 8
CHINESE 'BARBARIAN EXPERTS' IN EARLY
SINO-AMERICAN RELATIONS

A modern Chinese scholar has translated the diary of a minor official, named Chang Hsi, who played a significant, if not decisive role in the negotiations resulting in the Treaty of Nanking signed by China and Great Britain on August 29, 1842.[1] This diary reveals Chang Hsi as a presumptuous boasting, tippling and probably avaricious and scheming underling who made himself indispensable to the Manchu and Chinese officials who were faced with the thankless task of dealing with the "English barbarians." It is clear that the stereotyped Confucian bureaucrat was unequal to the new responsibilities of foreign relations and that Chang Hsi was in a position to take advantage of them. Just what he had to offer, is not at first obvious: he was not a merchant so had no extensive dealings with foreigners; he was not a Cantonese and knew neither English nor the pidgin of commercial intercourse; he was not a scholar who had probed into the strange customs of the West, although he did occasionally show a canny knowledge of "barbarian" customs. How, then, did he qualify as the first "barbarian expert" or specialist in the "management of barbarian affairs"?

A careful examination of Chang Hsi's diary reveals a number of qualifications. In the first place, he was "seven feet tall," which, although obviously a gross exaggeration, at least indicated that he was a prepossessing figure who could "face up" to the tall and awesome foreigners better than the characteristically small Chinese or Manchu. Moreover, he had a capacity for frank, bold talk, and could, on occasion, "burst into a rage and beat the table and shout."[2] This was meeting fire with fire and obviously fill the timid officials with admiration.

It also indicated the contempt the Chinese had for the "barbarians", because they were not willing to lower themselves to this crude conduct but felt that it was necessary in dealing with those outside the pale of Chinese civilization. Besides, Chang Hsi did have some knowledge of the West. On one occasion he was able to assure his superiors that the British warships would not open fire on a certain day because it was Sunday.[3] Again, he explained to a Nanking official the principle of the steam engine. His superior refused to believe him and insisted that the paddle-wheels of the British ships were turned by oxen concealed in the hold. Only after he went on board a steamer and was shown the engines was he convinced that Chang Hsi knew what he was talking about.[4] This knowledge of the West gave Chang Hsi a respect for the barbarians which was unusual in this period. This and his weakness for alcohol got him into trouble. He persuaded his master, who was suffering from hookworm that "barbarian" medicine would cure him. When he was sent on board a British ship to secure the drug, according to English accounts, he got drunk in the gunroom and lost the doctor's instructions which accompanied the prescription. As a consequence, his master "swallowed at once what should have lasted three days."[5]

Whatever his real or imagined qualifications, it is clear from both English and Chinese records that Chang Hsi was regarded by the British as a jovial, frank, slightly ludicrous fellow whose drinking capacity they admired; by the Chinese he was held somewhat in contempt and somewhat in awe--recognizing that he had "a glib tongue and thoroughly understood the general situation."[6] That is to say, he recognized the superior strength and the necessity of making peace on the best terms possible. On the other hand both Chang Hsi and his appeasing superiors were slandered by the "war party" at court who favored a militant but unrealistic policy of sweeping the barbarians out of the country and settling the matter once and for all.

The diary of Chang Hsi throws light upon an obscure phase in the opening of diplomatic relations between China and the West in the midnineteenth century, namely, the role of the obscure underling who met the barbarian on his own level and did the dirty work for his refined superiors. On the whole, this new group of Chinese, who anticipated the returned student, liberal reformer, and revolutionary by two or more generations, must always remain anonymous. Undoubtedly hundreds of Chinese in Canton and Shanghai were getting new ideas and forming new attachments during this period down to 1861, and their names will never be known.

However, in the Chinese documents of this period dealing with the United States, more than forty "barbarian experts" are mentioned at least by name, and some of their activities show a pattern of early Chinese adaptation to the West. Naturally, hardly a one of these humble people has a biography or any mention in Chinese history, and so far Chang Hsi's is the only diary to appear. Whatever is known of them has to be gleaned from the context of the memorials of the period.

The first occasion of American official contact with China was the Opium War and the Treaty of Nanking which concluded it in 1842. The principal figure on the Chinese side was Ch'i-ying, imperial commissioner who negotiated with the British. Ch'i-ying was keenly aware of the value of specialists in dealing with foreigners, although he seemed somewhat contemptuous of Chang Hsi and preferred "barbarian experts" of his own choosing. For instance, one Ch'en Pai-ling, who was active in the British negotiations in 1842[7] and as garrison officer at Canton, assisted Ch'i-ying in his negotiation of the supplementary treaty of Bogue with the British in 1843. Later, when Ch'i-ying was governor general of Liang-chiang, he recalled that Ch'en was "thoroughly familiar with the barbarian temper," found him serving as chiliarch of the Hung-hu (Hunan) regiment, and drafted him to investigate the foreign situation on the Kiangsu seaboard and on the island of Chusan.[8] At the same time he recognized in Ch'in Yung-an, a sergeant in the Nanking garrison, another "barbarian expert" and sent him along with Ch'en Pai-ling. The most we can say of their possible competence is that they had had experience in dealing with the British at Nanking.

As soon as Ch'i-ying was ordered to return to Canton to meet the American minister, Caleb Cushing, he began to look around for experts who had helped him during his negotiations with England in 1842 and 1843. At Nan-hsiung, Kwangtung, en route to Canton, he met Chao Ch'ang-ling, a Cantonese, one-time prefect of Chao-ch'ing, Kwangtung, and expectant ministerial secretary. Chao had worked closely with

Ch'i-ying at Canton in 1843, and was regarded as an expert on barbarian affairs. Ch'i-ying was delighted to meet him at this opportune time and promptly drafted him to assist in negotiating the American treaty. Chao went to Canton with Ch'i-ying and served throughout the negotiations, and Cushing refers to him as "Chow, a member of the Han-lin College."[9] Ch'i-ying also mentions Ch'en Chih-kang, who had been a principal intermediary with the British at Nanking, to whom he was known as "Corporal White,"[10] and later, as garrison officer at Canton, had assisted in the 1843 negotiations. Ch'i-ying was disappointed to find that "Corporal White" was not available in 1844. Ch'i-ying turned for assistance to P'an Shih-ch'ing, wealthy hong merchant, expectant tao-t'ai and honorary Board president. Ch'i-ying said of him: "he has exceptional judgment, was born and reared in Canton and is well-versed in the local dialect. Moreover in the adjustment, of postwar issues for several years, in connection with the purchase of barbarian cannon and the employment of barbarian artisans to construct torpedoes, he has become well acquainted with a considerable number of American merchants and is generally respected by the barbarians of the said country."[11] This judgment is corroborated by Cushing who said of P'an Shih-ch'ing, that "be reason of his parentage, he being the son of an opulent Hong merchant, [is] understood to possess very liberal views in regard to the foreign relations of China."[12]

Another whose aid Ch'i-ying sought in 1844, was in a different category. Wen-feng (died 1860) was a Chinese plain yellow bannerman, whose original Chinese surname was T'ung. He was Canton customs superentendent (hoppo) and as early as 1842 became interested in a project to build or purchase Western-type warships. He assisted Ch'i-ying in the negotiation of the supplementary treaty of the Bogue in 1843 and had contacts with Commodore Kearny.[13] This was not his last appearance in the foreign relations field, however. In 1860, when the emperor fled before the British and French armies, Wen-feng was left behind to defend the Summer Palace. When the allies sacked and burned the palace, Wen-feng drowned himself in the artificial lake in the imperial garden, and thus achieved immortality as a loyal, though ineffective minister.[14]

In the later Canton period, 1856-1858, other specialists in barbarian affairs were sought out and utilized. In 1856, after the breakdown of negotiations following the Arrow incident and the bombardment of Canton by British naval units, two Cantonese were employed by Imperial Commissioner Yeh Ming-ch'en to treat with the British consul, Harry Parkes. One of these was a member of the Canton gentry named Su T'ing-k'uei, of whom nothing further is known. The other was Wu Ch'ung-yueh (1810-1863), fifth son of Wu Ping-chien, and, like his father, a hong merchant known to foreigners as Houqua, and head of the I-ho Company (known in contemporary literature as Ewo Hong). Wu Ch'ung-yueh was the wealthiest member of the Co-hong and the particular friend and patron of American merchants. His career is indicative of the rise of the Canton bourgeoisie and the dependence of Chinese officialdom upon this new class. He obtained by purchase his hsiu-ts'ai degree at the age of thirteen sui and his chu-jen degree in 1831, as a result of his father's contribution of 30,000 taels for flood control. During the next sixteen years, he competed four times for his chin-shih degree, but failed every time. In 1833 he entered the Co-hong, and in 1843 inherited his father's immense fortune. His policy in dealing with the British was literally "peace at any price" and he was willing to pay the price out of his pocket. For his diplomatic efforts and his generous contributions, Houqua was awarded the red coral button of a second class official and the brevet rank of financial commissioner.

Imperial Commissioner Yeh Ming-ch'en employed a man named Hsu Wen-shen as a kind of major domo for his meeting with British and French military officers representing Lord Elgin and Baron Gros aboard ship at White Goose Tything, opposite the Canton Bund, December 12, 1857. Hsu was expectant assistant subprefect of Nan-hai (Canton) and for years had handled the Canton government's communications with barbarians. He had previously been deputy magistrate of Kowloon, opposite Hong Kong. Yeh Ming-ch'en regarded him as invaluable because he was generally recognized and trusted by Hong Kong officials and merchants. Although no specific mention is made of it, he probably knew at least pidgin English.

Another type of extra-official function was performed by Lo Tun-yen. Because of the practice of the Chinese government never to employ an official in his native province, regular magistrates and prefects were always aliens and had little personal influence with the people. Consequently, when a native local leader was needed to stir up the people, an expectant, degraded, or retired official was called for. Lo Tun-yen was a native Cantonese, had served as board vice-president in Peking, but was on leave. In 1858, he was ordered by edict to enlist local militia and trainbands to drive the British from Canton. Such a person, who both knew the barbarians and had the respect of his fellow countrymen, was regarded as particularly suitable for this important service.

In Shanghai, where no tradition of foreign trade existed, experts on barbarian affairs were particularly in demand. Cantonese, especially, capitalized on their long experience in dealing with foreigners, their knowledge of English, and their business connections. When Shanghai officials wanted to charter foreign warships to use against the Taiping rebels in 1853, they employed Lieutenant Colonel Chang P'an-lung. He was regarded as an expert because as a petty officer he had acted as deputy for Commissioner Niu Chien at Nanking in 1842. Two Ningpo merchants were employed by the Shanghai tao-t'ai to negotiate with the foreign consuls in 1854 to secure their cooperation in defense against the rebels. Chang T'ing-hsueh, Hanlin bachelor and expectant magistrate, was operating a foreign goods store. He was regarded as a specialist on foreign affairs, and with his relative, Yang Fang, was deputized to carry out negotiations for the charter and purchase of foreign ships. Similarly, one Liang Chih, Cantonese expert, was sought out by Shanghai officials to "manage" the foreigners in 1858. Shanghai Tao-t'ai Wu Hsu, in 1859, made use of a merchant named Hsi K'uan in an attempt to persuade the foreign envoys to exchange ratifications in Changhai and possibly to agree to some modification of the Tientsin treaties. Ts'ai Chen-wu, Cantonese resident of Shanghai, who had purchased the brevet rank of tao-t'ai, was reported by memorial to be "thoroughly familiar with barbarian affairs." He was ordered by edict, September 24, 1858, to report to the Board of Civil Office at Peking for appointment to assist in the negotiations at Shanghai following the Tientsin treaties.

The profession of barbarian expert invited fraud. One Huang Chung-yu, Cantonese specialist in foreign affairs, was sought in 1859 to assist the imperial commissioners at Shanghai. He could not be located but was reported to be in Canton "wearing the button and sash of the fifth rank and conducting separate negotiations." Actually, he was a brevet first-class sub-prefect and district magistrate. He arrived in Shanghai, January 1, 1859, and enjoyed the full confidence of Kuei-liang. When the foreign envoys became difficult, he was ordered to talk them out of going to Peking--with what effect, is a matter of history. The use of these mountebanks was indicative of the contempt in which foreigners were held. They were supposed to meet the barbarian on his own level, to which the scholar-official could not stoop. It was a part of the classical axiom to "rule barbarians with misrule."

When negotiations shifted to Tientsin, Cantonese proficiency in barbarian affairs was even more in demand. Ch'en Chao-lin, native of Kwangtung, was local magistrate and director of the Fukien-Kwangtung Guildhall in Tientsin in 1858. He was recognized by Governor General T'an T'ing-hsiang as an expert on barbarian affairs and charged with the responsibility of raising trainbands to resist foreign invasion. Ch'en was also expected to check on his Cantonese and Fukienese compatriots in Tientsin, whose loyalty was somewhat suspect. To check on Ch'en and to assist in training local militia, the governor general appointed three natives of Chihli (Hopei), who were either expectants or officials on leave: Chen-lin, Ch'un-pao, and Fei Yin-chang.

Two officials who had participated in the negotiations with the British in 1850, Chang Ch'i-yuan and Chang Tien-yuan, were both regarded as "old barbarian hands" but were excused in 1854, when Bowring and McLane arrived, because of military responsibilities. Any contact with foreigners marked an official for further diplomatic duty, as well as for official suspicion. Ch'ing-ming, a Manchu, was director of the Board of Punishments in 1859. Because he had been associated with the imperial commission at Shanghai in 1858, he was delegated to assist in the exchange of ratifications with Ward at Pei-t'ang, August 16, 1859. Similarly, Ch'un Hsin-ho was one of the local officials who met the British in Tientsin in 1850. When Bowring and McLane came in 1854, he carried on the preliminary negotiations with Medhurst and Parker. By this time he was a veteran of foreign affairs and in 1858, now financial

commissioner of Chihli (Hopei), he was summoned to
assist in the negotiations before and after hostilities. His name appears on all the memorials up to
the arrival of Kuei-liang and Hua-sha-na. Although
he did not continue as a memorialist, his name is
mentioned later so it is apparent that his advice was
still sought by the imperial commissioners. Huang
Hui-lien, a Cantonese who came to Tientsin with the
British in 1858 and remained after the hostilities,
spoke "fluent" English and was regarded as an authority on the West. He advised Prince Seng-ko-lin-ch'in
on the Western practice of requiring indemnity of the
party which asked for terms. In 1859, Huang was ordered to fraternize with the two British prisoners
taken by Prince Seng, one of whom was thought to be
an American but was actually a Canadian, in the hope
of utilizing them to get terms from the British and
French.

Incidentally, there is one expert on Russian
affairs mentioned in the documents. Te-hsiang, a
Manchu, assistant department director, apparently
spoke Russian and was used as officer messenger and
major domo in negotiations with the Russians in 1860.
He became suspect, however, because he was too "intimate" with the Russians and was dismissed.

A final and quite different category of barbarian experts is represented by Chinese officials and
merchants who recognized the weakness of China and
the strength of Europe and consciously set out to do
something about it. Some of these were academicians
who advocated the acquisition of knowledge of the
West; others were practical people who bought Western ships and guns, experimented in shipbuilding and
munitions making, and emulated Western military and
naval tactics. These were the pioneers who were to
assume great prominence after 1860. During this
earlier period, however, these men were ahead of
their times and were going against, but trying to
change, the tide. Only those pioneers who are mentioned in the documents dealing with the United
States will be discussed here.

It is interesting to note, in this connection,
that the two Chinese officials whom the foreigners
regarded as the most virulent barbarian haters, Lin
Tse-hsu and Yeh Ming-ch'en, were both intelligent
students of the West and pioneers in the utilization
of Western knowledge in China.

Imperial Commissioner Lin Tse-hsu (1785-1850) is best known for his vigorous enforcement of opium prohibition from 1839 to 1840, which provoked the first Anglo-Chinese war. During his Canton administration, however, he was impressed by Western knowledge and weapons. He employed a staff at his yamen to collect and translate such Western materials as were available, mostly periodicals. His principal interests were geography and science; in the latter field he concentrated on weapons and maritime defense.

The results of his researches were published under the title Ssu-Chou Chih or "World Gazetteer," which was a pioneer work in the field. Lin's work stimulated Wei Yuan (1794-1856), China's first scholar-geographer of the West, to comple his famous Kai Kuo T'u Chih, "Atlas and Gazetteer of Foreign Countries," which appeared in 1844. The practical importance of these studies is indicated in Wei Yuan's statement in his preface that "he compiled the Hai Kuo T'u Chih in the hope that it would be of service to his country in dealing with foreign nations."15

Wei acknowledges Lin's Ssu Chou Chih as one of his sources. The real significance of Wei's work was only gradually realized by the Chinese. In 1858, when Peking was threatened by Allied forces, Wang Mao-yin, senior vice president of the Board of War, memorialized, July 9th, recommending that the Hai Kuo T'u Chih be made required reading for all officials entrusted with foreign affairs. He urged that the atlas and gazetteer be republished by the government and distributed to all officials.

The notorious Viceroy Yeh was less of a scholar than Lin Tse-hsu, but he did employ translators to extract and make available materials from Hong Kong newspapers and other English materials in China. He showed a keen, if scornful, interest in British affairs and during his long exile in India, studied the London Times and the Parliamentary Debates.

Another pioneer geographer was Hsu Chi-yu (1795-1873), who was appointed financial commissioner of Fukien province. Here he met the American missionary, David Abeel, who gave him a world atlas. After five years of studying this and other sources, Hsu published, in 1850, his Ying Huan Chih Luen or "World

Geography." He was denounced in 1851 for being too friendly with foreigners, and spent several years in retirement. He was eventually vindicated, however, and called to Peking, where he was appointed to the Tsung-li Yamen in 1865, while his "World Geography" was reprinted the following year by the Chinese Foreign Office. His work was twice reprinted in Japan, 1859 and 1861. He served in the Tsung-li Yamen until 1869.

Another academic pioneer was Lo Ping-chang (1793-1867), Cantonese authority on foreign affairs. Chin-shih of 1832 and Hanlin academician, Lo Ping-chang came to be regarded as an expert on Western naval warfare and armament. More scholastic was Chin Ying-lin, sub-director of the Grand Court of Revision, who memorialized on the strength of Western fleets and the necessity of building up a strong Chinese navy. Chin's knowledge, however, was strictly from the book. After reading descriptions of Western ships, he decided that they were no improvement over Chinese models. He recommended building up a strong navy composed of ships of various types drawn from Chinese history. Nevertheless, he was a forerunner of the later nineteenth century reformers, and his published writings, Ch'ih Hua T'ang and Shih Wen Chi, are important contributions.

In Canton, however, more practical pioneers were at work. Fang Hsiung-fei, undergraduate at Canton in 1842, advised General I-shan on the corruption involved in the building of Chinese warjunks, and urged the use of foreign ships. The real promoters were a group of wealthy and patriotic hong merchants. P'an Shih-ch'eng, well known to Americans in Canton as Puan Kei-qua, a member of the T'ung-wen Hong and descendant of the famous hong merchant, P'an Chen-ch'eng, was a recognized authority on foreign affairs and a trusted advisor of Ch'i-ying. In 1841-1842, P'an Shih-ch'eng built a Western-type warship at his own expense. He also later undertook to build a squadron to patrol the South China Sea, but after the hostilities of 1839-1842 were concluded, China lost interest in his project. He did succeed in interesting, temporarily, the Manchu general, Na-erh-ching-e, in building ships on Western models. Another of the Canton merchants, P'an Shih-jung, built a small steamer near Canton and launched it in 1842, in inland waters. He was convinced, however, that the machinery was too complicated for native workmen. Hence he recommended, if further steam navigation were to be attempted, that foreign artisans be recruited in Macao. Another hong merchant of the same firm, P'an Cheng-wei, who was the third Puan Kei-qua, collaborated with Wu Ping-chien (Houqua) of Ewo Hong, in the purchase of one American and one Spanish ship in 1843, and turned them over to the Canton authorities. Official interest had already waned, however, and the two foreign ships were reported as being good but too small and rather old. Monarchies as well as democracies are ungrateful.

In dealing with the United States, at least, the use of the "barbarian expert" was well established by 1861. The pattern is somewhat different from the isolated example of Chang Hsi. Perhaps the Americans were more receptive of the unorthodox Chinese opportunist whom the British were inclined to hold in contempt. At any rate, the pidgin-speaking linguist, the opulent hong merchant, the curious scholar, the scientific minded pioneer experimenting in torpedoes and steam engines all played their part in Sino-American relations before 1861. These are obviously the forerunners of the reformers, industrialists, and revolutionaries who were to become prominent in China in the second half of the 19th and the early 20th centuries. The beginnings of this new class of Chinese are the "barbarian experts" of the 1841-1861 period.

CHAPTER 9

CHINESE REPRESENTATION IN THE UNITED STATES,
1861-1912

The development of diplomatic relations between China and the United States was a gradual, not to say tortuous affair extending over a period of a hundred years, with two preliminary stages before a third period during which formal and increasingly satisfactory diplomatic relations were established. As far as China and the United States are concerned, these periods can be designated as follows: the Canton Trade Period, 1784-1844; the First Treaty Period, 1844-1861; and the Tsung-li Yamen--Foreign Office Period, 1861-1912. As this paper is concerned with the third period, the previous two will be sketched in roughly; just enough to give some basis for an understanding of the later one.

The first period was inaugurated in 1784, when the American merchant ship, the Empress of China, sailed from New York to Canton to join the British, Dutch, German, Spanish, and other traders at China's only port open to the West. During this period, the relationship was strictly commercial and even the trade was jealously guarded by the emperor's court in Peking, two thousand miles away by sea, three to four weeks away by the fastest "pony express." On the Chinese side the foreign trade was restricted to the Co-hong, a loose corporation of "Thirteen" (actually, the number varied from nine to seventeen) hong merchants, by an imperial charter. The Americans, like the other foreign merchants, lived in the Factories along the Canton Bund during the three-month trading seas. They dealt with one or another of

Earl Swisher, "Chinese Representation in the United States, 1861-1912," University of Colorado Studies (Series in History, No. 5, 1967),pp. 1-35. Reprinted with permission of the University of Colorado.

the hong merchants, talked through "linguists" to coolies and compradors, and occasionally heard vaguely of a Chinese official called the hoppo (customs collector), or the magistrate, but had no formal relations with the three highest officials at Canton, the viceroy (governor general), the governor, or the Tartar General. During this period, the only American official at Canton was a merchant consul, designated by the Secretary of State to look after the interests of the other American traders and to make periodic reports to Washington. This was a good time for Americans, pleasantly spiced with profit and graft, unencumbered by politics or diplomacy.[1]

This idyllic period was brought to a rude close by the Opium War, fought by England against China, 1838-1842, culminating in the Treaty of Nanking and followed by the Treaty of Wang-hsia signed between the United States and China in 1844. The war destroyed the Co-hong monopoly system and the treaties opened four additional ports along the South China coast, Swatow, Amoy, Foochow, and Shanghai, to foreign trade. The customs schedule was incorporated into the treaties and specific provision was made for the official relations between Westerners and Chinese. As the Chinese stubbornly refused to open Peking to foreigners, the arrangements fell short of diplomatic relations, but the British governor of Hong Kong and commissioner of China Trade and the American commissioner were allowed to deal officially with viceroys (governors general) and governors of the provinces in which treaty ports were located; and American and British consuls appointed to the various ports could deal with the local officials. There were no ministers or ambassadors to China, no Foreign Office or Department of State in Peking, and, naturally, no Chinese representation in any of the Western capitals. The nearest thing to a Chinese foreign minister was a newly-created imperial commissioner of foreign trade assigned first to Canton, the old center of trade, and later moved to Shanghai when it became the entrepot of world trade.

In this limbo between Chinese isolation and full acceptance of membership in the family of nations, some strange and wonderful things happened. Local magistrates (tao-t'ai) at the treaty ports found new outlets for their energies and abilities in the new rush of foreign trade, in the hundreds of new private companies and business houses, in the expaned customs revenues, and the greatly increased contacts with Westerners, with

business methods and with machines. A few of these
local officials became proficient in things Western--
even more of them waxed wealthy. An occasional provincial official became involved in foreign affairs
and developed ideas on policy, on strategy, on
methodology--a specialist on the handling of the
English barbarians, the American barbarians, and
assorted other tribes from places like France, Holland,
and Russia. The memorials sent to Peking by these
enlightened officials constitute the first source
materials on modern China's foreign policy.[2]

On the lowest level this period produced China's
first unofficial foreign service in the persons of
linguists (pidgin-English interpreters), compradors, and
servants in foreign firms and households. On the basis
of superficial contacts with Westerners and a smattering
of English, these "coolies" became self-styled "barbarian
experts," always ready to sell their expertise to the
highest bidder."

From all the above levels of Chinese who became
interested in Western trade and gained some knowledge
of the language, values, and material culture of the
West, came China's first modernizers and innovators.
Even the crudest and most naive of these early enthusiast
introduced changes and new ideas into China which were
to rock her to the very foundations. Unwittingly, they
brought on the deluge of Westernization and modernization

This transitional period was obviously unsatisfactor
to both Chinese and Westerners in China. Most Chinese
were alarmed by the expansion of trade and influx of
businessmen and missionaries, material goods and ideas.
They would have liked to have the treaties revised and
limited or even abolished, so that the dangers to China
could be minimized or postponed. The foreigners were
also in favor of treaty revision, but in the direction
of expansion: increasing the number of ports, opening
up the interior and the north of China to trade,
legalizations of the opium trade, and access to Peking
for full diplomatic representation which would force
the emperor and the court to receive foreign embassies,
to allow them to reside in the capital, and even to send
Chinese missions to the courts of the West. This last
objective--the establishment of diplomatic relations--
seems to us to be the least oppressive of the foreign
demands, but to the Chinese court and bureaucracy it
was by far the most repulsive and abhorrent.

The initiative for treaty revision was taken
by the Western countries rather than by the Chinese,

165

so naturally it was the Western demands, backed by superior military force, that prevailed over Chinese apprehensions. The means employed was a new series of wars against China between 1858 and 1860 carried out by the combined British and French fleets, with supporting armies. In three major operations, the river ports guarding the entrance to Tientsin were destroyed, Tientsin occupied, Peking stormed and captured, the Imperial Palace occupied and the Summer Palace bombarded, looted, and burned to the ground.

The United States was not involved in the hostilities but American ministers and units of the American navy accompanied the first two stages in the Allied operations against China and shared equally, through the convenient device of the most-favored-nation clause, in all the treaty revision and expansion resulting from the so-called Second Opium War-- among other provisions the import of opium to China was legalized in this second round of treaties.[3]

Among the Peking officials who realized most keenly the unwelcome but clearly inescapable fact that China had been forced to assume diplomatic relations with the West when she signed the Tientsin treaties and the subsequent Peking convention, were three capable Manchu statesmen who were destined to become key figures in the articulation of China's first step forward toward the West.

The first of these Manchu officials was always known to foreigners by his title, Prince Kung. He was the sixth son of the Tao-kuang emperor (1821-1851), half-brother of the then ruling Hsien-feng emperor (1851-1862) and uncle of the T'ung-chih emperor (1862-1875). When the emperor fled the Summer Palace at the arrival of the British and French armies, September 22, 1860, he authorized Prince Kung to make China's peace with them. Actually, Prince Kung, who had never seen an European, panicked and fled to the Marco Polo Bridge. His instinctive attitude toward foreigners has been described as "disdain mingled with hatred and fear."[4] After the Allies had settled down in Peking, Prince Kung appeared and took the lead in the negotiation of the Conventions of Peking which followed the dreary pattern of the previous treaties: indemnities, more concessions--including Kowloon, opposite Hong Kong-- but the most humiliating provision was the opening of Peking to the permanent residence of foreign diplomats and the obligation of the Manchu and Chinese court officials to deal with barbarians on a day-to-day basis. But, strange as it may seem, familiarity bred respect and by the time the conventions were signed Prince Kung began to understand and like the British and later was to become personally friendly with a series of American ministers. He was destined to pilot China's foreign relations for a total of twenty-seven years with stability and dignity, although many losses and further humiliations cluttered the way. Prince Kung dies in 1898.[5]

The second figure at this ground-breaking ceremony was Kuei-liang, another Manchu but a Plain Red Bannerman, rather than a prince. Forty-eight years older than Prince Kung, Kuei-liang had followed a common practice of the time by buying local and provincial posts where he could gain experience and prove his ability, which he seemed to prefer to the conventional scholar-examination procedure, until he attained office as high as governor general (viceroy). He then turned to Peking, where his real ambition lay, and by 1857 was a grand secretary. He got some military experience when he defended Paoting, thirty miles from Peking, against the Taiping rebels and thus saved the capital from the tide of Taiping advance. His introduction to foreigners was his role in assisting Prince Kung in the Peking negotiations with the British and the French. Unlike the young and rather debonair Prince Kung, Kuei-liang was a tall, stooped, kindly old man with quavering voice.[6]

Between these two was middle-aged Wen-hsiang, also a Manchu Plain Red Bannerman. Wen-hsiang was born in Mukden and first purchased rank in the Imperial (Manchu) Academy there, but he soon went to Peking where he took the regular examinations, earning his chin-shih (Ph.D.) in 1845. He had already served on several boards in Peking when he was named to work with Kuei-liang, under the leadership of Prince Kung, in the negotiations with the British and French. Wen-hsiang became an enthusiastic Westernizer. He recommended the training of a corps of Manchu Bannermen in the use of Western (Russian) firearms, is recognized as the founder of the T'ung-wen Kuan or Translators School to supply the new foreign service, and proved his theories by leading his Bannermen fusiliers in a successful campaign against bandits in Manchuria. Stocky, blustery Wen-hsiang became the best-liked of the new breed of Chinese official. Both Sir Frederick Bruce, brother of Lord Elgin and British minister to Peking, and the American diplomat,

George F. Seward, nephew of the secretary of state, consul general at Shanghai and later United States Minister to Peking, were devoted to him, admiring "his straight-forwardness and honesty." Wen-hsiang in turn admired Anson Burlingame and initiated his mission to the Western world on behalf of China; he also sponsored the first educational mission to the United States, which brought Chinese youth to live with New England families and eventually to study at Yale University.[7]

January 13, 1861, Prince Kung, Grand Secretary Kuei-liang and Senior Vice President of the Board of Revenue Wen-hsiang memorialized their proposal for the establishment of a new department in the Peking government to take charge of foreign affairs. They approached this task imposed on them by the treaties with considerable distaste, but with few illusions. The problem of handling barbarians runs all through Chinese history and there had been periodic climaxes when barbarians became such a threat that all efforts had to be concentrated on the problem. This was such a time. The barbarians were in Peking. "But as we, your ministers, analyse the present situation, among the barbarians the English are tyrannical, the Russians are inscrutable, while the French and Americans follow along after them."[8]

The policy they proposed was realistic--that is they recognized that China was helpless in the face of Allied arms, but that she still had a lot to lose that she might salvage with patience and a little dexterity. It was a policy of accommodation, the treaties must be accepted and carried out, but things still could be worse. "Since the barbarians did not take our territory or our people, if we are able to make use of good faith to bind them and subdue their natures, at the same time maneuvering to regain our prosperity, it would seem to be little different from previous situations."[9] The barbarians could be played off one against another. In the meantime, China was faced with the major Taiping Rebellion, controlling half of China with a rival capital in Nanking, plus a rising Nien Rebel menace in the north. She would have to learn to live with her barbarian enemies and deal with first things first. After all, they reminded the exiled emperor: "The ancients had a saying, 'treat peace as an expedient, war a fact.'"[10]

The prince and ministers proceeded to propose the establishment at Peking of a Tsung-li Yamen[11] with

exclusive responsibility for foreign affairs and a
separate building with a separate staff, parallel to
the Grand Council, the highest governing body of the
Empire. Whether naively or disarmingly they concluded this section with the plaintive note: "When the
military section has cleared up and foreign affairs
have quieted down, it (the Tsung-li-Yamen) will be
abolished and management will revert to the Grand
Council, in conformity with the old rule."[12]

Because the new treaties greatly increased the
number of ports open to foreign trade--from five to
sixteen--the Prince and ministers recommended replac-
ing the single imperial commissioner with two new
officers, Trade Commissioner for the Northern Ocean
at Tientsin and Trade Commissioner for the Southern
Ocean at Shanghai, each to supervise the trade, customs, and local officials handling foreign affairs
in the ports within his jurisdiction. For the latter
crucial post, they bypassed the prestigious Governor
General Tseng Kuo-fan as lacking "full comprehension
of barbarian temperament" in favor of Governor Hsieh
Huan, who had already proved his proficiency in trade
and foreign affairs over the years.[13] This bit of
administrative realism is an indication of the knowledge and practicality of these three Manchu statesmen. In the northern area, they were especially
concerned about Russian encroachment of the frontiers
and expansion of Russian trade, both the traditional
overland trade and the new ocean trade made possible
by the establishment of Vladivostok. They regarded
the prospects for trade expansion at the new port of
Tientsin as somewhat dim and proposed to abolish the
post of Trade Commissioner there if volume of trade
continued small.

The Prince and ministers were concerned about
translators and interpreters for the new Tsung-li
Yamen--"without an understanding of their language
and with their writing unintelligible to us, there
is a complete barrier; how can we expect to be able
to deal with them?"[14] They went back to the only
precedent Peking offered, the Russian Language
Mission set up in the eighteenth century to train
Russians in Chinese and Chinese in Russian. But this
had long since fallen into disuse and decay. They
recommended its revival, because Russian was now to
have new importance and went on to see what they
could do about English, their major concern, and
eventually about French and German, in that order.

They proposed various expedients. They knew that Canton and Shanghai firms employed linguists and writers of pidgin, i.e., "Business" English (rarely French), so two of these from each port were to be selected and sent up to Peking "bringing books of the various countries."[15] This was a naive device and obviously not very constructive.

In addition, four or five Manchu boys, fourteen years old or under, were to be selected from each of the Eight Banners to undertake foreign language studies, with generous allowances: they were to be weeded out periodically and the survivors rewarded after two years' trial. This was the germ which produced the T'ung-wen Kuan (Translators College), which will be considered later.

Great emphasis was placed on getting to the crux of foreign affairs; policies had failed because "rumors have been received from everywhere, but nothing is exact or accurate. The clue to the situation is newspapers." The newspapers of the various countries, "although not necessarily entirely reliable, but by inference and deduction the general picture can be grasped. Canton, Foochow, Ningpo, and Shanghai have long had publications, under different names. The newly opened ports will inevitably soon have publications. We urge that orders be sent to the Imperial Commissioner, the Trade Commissioners, as well as the provincial Tartar Generals, prefects, governors general and governors to transmit all publications, whether in Chinese characters or foreign writing, to the Tsung-li Yamen every month. In all Chinese-foreign matters, it is as clear as the palm of your hand, the way to correct abuses and avert prejudice is more and more detailed research."[16]

All the recommendations of the Prince and ministers were approved immediately and on January 20, the Imperial Edict establishing the Tsung-li Yamen and naming Prince Kung as its director with Kuei-liang and Wen-hsiang as his associates, was published. Quarters for the new department were found in the "Old Telegraph Building" on Tung-t'ang-tzu Hutung, in the East City, near the site of the later, well-remembered Foreign Office. The building was remodeled to suit the needs of the Tsung-li Yamen.

The organization of the Yamen was very simple. It started with Prince Kung and his two minister-rank associates, Kuei-liang and Wen-Hsiang, and remained at this modest number until 1885, when the membership was increased to fourteen.[17] In 1899, at the height of Chinese indignation at incessant foreign demands and indignities, the so-called "Battle for Concessions" which aroused nationwide anti-foreign feeling, an Imperial Edict ordered all governors general and governors to serve concurrently in the Tsung-li Yamen, so the list was greatly increased.

Below the Prince and ministers were secretaries (chang-ching), originally eight each of Manchus and Chinese, all recommended by the Grand Secretariat and the boards and taken into the Tsung-li Yamen after a special examination.

The Tsung-li Yamen took the general structural pattern of its contemporary opposite numbers, the British Foreign Office and the American Department of State. It was divided into five Divisions, one Court, the Archives Section, and the T'ung-wen Kuan.

The Divisions were geographical and grouped the countries of the world which China expected to deal with or was already involved with in treaty relationship. To appreciate the revolutionary change involved it should be noted that up to this time all the "foreign affairs" of the Central Government and Court of the Ch'ing (Manchu) Dynasty were handled by the Board of Rites (Li Pu), which laid down the terms of the reception (rare) of ambassadors and missions from the West, including the famed kowtow (k'e-t'ou). The requirements of this form of obeisance before the emperor and the throne had been a major stumbling block for Sino-Western relations for a hundred years. The Board of Rites also supervised relations with tributary states, such as Annam (Vietnam), Siam, Burma, Nepal, Korea, and the Liu-ch'iu Islands (Okinawa), with which the Western states refused to be classified.[18] The other predecessor of the Tsung-li Yamen was the Board of Dependencies (Li Fan Yuan), which handled China's relations with Central Asian and Mohammedan princedoms in western China. Until the establishment of the Tsung-li Yamen, all relations with Russia were supervised by the Board of Dependencies.[19] Again, the Western countries consistently refused this approach to the Chinese Court and Russia was no longer willing to accept it.

The new categorization of the world established at this time by the Tsung-li Yamen was: (1) the

English Division which had charge of relations with England and Austria-Hungary, including trade and tariff matters with both countries; (2) the French Division included France, Holland, Spain, and Brazil and also had charge of all matters of protection of missionaries and recruitment of laborers; (3) the Russian Division comprised Russia and Japan and had charge of all trade by land routes and of all land frontier defenses; (4) the American Division included, besides the United States, Germany, Peru, Italy, Sweden, Norway, Belgium, Denmark, and Portugal and all matters regarding protection of (Chinese) laborers abroad; (5) the Sea Defense (Coast Guard) Division, established in 1884 and added to the Tsung-li Yamen, had charge of both northern and southern coastal defense, the Yangtse Marine Patrol, coastal forts, shipbuilding, purchase of steamers and munitions, machine building, telegraphs, railroads, and mining operations in the various provinces. This identification of many of the early aspects of Chinese "modernization"--steamships, railroads, telegraphs, arsenals, et cetera--is an interesting recognition of the important role played by the Tsung-li Yamen and by the foreign diplomats who came into direct contact with the central government of China in Peking.

The Chancery (Ssu-su T'ing) was a court of equity dealing with internal matters of the Tsung-li Yamen and had charge of investigating all such matters.

The Archives (Ch'ing-tang Fang) had charge of arranging and keeping the department files, collating and cross-indexing them, and was also charged with investigating and decoding secret dispatches.

The T'ung-wen Kuan was established in 1863, at the instigation of and with the loyal support of Wen-hsiang, as a training school for interpreters and translators for the Tsung-li Yamen and later to staff the legations and consulates which China was eventually to set up in many countries of the Western world.[20] From the beginning it was headed by Dr. W. A. P. Martin, an American Presbyterian missionary from Indiana. From training interpreters, it gradually expanded into China's first college of Western studies. It was strongly supported by Sir Robert Hart, Inspector General of Chinese Maritime Customs, and eventually merged with another Peking school to form Peking Imperial University, of which Dr. Martin was the first president.

During the forty years of its existence, the Tsung-li Yamen underwent several changes of both personnel and policy which can best be identified by the leadership at the top, the series of prime commissioners who gave their successive characterizations to the Yamen.

The first period bears the stamp of Prince Kung and coincides with this initial period of hardship of the Tsung-li Yamen, comprising twenty-four years. In this period, there were, altogether, more than twenty-five men appointed to serve as ministers in the Tsung-li Yamen. Except for one or two persons, they all belonged to the "self-strengthening" group in principle. This means that the Yamen was filled at the top with pioneering, progressive, possibly in some respects even liberal, persons who believed that the answer to China's ills was to be found in the material and scientific knowledge, especially applied knowledge, of the West. The term "self-strengthening," which was to become the shibboleth of the small minority of progressive Chinese for the remainder of the 19th century, may well have originated right in the Tsung-li Yamen itself, possibly the coinage of the ebullient Wen-hsiang. In 1884, faced with French defiance of China's claim of tributary status for Annam, Prince Kung and his ministers of the Tsung-li Yamen argued against plunging into a war which China was sure to lose and favored negotiation for whatever China might salvage out of a hopeless situation. The entire court was in favor of war so Prince Kung was impeached and removed from office, along with most of the handpicked ministers he had brought in over the years. This ended the first period of the Tsung-li Yamen.

Prince Kung was succeeded by another Manchu scion of the imperial family, Bei-lo I-k'uang, with the brevet rank of prince of the first degree. By juggling the succession, he received the family designation, Ch'ing, and so became generally known as Prince Ch'ing,[22] but he had none of the qualities of mind or character which Prince Kung possessed. Prince Ch'ing was strongly supported by Yuan Shih-k'ai, whose star was in the ascendancy and was a favorite of the Empress Dowager, so he was safe in his rank and high government office, but he was not a grand councilor in his own right so the relationship between Tsung-li Yamen and the Grand Council was not as intimate as heretofore. Prince Ch'ing repeatedly memorialized and explained his policies in detail but they were seldom accepted by the Grand Council. On the contrary, edicts were issued from time to time reprimanding him, but with that kind of backing, he could not be budged. Nor was his personal integrity above reproach. His biographer says that "he was several times accused of corruption and of hording great wealth. It is reported that whereas other corrupt officials received bribes through intermediaries, he insisted on personally negotiating every such transaction."[23] When the Sino-Japanese War broke out in 1894, Prince Ch'ing was hopelessly unequal to the responsibilities of the office and resigned, bringing to a close the second period of the Tsung-li Yamen.

The third period was instituted by the return of Prince Kung to office for his second term of service, which was to last four years. The conciliatory and realistic policies of Prince Kung might have staved off Japanese aggression by concession and appeasement but by the time he came back to office it was too late to save or even salvage the situation. China could not win and had no alternative to defeat and humiliation. Prince Kung by now realized that the old formula of "using barbarians to control barbarians" was no longer efficacious. Among the ministers now influential in the Tsung-li Yamen, Li Hung-chang,[24] rapidly becoming one of the most powerful leaders of China, advocated alliance with Russia and Weng T'ung-ho[25] advocated reform and the establishment of a constitutional monarchy. As tutor to the young emperor, Weng was teaching him world history and Western science as a basis for eventual reform of China. Weng's faction, however, steadily lost power in the Tsung-li Yamen and the court and finally resigned leaving the Li Hung-chang faction in control. Then, just as his policy of alliance with Russia was instituted, the Western powers occupied the ports and Chinese affairs went from bad to catastrophic. Prince Kung died May 29, 1898,[26] and the third and tragic period of the Tsung-li Yamen came to an end.

Again Prince Kung was succeeded by I-k'uang Prince Ch'ing and his final two-year stint constitutes the fourth period of the Tsung-li Yamen. Prince Ch'ing returned to face the clamorous demands of the Western powers for k'ua-fen ("dividing up the melon") or the partitioning of China with echoes of the recent infamous partitioning of Poland by the same European powers. A Foreign Office statement oversimplifies the situation but offers a refreshing contrast to some American opinion, by saying flatly that "thanks to the American proposal of the Open Door Policy the disaster was averted."[27] But China's problems were not solved or even alleviated by the postponement of territorial partition. Many of the Western-influenced developments of the last decades, road-building, introduction of machines and factories, shipbuilding, railroad construction, et cetera, tended to increase the wealth and independence of the provinces and the arrogance of provincial governors general and governors. A strong national and foreign policy demanded a centralized government in control of the country's wealth and power but China's early modernization had a sharply decentralizing influence. This degeneration was reflected in the Tsung-li Yamen, when provincial officials were given concurrent posts and ministerial rank in the Tsung-li Yamen. This move only diffused and weakened its prestige without in any way diminishing the power of the provinces. As a consequence, the center of gravity in the court shifted away from the Tsung-li Yamen, back to the Grand Council. When the Boxer Rebels attacked in 1900, Prince Ch'ing and his followers in the Tsung-li Yamen favored their repudiation and extermination, contrary to the policy of the Empress Dowager and the powerful court faction. Because of Prince Ch'ing's personal favor, he was saved from arrest and punishment but he was forced to resign and thus terminate the fourth period of the Tsung-li Yamen.

During its fifth and final period of existence, the Tsung-li Yamen was headed by Ts'ai-i Prince Tuan, the darling of the Empress Dowager and the principal author of the policy of using the Boxers to exterminate all the foreigners in China, missionaries, traders, and diplomats alike, and thus solving her problems once and for all. But Prince Tuan was not long in office before the eight-power Allied army fought its way into Peking. Prince Tuan fled with the Empress Dowager and her court. The Allies insisted on his execution as an anti-foreign criminal but the Empress Dowager commuted the sentence to exile to Ili and life-imprisonment. He went cheerfully into exile, grateful to have his life spared, and when the Revolution broke out in 1911, he returned to China and became a republican.[28] So the Tsung-li Yamen came to a timely end, having served a useful purpose in modern Chinese history largely due to the extraordinary character and intuitive judgment of I'hsin Prince Kung, who headed it for twenty-seven of its total forty years of existence.

When the Boxer uprising was smothered under a barrage of foreign guns and an international army, the Final Protocol, signed September 7, 1901, provided that the Tsung-li Yamen be transformed into a Ministry of Foreign Affairs (Wai-wu Pu) which would take precedence over the six other Ministries of State and our old friend I-k'uang Prince Ch'ing was named as the first Foreign Minister. Prince Ch'ing continued in office until 1911, when he was forced by the rising tide of revolution to resign. He was elevated to prime minister but in a few months, the emperor abdicted and the dynasty came to an end.

The new Ministry of Foreign Affairs reflected the overwhelming importance foreign relations had assumed in Chinese government but it was badly organized and burdened with many matters not strictly related to foreign affairs. Its four bureaus were: (1) Bureau of Harmonious Intercourse, in charge of all foreign correspondence, envoys abroad, ministers and ambassadors in Peking, et cetera; (2) Bureau of Industrial Affairs, dealing with railways, mines, telegraph, machinery and manufacture, shipping, foreign employees, labor emigration, and educational missions abroad; (3) Bureau of Customs and Accountancy, in charge of maritime customs, commercial affairs, navigation, domestic and foreign loans, currency, postal service, expenditure of the ministry and of legations and consulates abroad; and (4) Bureau of Miscellanea, in charge of boundaries, coastal defense, missionary cases, travel, protection, foreign claims, contraband, police, and mixed cases.[29]

The only noticeable improvement of the Ministry of Foreign Affairs over the old Tsung-li Yamen was its elevation to pre-eminence in the government, thus freeing it from its dependence on the Grand Council. But actually, no organizational change could have done much to improve China's foreign relations for the next sixteen years (1912-1928) because during most of that time rival governments, local, provincial and regional warlords, constant shuffling and continual civil war--prevented the Peking government from ruling China, and reduced its foreign relations to a kind of shadow play, devoid of reality. Efforts were made from time to time to speak outwardly for all of China, despite internal strife and chaos, but this voice of China was often strident, contradictory, and lacking in dignity.

The Tsung-li Yamen made it possible for European and American diplomats to realize their cherished

dream of living in Peking--cherished, perhaps, because it was forbidden--and they lost no time in taking advantage of the opportunity. The first American
minister appointed to reside at the capital, Anson
Burlingame, arrived in China, October, 1861, and took
up residence in Peking the following summer. British,
French, and Russian ministers were already there and
the fame of Peking as an urbane cosmopolitan capital
was in the making. But China was not so avid to reciprocate by sending Chinese representatives to reside in London, St. Petersburg, Paris or Washington.
Her involvement in two major rebellions--the Taiping
and the Nien--of civil war proportions, the conser-
vativism and inherent contempt for barbarians retained by many Chinese officials, high and low, and the
lack of personnel fluent in Western languages as well
as the comparative ignorance and lack of curiosity
concerning the West, all probably contributed to this
reluctance, even on the part of the "liberal" Tsung-
li Yamen, to institute Chinese representation to the
West. But sooner or later it had to come.

It has been generally assumed by Western observ-
ers that Chinese ignorance and conservative adherence
to tradition and established custom prevented the establishment of diplomatic missions abroad. This was
undoubtedly true of Chinese people in general and
even of the great majority of Chinese officials and
literati but it was definitely not the attitude of
the Prince and ministers of the Tsung-li Yamen nor of
the better informed provincial officials.

In 1867 and 1868, the Tsung-li Yamen took the
initiative of formulating its own position on the
question of Chinese representation abroad and then
undertook to poll the opinions of provincial authorities. The secluded and suspicious court argued that
the foreign countries had eagerly sought representation in Peking but that China was self-sufficient and
neither had nor needed to develop interests in foreign
countries. It was pointed out that Great Britain,
the United States and France had both trade and missionary interests in China but that the emperor was
not concerned about sending either Chinese merchants
or Confucian missionaries to the West.[30]

The Tsung-li Yamen, however, insisted that certain advantages would accrue to China from maintaining Chinese ministers and consuls in foreign countries. It is interesting to note that the advantages
listed are political and diplomatic rather than

commercial--the actual area in which the future gen-
ius of the Chinese was to express itself in Hong Kong,
Singapore, San Francisco, and New York. The Tsung-li
Yamen pointed out that it would be advantageous for
China to be able to study foreign policies of Western
countries at first hand in the foreign capitals, to
learn the secrets of the Western military and naval
power that had already harrassed China's ports and
continued to threaten China's security ("know your
enemy"), and finally it would be helpful to China to
have direct access to foreign governments over the
heads of the foreign representatives resident in
Peking, who could not always be trusted.

On the other hand, the Tsung-li Yamen pointed
out certain practical difficulties which would have
to be overcome before China could be represented in
foreign capitals, namely, the complete lack of trained or experienced foreign service personnel and the
almost complete ignorance of Western languages on the
part of Chinese officials.[31]

In order to strengthen its hand against the
court, the Tsung-li Yamen sent out a "Secret Letter"
asking for the opinions of provincial officials on
matters of foreign policy. Seventeen governors general and governors responded with learned and surprisingly "liberal" views, generally favorable to the
gradual development of Chinese diplomatic relations
with the West. Some favored occasional missions of
inquiry and investigation abroad; one proposed recruitment for the foreign service among Western-
educated Chinese in the port cities, outside the
traditional scholar-official tradition; another mentioned China's responsibility to the new class of
overseas Chinese whose existence was just beginning
to register on official consciousness. Already the
"coolie trade" was carrying tens of thousands of
Chinese laborers to California, Mexico, Peru, and
Cuba and Chinese emigrants were beginning to settle
in Singapore, Malaya, and Indonesia.

The seventeen memorialists who responded to the
"Secret Letter" in 1867-1868, showed surprisingly
little opposition to the idea of establishing diplomatic relations with the West. This may have been
because they were mostly relatively sophisticated
high officials, many of whom had already had some
dealings with Western diplomats, businessmen, customs officials, and missionaries. Perhaps also, the
Tsung-li Yamen did some selection of officials known

to be sympathetic toward their own point of view. Despite the general acceptance of the idea of dealing with the West, there occurred in these memorials a vague, haunting fear that Chinese officials sent to Western countries might bring disgrace to China, that Chinese envoys might be humiliated or rebuffed by Western governments, or that Chinese officials, through ignorance of foreign customs and etiquette, might not conduct themselves properly.[32] This might be interpreted to mean that the pride and self-confidence of the Confucian-educated Chinese was beginning to crack. Certainly, the arrogant and smug Victorians from England and the United States took little pains to conceal their contempt and condescension for the Chinese.

The first minister China sent to the United States was an American. On November 21, 1867, Anson Burlingame resigned as American minister to China, explaining in his natural oratory that "in the interests of my country and civilization," he had been persuaded to accept "the position of envoy of the Empire to all the Western powers then having treaties with China."[33] Burlingame set out from Peking with two officials from the Tsung-li Yamen, a Manchu named Chih-kang and a Chinese named Sun Chia-ku, British, French and Chinese secretaries, and a retinue of thirty--servants, students, and curious relatives. In Washington, Burlingame negotiated eight supplementary articles to the Treaty of Tientsin (1859), clarifying American policy on Chinese sovereignty and providing for the emigration of Chinese laborers to California, among other things. These ratified supplements were exchanged the following year in Peking and became a part of the treaty. The party moved on to London where an agreement clarifying some points in British policy was signed with Lord Clarendon, Foreign Secretary of the first Gladstone Ministry. Burlingame and his retinue visited and were feted in several capitals on the continent before proceeding to Russia early in 1870. Here Burlingame died of pneumonia, February 23, 1870, "thus terminating before the age of fifty a truly brilliant career."

Tyler Dennett is of the opinion, probably justified, that Burlingame was "easily the most capable American diplomatic representative in China since Caleb Cushing who though superior to him in intellect, lacked his unselfish idealism and breadth of statemanship."[34] He may also have been the most capable representative of China to the United States in the

179

nineteenth century. But neither Williams nor Dennett has any more to say of the two Chinese associates of Burlingame than that they were along.

Chinese documents which became available to modern scholars in 1931, long after the Manchu dynasty was overthrown and replaced by the Republic of China, bring to light new details of the Burlingame mission and give it much greater significance as an important step in the evolution of a Chinese foreign policy and as an advance toward the inauguration of Chinese diplomatic representation in the United States.

In Burlingame's official instructions, the Prince and ministers of the Tsung-li Yamen stated clearly that they had "long desired to request the appointment of Chinese officials to proceed to the treaty powers, but without training and experience it was feared that they would not be at all familiar with foreign manners and customs." Consequently they entrusted this first mission to Burlingame. "But at the same time it is still necessary for China to send her own officials to consult with Your Excellency, both to expedite matters and to enable Chinese officials to secure thorough training and experience. All details are to be clearly set forth in their presence." They also made clear that Burlingame's two associates, the Manchu Chih-kang and the Chinese Sun Chia-ku, ". . .must, according to Chinese usage, be on an equal footing both with Your Excellency and with the high officials of the treaty powers no matter what their rank."[35] Thus this first Chinese venture into Western diplomacy was clearly a training mission for future, permanent Chinese representation in foreign countries, but also these official instructions to Burlingame make clear that the Chinese and Manchu envoys were imperial commissioners, equal to Burlingame in rank, and actually China's first official envoys to the United States and to the other Western powers.

The Tsung-li Yamen also clearly wrote policy into Burlingame's instructions, saying: "The Imperial appointment of Chinese officials (to go abroad) is an experiment, and definitely does not constitute an appointment of resident envoys to the treaty powers. . . .If after they return a thorough investigation of the experiment shows that it has yielded effective results, the matter of a permanent system will again be considered."[36]

After the instructions to Burlingame had been issued, an Imperial Rescript announced the appointment of two "Ministers for the Management of Chinese Diplomatic Relations," titles identical in meaning and rank with that of Burlingame.[37]

Chih-kang, the Manchu envoy, and Sun Chia-ku, the Chinese envoy, had both served in the Tsung-li Yamen as secretaries for several years and were well acquainted with Chinese foreign relations. Chih-kang wore the decoration of the peacock feather and held the official position of an intendant of the Maritime Customs awaiting assignment to a post (i.e., an "expectant") and Sun Chia-ku was a brevet intendant of circuit and had the actual status of prefect awaiting assignment to a major post of senior secretary in the Board of Rites. With their new appointment as envoys, both Chih-kang and Sun Chia-ku were elevated to the second official rank and Sun was given the peacock feather decoration to match that already held by Chih-kang.[38] This practice of appointing to ministerial posts in Western countries, Chinese officials of low rank and then awarding them some honorific elevation of rank and decoration to give them additional status in foreign courts, was to become standard operating procedure of the Chinese government throughout the period under study. Besides the obvious under-rating of the foreign service implied in staffing it with low-ranking officials, there seems to be some logic in it in the fact that the rigid Confucian discipline of the Chinese scholar-official provided no training for foreign service officers and that lower, less encumbered officials with some practical experience in the Foreign Office, might be better qualified than high-ranking officials.

On January 4, 1868, Chih-kang and Sun Chia-ku were received in audience by the Empresses Dowager, who were acting as regent for the minor T'ung-chih emperor, for their final oral instructions as China's first official envoys to the West. "When asked a question concerning audiences with foreign rulers, they replied that the matter depended upon the rulers--that they themselves would not request such interviews. In reply to an admonition, they promised to see that their attendants behaved themselves, thus avoiding disgrace to themselves and to their country."[39]

Contrary to the clear wording and obvious intent of his instructions, Burlingame signed the Eight Supplementary Articles of the Treaty of Tientsin, commonly referred to as the "Treaty of Washington." in the following presumptuous manner: "Anson Burlingame, Envoy Extraordinary and Minister Plenipotentiary, and Chih-kang, and Sun Chia-ku, of the Second Chinese rank, associated high Envoys and Ministers of his said Majesty."[40]

A specific evidence of the full diplomatic status of Chih-kang and Sun Chia-ku is their independent action after Burlingame contracted pneumonia and died in St. Petersburg, February 23, 1870. The mission, now led by Chih-kang and Sun Chia-ku, left Russia April 20, after funeral arrangements for Burlingame were completed, and visited Berlin, Brussels, Paris, Florence, and then returned to Paris. Here they received word of the Tientsin Massacre and Chih-kang recorded in his diary the bitter feeling against the Chinese expressed in the French press. During this period, the two envoys presented their credentials to the various European courts to which they were accredited, were received by kings and queens, attended various state function in their honor, and reported their activities and observations back to the Tsung-li Yamen like the experienced diplomats they had become. The mission returned to Peking, November 18 having been abroad for nearly three years and having traveled some 42,000 miles.[41]

One of the incidental provisions of the Burlingame treaty was that "the Emperor of China shall have the right to appoint consuls at ports of the United States." When Chih-kang and Sun Chia-ku endorsed the treaty to the Tsung-li Yamen and recommended its ratification by the emperor, they showed the results of their diplomatic experience in the United States by pointing out that "there were many thousands of Chinese merchants and laborers living in California, and that it was advisable to appoint Chinese officials to look after them, not only to see that they conducted themselves properly, but also to make sure that they did not lose their nationality."[42] This was to become a major concern of Chinese diplomacy in the years to come.

The second phase of Chinese representation in the United States is closely identified with the Chinese Educational Mission to the United States, the brain child of Yung Wing (Mandarin spelling, Jung Yung)

who as a protege of Protestant missionaries in
Canton became the first Chinese to graduate from
an American university (Yale, 1854). When Yung
Wing's proposal received the support of Viceroy Tseng
Kuo-fan in 1870, its success was assured, and in 1872,
he and one Ch'en Lan-pin were made joint commissioners
to the Educational Missions. The first group of
thirty Chinese students left Shanghai in 1872 with
Ch'en Lan-pin as their leader and were met by Yung
Wing at Hartford, Connecticut, where arrangements
had been made for them to live with American families
for the first part of their program.[43] Ch'en Lan-pin
had been appointed as a conservative counterbalance
to the Western educated and aggressively progressive
Yung Wing. He was a member of the Hanlin Academy
and had served twenty years as a clerk on the Board
of Punishments. Later when he was made minister
plenipotentiary he was awarded the honorary rank of
expectant assistant grand secretary.[44] His patron
was first Tseng Kuo-fan and after his death, his
successor, Li Hung-chang. He is described as a great
scholar but timid and increasingly conservative. He
and Yung Wing eventually became emplacable enemies
and the latter held Ch'en Lan-pin chiefly responsible for the eventual withdrawal of the Educational
Mission. While he was educational commissioner
he was called upon to head a mission to investigate
the uprising of Chinese coolies in Cuba and even
through the prejudiced account of Yung Wing the
talent of Ch'en Lan-pin for administration and efficiency can be seen. Yung Wing wrote bitterly:

> He sent Yeh Shu Tung (Yeh Shu-t'ung) and one
> of the teachers of the Mission accompanied by
> a young American lawyer and interpreter to
> Cuba, which party did the burden of work and
> thus paved the way for Chin Lan Pin (Ch'en
> Lan-pin) and made the work easy for him. All
> he had to do was to take a trip down to Cuba
> and return, fulfilling his mission in a per-
> functory way. . . . Chin Lan Pin gathered in the
> laurel and was made a minister plenipotentiary.[45]

In 1875, Ch'en Lan-pin returned to China on leave
of absence taking the teacher, Yeh Shu-t'ung, who had
served him well in Cuba, with him. Three months later, the Tsung-li Yamen announced that Ch'en Lan-pin
and Yung Wing had been appointed joint Chinese ministers to Washington. The Imperial Edict read:

Ch'en Lan-pin, a third/fourth grade expectant Director of one of the Four Minor Courts, a Secretary of the Grand Council, a Senior Secretary of the Board of Punishments, and wearer of the button of the second rank, and Yung Wing, a brevet third grade sub-prefect, shall be imperial commissioners to go to the United States, Spain, and Peru as envoys. Yung Wing shall be promoted to an intendantship and shall receive the button of the second rank.[46]

Yung Wing, back in Hartford, according to his own statement, asked to be excused to continue as educational commissioner, generously conceding that Ch'en Lan-pin would ". . . doubtless be able alone to meet the expectations of the government in his diplomatic capacity."[47] Peking complied and Ch'en Lan-pin was made minister plenipotentiary with his faithful Yeh Shu-t'ung as first secretary, while Yung Wing became associate minister, retaining his duties as educational commissioner in Hartford.

The actual establishment of the first Chinese legation in the United States was plagued with still further delay. The minister designate, Ch'en Lan-pin, did not leave China until more than two years after his appointment was published. He finally received his farewell audience with the Empress Dowager Tzu-hsi, regent for the infant Kuang-hsu Emperor, on March 12, 1878, and left Peking on March 27. Traveling _via_ Shanghai, Hong Kong, Japan and San Francisco, he proceeded to the headquarters of the Chinese Educational Mission in Hartford, Connecticut. From there, he sent his associate minister, Yung Wing, and an attache ahead on August 27, to secure quarters for his large suite of officers who were to constitute his legation staff. They purchased the large mansion on 19th Street, NW (Dupont Circle) in what was then a fashionable district of Washington, and which the Chinese government still owns, although the new Embassy offices and Chancery have long since been moved to Massachusetts Avenue and the Embassy is housed in the spacious Twin Oaks Estate, acquired since World War II.

Ch'en Lan-pin himself did not follow Yung Wing to Washington until three weeks later, reaching the capital on September 19. The envoy and his associate minister presented their credentials to President Hayes on September 28, 1878, and with this ceremony

the first Chinese legation in the United States officially came into being. Yung Wing, a graduate of
Yale University of 1854, and completely bilingual,
naturally assumed the role of Councillor of Embassy
and for long periods of Ch'en Lan-pin's absence from
Washington, was acting minister but he was never
accredited as Minister to the United States.

Leaving Yung Wing and most of his staff in Washington, Ch'en Lan-pin set out early in 1879, to present his credentials to the governments of the other
two countries to which he was accredited. Going
first to Spain, by way of England and France, he presented his Letter of Credence to the King in Madrid
on May 24, 1879. Almost a year later, on April 17,
1880, he presented his credentials to the President
of Peru. In each country he left a charge d'affaires
to maintain the Chinese "legation,"[48] which had the
actual status of a consulate general. China's concern in Peru was limited to the interests of the several tens of thousands of Chinese coolies working in
the silver mines there.

The second Chinese minister resident in Washington, was Tseng Tsao-ju, who served from 1881 to
1886,[49] who had been Tientsin Customs Tao-t'ai, and
was given the rank of Third Grade Court Official in
accord with his office.[50]

From Washington Tseng Tsau-ju transmitted a
Chinese transcription of report prepared by an American living in Hawaii describing the myriad islands
of Polynesia, someday "destined" to become Hawaiian
and soliciting the protection of various great powers.
Tseng reports that this "archipelago" (transliterated
in Chinese characters) is some five thousand miles
northeast of Australia; Hawaii being another five
thousand miles northeast of them. They constitute
the "Micronesia" of the Pacific. He says that according to newspaper reports, Australia is interested in
annexing New Guinea to keep France from devouring it
and that Hawaii fears that she will also claim Micronesia and eventually threaten the independence of
Hawaii itself. He suggests that although China has
no treaty with Hawaii, there are numerous overseas
Chinese there and that she might do well to send a
consul to Honolulu and maintain trade relations
there. A subsequent letter in the same file from the
Hawaiian Foreign Office to the Tsung-li Yamen explains

that if Hawaii is to maintain her sovereignty and independence she must enlist the support of all the great powers.[51]

A letter from a Chinese merchant in Peru tells of revolutions, military juntas, and unsettled conditions which call for Chinese consular protection of Chinese nationals.[52]

Tseng Tsao-ju also reports to the Tsung-li Yamen the visit of a Korean envoy and vice minister to the United States, with one American and one Japanese in their entourage. They came to Washington, saw the president and were given red-carpet treatment, and they stayed awhile in New York. "The Vice Minister has now left for San Francisco where he will take a commercial steamer back to Korea. The Envoy will go by United States warship from New York to Hong Kong, Shanghai, and thence to Korea."[53]

Other enclosures in the file report United States, British, and Russian treaties with Japan. Tseng Tsao-ju's file indicates a growing interest in Pacific and Asian affairs, but the fact that he lists thirty-two items and only seven are extant also indicates the hazards of survival in the Tsung-li Yamen Archive. Tseng Tsao-ju became involved and personally concerned about the anti-Chinese riots in Rock Springs, Wyoming, in September 1885, when twenty-nine Chinese were killed. Tseng hired competent assessors and presented the United States with a bill of $147,748 for damage to Chinese property and indemnity for the families of the deceased. He also initiated negotiations with the State Department for revision of the Burlingame treaty provision on Chinese labor, limiting and then suspending Chinese immigration.[54] Neither of these issues was completed during Tseng Tsao-ju's term of office, but they were continued and brought to successful conclusion by his successor, Chang Yin-huan.

The third Chinese minister resident in Washington was Chang Yin-huan (he used the slightly different transcription, Chang Yin Hoon, in his papers) and he presented his credentials April 29, 1886, serving until May 8, 1889. He was a native of Fo-shan (Fatshan), near Canton and had been a member of the Tsung-li Yamen for two years immediately before being named to the Washington post. As a failed hsiu-ts'ai (provincial graduate) he had prepared himself for government office by purchasing the title of student in the Hanlin Academy and later purchased the rank of magistrate. When he was appointed minister, the usual practice was followed of awarding him Court Rank of the Third Grade. These were merely the inpedimenta of aspiring young officials, who had money but lacked a powerful patron to promote them. Actually, Chang Yin-huan was a well-educated and experienced foreign service officer of considerable talent. He had served with Ting Pao-chen and later Li Han-chang in military affairs and was a recognized specialist in foreign affairs, as well as an authority on Chinese coastal defense. In this letter connection he had an interview with the powerful Li Hung-chang who supported his appointment to the Tsung-li Yamen as a probationary member.

In 1884, apparently the victims of the strong "self-strengthening" group in the Tsung-li Yamen who in principle opposed any protege of Li Hung-chang, Chang Yin-huan and the first minister to Washington, Ch'en Lan-pin, were both discharged from Yamen service for sending an "inappropriate telegram." Chang was sent to Chihli as intendant of Ta-ming Circuit. Apparently his patronage was still strong enough to override Tsung-li Yamen opposition for after serving only one year as tao-t'ai, Chang Yin-huan was appointed minister to the United States, Peru, and Spain.

Before leaving for his new post, Chang Yin-huan visited Governor General Chang Chih-tung on the problem of Chinese coolie laborers, which was becoming of increasing Chinese concern. In March 1886, he left for the United States with Jui-yuan, Liang Ch'eng, who later himself became minister to the United States, and Hsu Chueh, who was to become minister to Italy, in his entourage. The mission arrived in Washington in April 1886.

Chang Yin-huan's first concern was to follow through on the overseas Chinese and immigration problems left over from the previous administration of Tseng Tsao-ju. He pressed the State Department for the damage claims and made history in a minor way, when he received payment for the full amount claimed, $147,748, in March 1887. China, who had paid so many indemnities to Western powers, actually received an indemnity payment herself. Chang Yin-huan sent the full amount to the San Francisco consulate for distribution to the claimants. When all the claims were satisfied, $480.75 was left over and was returned to

the State Department.[55] This unprecedented act provided a precedent for President Roosevelt's return
of the unexpected balance of the Boxer indemnity to
China, which provided for the American education of
thousands of Chinese students.

Chang Yin-huan spent May and July in Spain
where he set up a permanent Chinese consulate, administered and staffed by the Washington legation.
On his return to the United States in August, he took
up in earnest with Secretary of State Bayard the negotiations leading to a new Chinese immigration treaty, which was signed March 12, 1888. It provided
for the prohibition of the immigration of Chinese
laborers or coolies for a period of twenty years,
but provided for entry of students, travelers, and
merchants with proper qualifications and passports.
It seems strange that as Chinese ministers in Washington, both Tseng Tsao-ju and Chang Yin-huan should
consent so readily to virtual repudiation by the
United States of the Burlingame treaty. The answer
can only by found in the fact that both ministers represented extreme conservative wings of Chinese
officialdom and disapproved of Chinese emigration
which violated Confucian family responsibilities and
opened the way to modernizing and Westernizing influences. This group was glad to keep Chinese
people at home and their position just happened to
coincide with the interests of the United States.
Hence, the comparative ease in renegotiating the
treaties.

In the meantime, new riots occurred in Denver,
Carson City, Sacramento, and several other western
mining and railroad communities where Chinese settle-
ments had developed, and new Chinese claims for damage against the United States under the treaties.
Chang Yin-huan was able to collect $276,61975 indem-
nity, again the full amount claimed.

Chang Yin-huan also spent several months in
Lima, Peru, where large numbers of Chinese coolies
had gone to work in the mines. Here, he set up a
permanent Chinese consulate with a small staff,
staffed and controlled by the legation in Washington.[56]

When he completed his term in Washington, May 8,
1889, Chang Yin-huan had definitely established himself as the ablest, most active, and the most constructive Chinese diplomat sent to Washington to

date. His vigilance in the interest of Chinese laborers in the western mining communities, his negotiation of treaties, organization of the legation,
establishment of consulates, concern for Chinese
interests in Spain and Peru, constitute a very re-
spectable record for only a little more than three
years in the Washington post.

Personally, Chang Yin-huan made the Chinese legation known to Washington society. During his more
than three years there, he and his staff lived luxur-
iously at the legation on Dupont Circle. He made
many friends and gave large parties with guest lists
up to one thousand. He enjoyed travel, frequently
held a box in the theatre, and generally lived the
good life. It is not surprising, therefore, that Li
Hung-chang wrote to the next minister, Tsui Kuo-yin,
that Chang had lived extravagantly and beyond his
means. His biographer, however, believes that this
charge is not wholly justified because "Chang thus
learned much about American life and about foreign
relations" by participating in the Washington merry-
go-round.[57]

After he retired, Chang Yin-huan extended his
influence and reputation by writing his memoirs in
seven volumes under the title Diary of Three Contin-
ents,[58] although this has done little to make him
better known in the United States due to the fact
that it is written in literary Chinese and has never
been translated or even reviewed or summarized in
English. The Diary reveals Chang Yin-huan as an
observant and refined Chinese gentleman-scholar.
With little or no knowledge of English, he depended
on his staff for interpreting and translations. He
belonged to the "self-strengthening" school, but on
the Chang Chih-tung side of the fence--putting heavy
emphasis on the preservation of Chinese character,
morals, social, and philosophical standards and lim-
iting Western influence to machinery and military
hardware. He was scornful of missionary work in
China and when an American preacher asked him about
Christianity in China, according to his diary, he
retorted with some feeling that "Jesus Christ, would
be ashamed of the way Christians treat Chinese in
Rock Springs."

But Chang Yin-huan was receptive to the new
world scene, too. He appreciated American democracy
but realized that it was not for China. He deplored
the slowness of administrative processes, found our

189

national defense loose, "but adequate because there was no enemy." He praised the speed and service of the transcontinetal railway and admired our judicial system. He was most favorably impressed by American business methods and the opportunities for making money.[59] On the whole his attitude was relaxed and he was clearly something less than overwhelmed by the United States in particular and Western civilization in general. China and America each had their points but it is pretty evident that he preferred China.

Chang Yin-huan completed his term in Washington, May 8, 1889, and returned to China, resumed his duties in the Tsung-li Yamen with the rank of Director of the Imperial Stud, and in 1892 was made vice president of the Board of Revenue.[60] Two years later he was sent to Japan by the Tsung-li Yamen to negotiate the ending of the war, but his mission was rejected by Japan because of insufficient powers. In 1896, he was appointed Envoy Plenipotentiary to Japan and signed the Commercial Treaty, July 21, 1896. The following year he represented China at Queen Victoria's Diamond Jubilee and remained in London to negotiate a British loan for the payment of the Japanese indemnity. In 1898, in the process of negotiating a loan from the Hong Kong and Shanghai Bank, he was reported to have received a bribe of a quarter of a million dollars from Count Witte for his support of Russia's lease of the Liaotung Peninsula (according to the same rumor, Li Hung-chang got $500,000). But Chang Yin-huan rode it out and remained a powerful figure in the Tsung-li Yamen. He supported the Reform Movement of 1898, but when the Empress Dowager returned to power his opportunism finally caught up with him. He was exiled to Sinkiang, spent two years at Urumchi, and was finally executed.[61]

Chang Yin-huan ended a period of Cantonese domination of the Chinese post in Washington, for the first three ministers, Ch'en Lan-pin, Cheng Tsao-ju and Chang Yin-huan were all natives of Kwangtung. This was at least partially justified by the fact that most of the overseas Chinese, with whom the minister at Washington would have to deal, were Cantonese and a common language and background would be an advantage to both. The charm was broken, however, with the appointment of the next minister, Ts'ui Kuo-yin, who was a native of T'ai-p'ing, Anhuei Province. Ts'ui Kuo-yin presented his credentials October 3, 1889 and remained in office until 1892. He was a chin-shih (Ph.D.) of 1871,[62] and served as a reader in the Hanlin Academy before his appointment.[63] As noted above, in connection with Chang Yin-huan's extravagance, Li Hung-chang warned his successor, Ts'ui Kuo-yin, to be careful when he got to Washington. Apparently, this advice was not heeded for after only a short stay in the United States, Ts'ui Kuo-yin was impeached. He returned to China in 1894 to defend himself, but died before his case came to trial.[64] It is evident, however, that Ts'ui Kuo-yin did not waste all his time in the United States, because in 1894, he published a book entitled Diary of an Envoy to the United States, Peru, and Spain in 12 volumes.[65]

Ts'ui Kuo-yin's voluminous Diary is a compendium of information, descriptions and impressions of the United States, Peru, and Spain, although understandably, the emphasis is on the United States. He traveled widely, used an interpreter from the legation to enable him to interview all kinds of American people and legation translators to clip and translate a wide range of materials from American newspapers and magazines--but mostly newspapers. There is no indication that he knew any English at all, himself.

Ts'ui's catholic tastes led him to explore American politics, economy, inventions, weaponry, the precarious situation of the overseas Chinese in the United States, and he did not hesitate to expound his theories on the world situation in general and the trends that pointed to the future.

He was impressed with the vast proportions of American territory, the great areas for future development, the thinness of the population--all of which he saw as a bright, unlimited future for the United States. He admired the United States already as a great power, destined to be greater. Her great production of gold, steel, petroleum, munitions, heavy machinery and many other things, he said, placed the United States "without a rival in the world." Much of this success he attributed to the government's policy of issuing patents for inventions and thus rewarding ingenuity and originality and stimulating new inventions. He seems to have been completely enthralled by the image of Thomas A. Edison and by the gospel of the Scientific American.

191

He regarded the United States as already highly
mechanized and admired the railroad trains, especially
the transcontiental service from San Francisco to
New York and Washington, the electric trams and
early electric carriages, the elevator, and many
other marvels.

He reserved a very special admiration for the
successful control of the Mississippi River from
disastrous floods, especially because this was
largely a federal government project which, being
Chinese, he could understand and appreciate, as well
as for its applicability to the Yellow River in China.
He did not hesitate to express his sorrow that China
over the millenia had failed to control the Yellow
River and in modern times had failed to take advantage of Western knowledge of engineering to do so.

As a Chinese he could not fail to be interested
in education, which he found to be a very popular
field in the United States. He noted that students
in American studied all fields, including science,
engineering, modern medicine, chemistry, and mathematics. On the contrary, he said, Chinese students
were exclusively taught the Classics which were not
concerned with progress.

Ts'ui Kuo-yin waxed enthusiastic about the
status of women in the United States. It is apparent
that his observation that men and women are equal
in the United States came as a complete surprise to
him. He praises this system but explains that it is
the result of special conditions and environment in
the West, completely different from those of China.
He shows no sympathy for and expressed no hope of
improvement of the fate of the poor Chinese women,
because that is inevitable in China.

Compared to the diary of his predecessor, Chang
Yin-huan, Ts'ui Kuo-yin is revealed as a much more
receptive observer and as a person prepared to make
at least limited and tentative value judgments.
Although never losing his Chinese pride and Chinese
loyalty, he is more ready to admit mistakes and
failures and to advocate utilization and adaptation
of Western material culture and, in a very tentative
way, even to see some virtue in a few Western ideas.
Perhaps his greatest enthusiasm was for invention,
new gadgets and machinery to improve the condition
of the people. At most, his writings put him in the

still small group of Chinese official "self-strength-eners," even though politically he was in the con-servative wing.

The next Chinese minister to reside in Washington was a Chinese Bannerman, Yang Ju, who served the legation from 1892 to 1897. He came to the high post from a very modest background, having served as tao-t'ai (district magistrate) in Kiangsu province in 1888, in Wenchow, Chekiang province in 1891, and in Wuhu, Anhuei province in 1892.[66] On his appoint-ment as minister he was given the rank of expectant assistant grand secretary. At the end of his Wash-inton stint, Yang Ju was made Chinese Minister to Russia, Austria and Holland and in this capacity was one of the co-signers of the contract with Russia, July 6, 1898, to build the South Manchurian Railway, from Harbin, south through Changchun and Mukden, to Dairen and Port Arthur. This is sometimes called the Changchun line and connects Manchuria to the Russian Chinese Eastern Railway, which is a cutoff of the main line of the Trans-Siberian Railway, connecting Vladivostok and Chita.[67] The only publication of Yang Ju is a collection of documents dealing with a Sino-Russian conference on the return of telegraphs in Manchuria.[68]

If Yang Ju's record of his mission to Washing-ton, at least in surviving Chinese documents, is slight or virtually nil, the lack of more than made up by the voluminous record, in both Chinese and English sources, of his successor. Wo T'ing-fang, a Cantonese born in Singapore and educated in Chi-nese schools in Canton and St. Paul's College in Hong Kong, got his career started by serving as interpreter in the law courts of the British Crown Colony. In 1874, he went to England, entered Lincoln's Inn, and was called to the Bar in 1877. After prac-ticing law as a barrister in Hong Kong until 1882, he turned his attention to Chinese officialdom and joined the staff of the powerful viceroy, Li Hung-chang. With this kind of sponsorship, his future in the Chinese bureaucracy was assured. With his Western, as well as Chinese, education and his complete fluency in Chinese and English, his interest naturally turned to foreign relations. He had his first opportunity when he was named to accompany Chang Yin-huan on the abortive peace mission to Japan in 1895. The next year, however, he was a member of the mission of Li Hung-chang and participated in the three-month-long negotiations which produced the Treaty of

Shimonoseki. As English was the medium of communication for the peace conference and both Japan and China had American advisers to safeguard their respective national interests, this was a valuable experience for Wu T'ing-fang and his subsequent writings indicate that he made the most of it. On returning to China, he was appointed Vice President of the Imperial Clan Court and soon afterwards was made one of the Senior Vice Presidents of the Board of War and Superintendent of Imperial Railways. In 1896, he was appointed Minister to the United States.[69]

Wu T'ing-fang served two terms in the Chinese legation in Washington, the first, May, 1897, to November 25, 1902, and the second, March 11, 1908, to December 14, 1909, totaling nearly seven years in the United States.[70] As the first English-speaking Chinese diplomat in Washington he made a tremendous impression. He traveled widely, was much in demand as a lecturer at universities and colleges and equally in demand as an after dinner speaker. He was witty and colorful and used these gifts to press China's claims and to improve American-Chinese relations. He was the source of a never-ending stream of anecdotes and aphorisms and virtually every Chinese story in popular currency in the United States has been attributed to Wu T'ing-fang, whether he ever told it or not.[71]

An incident reported to Tsung-li Yamen by Wu T'ing-fang toward the end of his first term (1902) sheds an interesting sidelight on the practical operation of the Chinese legation in Washington. He noted that his legal adviser, an American named Costello, had been with the legation for more than twenty years with a retaining fee of more than U.S. $4,000 a year, the equivalent in Chinese-treasury scale of more than six thousand ounces of silver. He had been generally faithful and loyal to China's interests but recently he had been away from Washington for long periods and inaccessible when needed. He was also getting old and was often ill. "In the past," Wu T'ing-fang writes, "a foreign adviser has been essential because neither the minister nor his Chinese staff was familiar with foreign relations and they needed outside assistance."[72] Minister Wu had for some time had the idea of dispensing with his services but had no particular occasion for doing so. Then, the previous summer, he had occasion to consult him on the Hawaiian exclusion of Chinese labor question and he suddenly

194

became hostile, lashing out that China was in the wrong and would have to pay the indemnity. Wu T'ing-fang was very shocked and indignant and instructed the counselor of the legation to dismiss Costello immediately, adding that it

> would save us several thousand dollars a year. If in the future we need a foreign staff member, there are plenty available in the United States. Besides the new minister Liang Ch'eng [to be sent to Washington as Wu T'ing-fang's successor] is an experienced diplomat and may not need a foreign adviser and if he does the Counselor of legation can get one for him.[73]

The extended services of lawyer Costello must have been a great help to the relatively isolated Chinese legation in Washington, but the Chinese record is silent except for the long, detailed, but vitriolic report of Wu T'ing-fang.

This incident brings to attention another unsung hero of Chinese representation in the United States. This was a Cantonese youth named Jung K'uei (Cantonese form Yung Kwai), 1861-1943, who was a member of the first group of students of the Chinese Educational Mission, mentioned previously in connection with Yung Wing and Ch'en Lan-pin. Jung K'uei lived with an American family in Hartford, attended the institute there and later entered Yale University. He joined the legation in Washington and was on its staff in one capacity or another for more than forty years.[74] He served as First Secretary, Counselor of Embassy and repeatedly as acting minister or charge d'affaires ad interim between the departure of one envoy and the arrival, sometimes months later, of his successor. As a modest, capable, self-effacing fixture of the Chinese legation in Washington, Jung K'uei probably deserves much of the credit for making it work, training the staff and the ministers in the American way of life, maintaining contacts with the State Department and the press, and giving it whatever continuity and efficiency it attained.

As noted above, Wu T'ing-fang recognized his successor in the Washington legation as an experienced diplomat.[75] Liang Ch'eng, who presented his credentials April 6, 1903, and remained until July 3, 1907, when he resigned and left Chow Tzu-ch'i as charge d'affaires ad interim--in this case more than nine months--until Wu T'ing-fang returned for his

195

second term as Minister to the United States.[76] He was probably the ablest diplomat China sent to the United States during the Empire. He was certainly the most prolific writer of dispatches; his file extant in the Foreign Office Archive at Academia Sinica is larger than those of all the other ministers to the United States, down to 1912, put together. During his term of office the jurisdiction of the Chinese minister resident in Washington was changed from the United States, Spain, and Peru, to the more reasonable and logical definition of the United States, Mexico, and Peru.[77] One suspects that the earlier usage resulted from a vague concept of Western geography, confusing Spain with Spanish America, where Chinese coolies had been sent for several decades and which was a major concern of nineteenth century Chinese diplomacy. Certainly Mexico, with some twenty thousand Chinese farm laborers and mine workers was a logical responsibility, along with Cuba and Peru, for the Chinese minister in Washington.

Liang Ch'eng, before entering the foreign service had been a district magistrate and was given the Third Grade Court Rank as minister.[78] His most important qualification was the fact that he was brought to the United States by Chang Yin-huan and had several years experience in the Washington legation.[79] He probably had a fair knowledge of English, although he still required the services of translators and interpreters.

In 1903, Liang Ch'eng, through his charge d'affaires Shen T'ung, reported the receipt of a cable reporting that the Chinese consul at Honolulu, Yang Wei-pin, had been repeatedly impeached for being out of sympathy with business interests and should be asked to resign. Similiar reports came from the Grand Council to the Foreign Office in Peking that Yang Wei-pin and his vice consul, Ku Chin-hui, "had joined with evil forces to tyrannize the overseas Chinese, that they were selling opium and trafficking in human beings, and various other charges, and requesting a strict investigation of the case."[80] The original memorial was forwarded to Liang Ch'eng by the Foreign Office, ordering action. Minister Liang found that his predecessor, Wu T'ing-fang, had already started proceedings and had ordered the San Francisco consul general and a consular officer from Manila to to to Honolulu for an on-the-spot investigation. In the meantime, the Honolulu consul, Yang Wei-pin, denied the charges but asked to be allowed to resign until his position could be vindicated. Wu T'ing-fang had summarily ordered the accused consul to take home leave until the investigation had been made. In the meantime, even the American minister in Peking, Edwin H. Conger, had received word from a Chinese-American in Honolulu, making new charges and repeating the old ones against Consul Yang and demanding his removal.

Taking his clue from an Imperial Edict issued in 1901, Liang Ch'eng reported to the effect that:

> The large numbers of Chinese from various local-ities who go abroad to engage in trade all cher-ished the homeland and respected the monarchy until Sun Yat-sen, K'ang Yu-wei and Liang Ch'i-ch'ao, all traitors, under the guize of 'pro-tecting the country' set up lottery societies, stirring up the overseas Chinese and collecting millions of dollars. They must be made to real-ize that these traitors, pretending to 'protect the nation,' are actually plotting traitorous schemes and taking advantage of confusion; it is really feared that the Overseas will accept their seduction, little by little contributing funds, more and more every day until there is a really great disaster.

Minister Liang Ch'eng promised to press the investi-gation.

The two investigators who had been appointed by Wu T'ing-fang found that the traitorous "Protect the Emperor Party," organized by K'ang Yu-wei and Liang Ch'i-ch'ao to promote the cause of constitutional monarchy after the Reform Movement of 1898 had col-lapsed and the Empress Dowager returned to power, was behind all the trouble in Honolulu. The various charges made against the consul general and consul were carefully investigated, with a committee of re-spectable businessmen going through the record and auditing the accounts, which were all found to be in order. On the positive side the consul had raised relief funds and had treated the people with "genuine kindness," and had instituted administrative reforms. All the charges were completely dismissed. They found that all the persons who made charges were directly connected with "Liang Ch'i-ch'ao who came to

Honolulu in 1900 and organized the Protect the Emperor Society, designed to fan the flames in men's hearts."[81]

The investigators found that the Protect the Emperor Party had established a newspaper in Honolulu called the "New China News" (Hsin Chung-kuo Pao), actually the mouthpiece of the Party, "to defame the Manchu Court and slander the government." The language was very violent. Their false charges against Consul Yang went on day after day. The other Chinese newspapers in Honolulu supported the consul. The Overseas Chinese were intrigued with the talk about "equal rights" and "freedom" and knew that they could attack the consul with impunity.[82]

The long and detailed dispatches on this topic are interesting as the response of Chinese officials representing the Manchu Court and government in Peking to the movement for constitutional monarchy led by the leading members of the Reform Party, K'ang Yu-wei and Liang Ch'i-ch'ao, and the early revolutionary movement led by Sun Yat-sen, all three to become national heroes within a few years.

Liang Ch'eng was also called upon to make the arrangements for Prince P'u-lun to present his credentials and be received in audience by the President of the United States. He described the ceremony and conveyed the felicitations of the President to the Empress Dowager and the emperor, which received the Vermilion Notation: "We have understood. Respect this!" Liang Ch'eng appears to have been completely satisfied with the ceremony and the respect shown for the Empress Dowager, for the emperor, and for China.[83]

In 1904, Minister Liang Ch'eng visited the newly established Chinese consulate in Mexico City and reported on improved conditions of Chinese laborers there, increased Chinese shipping to Mexican ports, and agreements on new immigration. During his stay in Mexico City he presented China's national letter to the President of Mexico for the first time. He gives a long description of his train trip to the Mexican border noting the deserts, the mountains, adobe houses, and his first contact with American Indians.

In August, 1905, Liang Ch'eng sent a special dispatch to the Foreign Office describing with great intimacy and deep feeling the death of Secretary of State John Hay, whom he greatly admired. Condolences, at his suggestion, were sent by the Empress Dowager and emperor via Imperial Edict and by the Foreign Ministry, which were much appreciated. "Everyone regarded John Hay as an exceptional person, unique in his humanity and pacifism. In his seven years in office, in problems of foreign relations, he placed great emphasis on Eastern Asia. Recent events make this apparent."[84]

Liang Ch'eng also transmitted to the court his comment on Elihu Root, who was to succeed Hay, with equal respect but without the feeling he expressed for Hay:

> When Root was under appointment as Secretary of State, he got all the records and files in order before he took the oath and assumed the post. In New York, Root's law practice brought him an income of a million several hundred thousand dollars a year. Now he has nonchalantly given this up for an annual salary of eight thousand dollars. Commentators often say that he may one day be president. Loyalty and partiotism like his are hard to come by.[85]

These observations of Minister Liang are not supposed to add anything to the record of John Hay or Elihu Root but they do give some idea of the distance the Chinese minister in Washington had gone from the isolation and ignorance of Western, including American, affairs before 1861 when the Tsung-li Yamen was formed and for years afterward. Liang Ch'eng represents a landmark on the road.

Later in 1905, Liang Ch'eng described the activities of the Hague Peace Conference and the Hague Court. He strongly recommended that China send a resident minister to the Hague as permanent representative to the Court, rather than merely be represented at meetings by the Chinese minister at Berlin acting concurrently. His dispatch is a lucid account of the functions and capabilities of the court and a cogent argument for China's full participation in its activities. His request was approved and a minister to Holland was appointed in the person of Lu Cheng-hsiang.

In 1906, Liang Ch'eng made elaborate arrangements for the reception of the special Chinese mission to study the United States government and industry and to make recommendations to the throne for the establishment of a constitutional monarchy and a wholesale modernization of Chinese industry. The mission was headed by a Chinese, Tai Hung-tz'u, and a Manchu, Tuan-fang. Minister Liang got the full support of state and Washington officials and handled the month-long tour like a professional impressario. They were met in San Francisco by a special Treasury Department official, provided with interpreters from the legation, greeted by the governor of California, banqueted for three days by the mayor of Chicago, presented their credentials to the president, who gave them a warship in which to visit Annapolis, were shown West Point by Lieutenant General Grant, son of the ex-president, met at the station by the mayor of Boston. When they entered the Massachusetts state capitol, the governor had the American flag lowered and the dragon flag of China raised; then they visited Harvard and Yale.[86] The indefatigable Minister Liang accompanied them everywhere. He felt that this was all important because

> our Nation is awakening to greatness, is dis-
> cussing constitutional government and causing
> the people of other countries to regard us with
> great respect, which shows up where least ex-
> pected. Some said that because of the Labor
> (Exclusion) Treaty, there had been a different
> attitude toward us, so this show of unusual
> friendliness was to cement relations. Although
> the State Department actions may have had this
> aspect, it could hardly account for the feelings
> of the entire nation.[87]

Tuan-fang and Tai Hung-tz'u presented a report to the throne on their return to Peking entitled "Essentials of Government of the Great Powers" (Lieh-kuo Cheng Yao), in 133 chapters. Unfortunately, this enthusiasm for constitutional government and for wholesale modernization was too late to stave off revolution in China.[88]

Minister Liang's final pyrotechnic to wind up a brilliant term of office was his reportage of the San Francisco earthquake and fire.

> As your Excellencies already know, America's
> San Francisco is the largest commercial port on
> the Pacific Ocean; her market place is jam-
> packed, people and goods helter-skelter, her

buildings are splendid, her assets rich and abundant. Besides New York, none can compare with her. The Chinese living in this city all regard it as the hub of the universe. Their shops are numbered by the hundreds, Chinese settlers by the tens of thousands have been living there happily for several decades.

On the 25th (Chinese date), we suddenly heard that that city had an earthquake. First, it was thought that in the seacoast district the impact was not great, but before long it was reported that in the whole market district, the buildings lay in ruins, amounting to a billion-dollar loss, with casualties innumerable. The next day it was also reported that once the earthquake stopped, fire broke out in the area where the Chinese people's houses are clustered. The disaster also extended to the cable car tracks which were severed. The Port Defense dispatched troops to keep order and to enforce martial law. The situation was critical, as you can well imagine. [89]

Liang sent repeated cables to the Chinese consul general in San Francisco but received no reply because, it was learned later, the consulate was destroyed and the consul had fled with others. The minister and the legation staff all contributed their salaries for relief and solicited funds from overseas Chinese all over the country. He ordered one of his attaches to proceed immediately to San Francisco to do whatever he could and to report back. He requested the Foreign Office to memorialize the Throne for a contribution to the relief chest, requesting 100,000 taels for general American relief and 40,000 taels for overseas Chinese relief, which was promptly granted by Special Imperial Edict from the throne. Later, he learned that the consulate was functioning in Oakland and the attache and the consul were doing all they could to help and reporting regularly to Washington. Minister Liang wrote to the Foreign Office in Peking: "At first I, Ch'eng, was fearful lest the Chinese resident sufferers would be treated differently from the Americans but there was no selfishness shown." He expressed great appreciation for the solicitude and efficiency of the American Red Cross and the United States Army which provided medicines, food, warm clothing, tents, cots, blankets and every need for the

hundreds of thousands of refugees. He also had
some harsh words for his own countrymen:

> The resident Chinese temperament is not
> uniform but generally if they can eat
> without doing anything they will not drive
> themselves to work. Now, there were
> several hundred persons who were previously
> fisherman. Once they were on relief they
> refused to go back to work and so remained
> idle and inevitably got into trouble.[90]

Minister Liang and Attache Chou had no patience
with this attitude and took drastic measures to
force them back to work or to deport them.

Minister Liang eventually went to San Francisco
himself, met the head of the Red Cross, the command-
ing general, the governor and the mayor and did
everything he could to assure full Chinese cooperation. He fought vigorously to save Chinatown in its
original strategic location near the heart of the
city and made plans to rebuild it as a modern city
to replace the destroyed slums of the old Chinatown.
His reports and comments are invariably clear, lively
and intelligent, showing full understanding of both
detail and principles. He felt impelled to stay
longer in San Francisco, but as "Legation business
was piling up and Congress was still in session" he
felt that he should return to Washington. His
excellency was really caught up in the Washington
merry-go-round.

Liang Ch'eng was called back to China to observe
mourning for his stepmother and, as noted above, left
the legation in the hands of an attache for nine
months. After Wu T'ing-fang's second term of office,
which has already been reported, China's representation
in Washington virtually came to a stand-still as
China moved inevitably toward revolution. Two
ministers were named to Washington, one of whom,
Chang Yin-t'ang, first deputy of the Foreign Office,
is indicated as serving a term of two years but nothing
is known of him beyond the fact that he presented his
credentials December 21, 1909. There is also a
shadowy figure named Shih Chao-chi, appointed just on
the eve of the Revolution, who apparently never presented his credentials at all.[91] China was falling
apart and it would take some time to put the pieces
back together.

In the fifty years from 1861 to 1911, China underwent an evolution from diplomatic isolation to complete understanding and participation in international relations on the diplomatic level. The progressive development of the Tsung-li Yamen, of the Burlingame Mission, the Educational Mission, the first minister resident in Washington, to culmination in the persons of two brilliant and versatile diplomats like Wu T'ing-fang and Liang Ch'eng provide a case study in the painful process of changing the entire outlook of an ancient nation and state, clinging to an untenable self-image as the world's only civilized nation surrounded by barbarian tribesmen of varying degrees of tribal organization, to acceptance of a world filled with a myriad of nation states, each sovereign and equal with relations one with another based on mutual respect and carried out according to agree-upon protocol. One can only wish that the world had reciprocated with a little more alacrity. At least the Chinese representatives in Washington, D.C., appear gradually to have accepted the idea and within the half century were clearly enthusiastically enjoying the experience. Just when it was getting to be fun, the Revolution occurred and the relationship had to be started all over again--but not from where it began in 1861. A great deal had been learned in those fifty years.

NOTES

Chapter 1: Early Formulation of China's
          Foreign Policy

1. Ch'ing Shih Kao (Draft History of the Ch'ing)
(Peiping, 1928), chuan 376, 3a-4b; Ch'ing Shih Lieh
Chuan (Biographical series of the History of the
Ch'ing Dynasty) (Shanghai, 1928), chuan 36, 36a-40b.
Kuo Ch'ao Ch'i Hsien Lei Cheng (Ch'ing Dynasty
Biographies Systematically Arranged) (Hsiang, Hunan,
1890), chuan 40, 10a.

2. Ch'ing Shih Kao, ch. 370; 1a-3a. Ch'ing Shih
Lieh Chuan, ch. 36; 18b.

3. The following biographical data taken from
Ch'ing Shih Lieh Chuan.

4. Hosea B. Morse, Chronicles of the East India
Company Trading to China, 1635-1834 (Oxford, 1929),
III, 305-306.

5. Ibid., IV, 60-62.

6. Ch'ing Shih Lieh Chuan, ch. 40; 8-11.

7. After some military service Ch'i-shan was impeached,
removed from office, and ordered to "shut his door
and think things over." Later in 1843 he was made
Imperial Resident of Tibet and in 1846, Acting Governor
General of Szechwan. After two years of commendable
service, he was restored to the First Button and given
the rank of Assistant Grand Secretary. In 1849, he
was transferred to Shen-kan (Shensi-Kansu) as governor
general, where he saw active service against the

Mohammedan tribes of Kokonor. In 1851, he was again impeached for maladministration of military affairs and in the following year he was exiled to Kirin, released later in the same year and made Acting Governor of Honan where the Taiping rebels were becoming a menace. He again distinguished himself and was made lieutenant general and imperial commissioner in sole charge of military affairs. Lack of success brought imperial censure and degradation but he continued to campaign against the Taiping rebels until he was killed in battle in mid-summer of 1854. Ch'ing Shih Lieh Chuan, ch. 40; 18a, 11-25b, 14.

8. Ch'ing Tai Ch'ou Pan I Wu Shih Mo (The Management of Barbarian Affairs of the Ch'ing Dynasty from Beginning to End) (Peiping, 1930), reign of Tao-kuang, ch. 21; 21b, 1-22b, 8. Hereafter cited as IWSM. TK.

9. Ibid., ch. 21; 38b, 1-8.

10. Ibid., ch. 23; 33a, 8-33b, 3.

11. Ch'ing Shih Kao, ch. 386; 5a.

12. Hosea B. Morse, The International Relations of the Chinese Empire (New York, 1910), I, 265.

13. Ibid., 291.

14. Posthumous honors were heaped on Yu-ch'ien. He was made Protector of the Heir Apparent, with the rank of Board President; his tablet was placed in the Temple of the Illustrious Loyal, alongside that of his great-grandfather who had likewise committed suicide for honor in Ili; and after hostilities were concluded, an individual temple was to be erected in his honor at Chen-hai, where he fell. As he had no son, his younger brother was ordered to proceed to Kiangsu to bring his bier to Peking, where full military honors were conferred. His younger brother inherited his dukeship and a nephew was delegated to serve his tablets in both temples. Ch'ing Shih Lieh Chuan, ch. 37; 46a, 13-52a, 14.

15. IWSM. TK, ch. 24; 36a, 9-37a, 6.

16. Ibid., 37a, 7-37b, 4.

17. Morse, International Relations, I, 263.

18. Ch'ing Shih Lieh Chuan, ch. 39; 6a, 3-12a, 3.

19. IWSM. TK, ch. 25; 39b, 8-40b, 10.

20. Ibid., 41b, 10-42b, 2.

21. Ibid., 42b, 6-43a, 3.

22. Ibid., ch. 26; 18a, 8-19b, 1.

23. Ibid., 22a, 2-10.

24. Ibid., 36a, 3-37a, 4.

25. Ibid., 37a, 5-38a, 10.

26. Ibid., 38b, 1-5.

27. Ibid., 38b, 6-39b, 2.

28. Ch'ing Shih Kao, ch. 379; Ch'ing Shih Lieh Chuan, ch. 160; 1a, 2-2b, 10.

29. Ch'ing Shih Kao, ch. 379; 2b, 10-3a, 1.

30. Morse, International Relations, I, 280-281.

31. IWSM. TK, ch. 26; 40b, 10-42b, 10.

32. Ibid., ch. 27; 14b, 9-15b, 4.

33. On the reach, across the inner harbor from the Factories, Elliot had moved ships up from Whampoa. On the 20th he agreed with Yang Fang to a suspension of hostilities and reopening of trade. Morse, International Relations, I, 282.

34. A Chinese native of Shan-yang, Kiangsu, Kuan T'ien-p'ei rose in ranks to become General-in-Chief of Kwangtung Marine Forces in 1834. He was active fortifying and defending the forts at the mouth of the Pearl River and in blocking the channel with piles and iron chains. He was killed in battle when Commodore Bremer captured Bocca Tigris (Hu-men) February 26, 1841. Although in disfavor at the time for failure to stop the English, General Kuan was given posthumous honors and his tablet placed in the Temple for the Illustrious Loyal. His mother, then over eighty years old, was ordered given money and rice for her support by the local officials for the

rest of her life. Ch'ing Shih Lieh Chuan, ch. 39;
31b, 10-33a, 6.

35. Liang Chang-chu, native of Chang-lo, Fukien, was
a chin-shih of 1802. He served in various capacities
in the Peking government until 1823 when he was
appointed to a post in the provinces. In that post
he was described as competent and reliable but not
recommended for a responsible post in the Yellow
River and Grand Canal Conservancy. Appointed
Governor of Kwangsi in 1836, he came in contact with
the opium problem. He memorialized that opium was
being smuggled across the borders from Canton and
also that the opium poppy was being extensively
grown in his province as well as in Yunnan and
Kweichow. He proposed drastic means to suppress the
trade and the production and was ordered to carry
then into effect to eradicate the evils. In 1841
he memorialized recommending a special type of ship,
apparently a kind of ram, as effective against the
English warships. Later the same year, he was
transferred to Kiangsu as governor and was active,
in the rear, in the campaign against the British,
his main interest being in the commissariat and in
the relief of Chinese sufferers. Early in 1842, he
resigned on account of ill health and died in 1849.
Ibid., ch. 38; 29a, 3-32a, 10; IWSM. TK, ch. 27;
15b, 5-16b, 1.

36. Commodore Bremer authorized merchant ships of
all countries to come up the river on the same day
that he captured Bocca Tigris, February 26. Morse,
International Relations, I, 280-281.

37. IWSM. TK, ch. 28; 4a, 4-5b, 5.

38. Henri Cordier, Histoire Generale de la Chine
(Paris, 1920), 22-23.

39. Pottinger returned south at the end of January,
and on February 27, transferred the staff of the
superintendency from Macao to Hong Kong, which he
had proclaimed a free port on February 16. Morse,
International Relations, I, 292.

40. IWSM. TK, ch. 45; 30a, 3-32a, 6.

41. Ibid., 36b, 6-37a, 3.

42. Ibid., ch. 59; 18b, 9-21a.

43. Ibid., ch. 59; 18b, 9-21a.

44. Ibid., 21b, 9-22b, 5.

Chapter 2: Beginnings of Westernization

1. Gideon Chen, Lin Tse-hsu: Pioneer Promoter of the
Adoption of Western Means of Maritime Defense in
China (Peiping, 1934), 61.

2. Ch'ing Shih Lieh Chuan (Shanghai, 1928), ch. 38;
5a, 13-11b, 1.

3. Chen, 7.

4. Ibid., 23.

5. Ibid., 11.

6. Ibid., 18f.

7. Ch'ing Shih Kao (Peiping, 1928), ch. 384; Ch'ing
Shih Lieh Chuan, ch. 165; 3a, 3-3b, 5.

8. IWSM. TK, ch. 58; 43a, 3-47a, 5.

9. Wen-feng, a Manchu Bannerman, was made Canton
customs superintendent or hoppo in 1841. He was
later associated with Ch'i-ying in negotiating the
supplementary treaty with England in 1843. His later
official service was in Jehol and in Peking. He was
in charge of the Yuan Ming Yuan or Summer Palace,
outside Peking, in 1860 when it was raided and
burned by the Allied armies. Failing to prevent
their entrance, he threw himself into the water and
committed suicide. For meeting difficulty with
dignity and not disgracing the robes of a gentleman,
the emperor conferred on him the posthumous title of
Chung-i, "Loyal and Brave." Ch'ing Shih Kao, ch. 499.

10. IWSM. TK, ch. 61; 38b, 10-40b, 9.

11. Chen, 36.

12. P'an Shih-ch'eng assisted in the negotiation of
the Treaty of Wanghia in 1844, and according to
Consul General Joseph W. Ballantine, was one of the
four conspicuously wealthy men of his time, was a
salt merchant, and held the important post of Salt
Commissioner. It was he with whom Commodore Biddle
exchanged ratifications at Poon Tang (P'an-t'ang)

in 1845. Mr. Ballantine says: "Mr. Poon owned considerable property in Poon Tang, a village which was situated on the river about two miles southwest of the Viceroy's Yamen, and which has now been absorbed into the city of Canton. Presumably on account of the inconvenience experienced in those days by foreigners in calling upon Chinese officials. It was arranged to have the ratifications exchanged at Mr. Poon's residence directly accessible to boats." Hunter Miller (ed.), Treaties and Other International Acts of the United States of America (Washington, 1934), IV, 636.

13. Chen, 37.

14. IWSM. TK, ch. 61; 40b, 10-42a, 4.

15. Ibid., ch. 63; 16a, 8-16b, 8.

16. Ibid., 16b, 9-17a, 3.

17. Ibid., ch. 64; 26b, 5-9.

18. Neither the person or the incident has been identified in Western sources.

19. IWSM. TK, ch. 63; 17a, 4-17b, 6.

20. Ibid., 18b, 4-10.

21. Chen, 45-46.

Chapter 3: The Most-Favored-Nation Policy

1. Carroll Stoors Alden, Lawrence Kearny: Sailor Diplomat (Princeton, 1936.

2. Chinese Repository, XI, 333-334.

3. IWSM. TK, ch. 63; 17a, 4-17b, 6.

4. Ibid.

5. Ibid., 18b, 4-10.

6. Ibid., 29a, 3-10.

7. Ibid., 29b, 1-30a, 4.

8. A native of Shantung, Liu Yun-k'o began his
official career in 1814. After holding various
offices in the capital and in the provinces, he
became governor of Chekiang in 1840, succeeding
the Manchu, Wu-erh-kung-e, who had been removed
for his failure to save Ting-hai from capture by
the English. When Ting-hai was recaptured by the
English in 1841, Liu Yun-k'o was likewise held
responsible and degraded but continued in office.
When Cha-pu fell he was again degraded and removed
from office but by Imperial Favor allowed to
continue at his post. After the war he was promoted
to governor general of Min-che and was active in
adjusting commercial and defense regulations in the
newly opened ports and in establishing the foreign
residence settlement at Kulangsu, Amoy. In this
post he was also brought in contact with the
problems of Catholic and Protestant missionaries
and of extraterritoriality and memorialized
extensively on these matters. In 1850 he was allowed
to resign on account of chronic illness and return
to his home to recuperate. In 1852 he was degraded
on account of the miscarriage of a case he decided
when in office but was gradually restored to rank
due to his activity in raising subscriptions for
government support. He was summoned to Peking in
1862 and in the following year was received in
audience and made an expectant official. On account
of his illness, however, he was allowed to return
home, where he died in 1864. Ch'ing Shih Lieh Chuan
(Shanghai, 1928), ch. 48; 28a, 4-30a, 12.

9. IWSM. TK, ch. 64; 39-5-4a, 10.

10. Ibid., 37a, 3-37b, 6.

11. Ibid., 38b, 2-39a, 5.

12. Ch'ing Shih Lieh Chuan, ch. 40; 35a, 8-41b, 14.

13. IWSM. TK, ch. 64; 43b, 1-46a, 1.

14. Ibid., 46a, 9-46b, 5.

15. Ibid., ch. 65; 8a, 10-8b, 7.

16. Ibid., 11a, 2-6.

17. Ibid., 27a, 1-5.

18. Ibid., 27b, 1-4.

19. Ibid., 45a, 3-6.

20. Ch'ing Shih Kao (Peiping, 1928), ch. 376; 3a, 13-4b, 2.

21. IWSM. TK, ch. 65; 27b, 5-33a, 8.

22. Ibid., 45a, 3-46b.

23. Ibid., ch. 66; 11a, 2-12b, 3.

24. Ibid., 13b, 5-10a, 10.

25. Ibid., ch. 67; 3b, 6-8.

26. Ibid., 8a, 9-9b, 2.

27. Ibid., 40b, 4-45b, 8.

28. Ibid., ch. 68; 24b, 5-28a, 3.

29. Ibid., 28a, 4-29a, 5.

30. Ibid., 29b, 2-6.

31. Ibid., ch. 69; 29a, 10-29b, 6.

32. Ibid., 34b, 5-37b, 3.

Chapter 4:   Treaty of Wanghia

1. J. D. Richardson, Messages and Papers of the Presidents (Washington, 1898), IV, 211-214.

2. Hunt's Merchants' Magazine, IX, 575; the official text of the supplementary treaty is given. Ibid., XI, 365-369.

3. Ibid., VIII (1843), 251-257.

4. See Adams' lecture before the Massachusetts Historical Society, December 1841, Memoirs (Philadelphia, 1875), II, 30.

5. House Report, No. 93, 27 Cong., 2 sess., 1-3.

6. Hunt's Merchants' Magazine, VIII (1843), 205-226.

7. Congressional Globe, xii, 323-325.

8. In the Senate the appropriation bill was caustically criticized. See C. M. Fuess, Life of Caleb Cushing (New York, 1923), I, 409.

9. Ibid., 410.

10. Ibid., 413.

11. Ibid., 270.

12. Ibid., 395.

13. Ibid., 407.

14. Congressional Globe, viii, 275.

15. Guess, 414-415.

16. Senate Doc., 138, 28 Cong., 2 sess., 1-5.

17. Ibid., 5.

18. Ibid., 8,9.

19. IWSM. TK, ch. 69; 34b, 5-37b, 3.

20. Ibid., 37b, 4-38b, 9.

21. Ibid., 38b, 10-39b, 1.

22. Ibid., ch. 70; 17b, 4-18b, 1.

23. Ibid., 19a, 5-19b, 3.

24. Ibid., ch. 71; 6b, 4-9b, 3. The text of Cushing's letter in literal Chinese translation follows, 9b, 3-10a, 9; then the text of the acting governor general's reply, 10a, 10-12b, 2.

25. Ch'ing Shih Lieh Chuan (Shanghai, 1928), ch. 42; 34a, 14-36b, 13.

26. IWSM. TK, ch. 71; 12b, 3-13a, 7.

27. Ibid., 13a, 8-14a, 1.

28. Ibid., 14a, 3-14b.

29. Ibid., 14b, 3-15a, 3-10.

30. Ibid., 15a, 3-10.

212

31. Ibid., 15b, 1-16b, 2.

32. Ibid., 17b, 3-18a, 4.

33. Ibid., 18a, 6-18b, 8.

34. Ibid., 18b, 9-19a, 1.

35. Ibid., 23a, 8-24a, 10.

36. Ibid., 30a, 2-30b, 3.

37. Ibid., 30b, 4-31a, 3.

38. Ibid., ch. 72; 3b, 1-4a, 5.

39. Ibid., 4a, 6-4b, 4.

40. Ibid., 5b, 7-7b, 2.

41. Ibid., 8a, 7-8b, 8.

42. Ibid., 13b, 8-15b, 2. See Kuo Ping Chia, "Caleb Cushing and the Treaty of Wanghia, 1844," Journal of Modern History, V (1933), 34-54.

43. Hunter Miller (ed.), Treaties and Other International Acts of the United States of America (Washington, 1934), IV, 644-645.

44. Miller says: "It does not appear that any very material changes were made in the American draft." Ibid., 646.

45. Ibid.

46. Ibid., 647.

47. Ibid., 649.

48. Ibid., 650.

49. Ibid., 650-651.

50. Ibid., 653.

51. Ibid., 658.

52. Ibid., 659.

53. Ibid., 575.

54. IWSM. TK, ch. 72; 15b, 3-18b, 5; see Kuo Ping-chia's translation, Journal of Modern History, V, 470-477.

55. Henri Cordier, Histoire de la Chine (Paris, 1920), 24.

56. IWSM. TK, ch. 72; 18b, 6-20b, 2.

57. Ibid., 20b, 3-21a, 5.

58. Ch'ing Shih Lieh Chuan, ch. 40; 29b, 4-35a, 7.

59. Miller, IV, 658-660.

60. IWSM. TK, ch. 72; 21a, 6-25a, 7.

61. Ibid., 33b, 4-34b, 6.

62. Ibid., 37b, 1-3.

63. Ibid., 38a, 3-9.

64. Ibid., 47a, 5-47b, 3.

65. Ibid., ch. 73; 18a, 8-20b, 2.

66. Ibid., 28a, 8-30a, 7.

Chapter 5:   Extraterritoriality and the Wabash Case*

*The Wabash case was the first case in which official Chinese documents give mention to the United States. Relative to the matter of extrality in China, it is the first case now known which presented Chinese court efficiency in a favorable light. It has here-tofore been unknown in available literature. The author translated the material himself from Manchu documents in Peking. The significance of the Wabash case was to set a negative precedent against extrality for China. American commercial elements in China were consistently against extrality, but official quarters in China joined the pro-foreign elements in the adoption of extrality after the Terranova and the Sue Aman cases. In the deliberations, the Wabash case did not enter into the discussions.

1. Treaty of Wang Hiya (Wang-hsia), Senate Doc., 58, 28 Cong., 2 sess.; also Hunter Miller, Treaties and Other International Acts of the United States of America (Washington, 1934), IV, 559-662.

2. Articles XXI and XXV.

3. Senate Doc., 58, 28 Cong., 2 sess.

4. Germany and Austria lost their extraterritorial rights in China in 1919. The Soviet Union relinquished hers in 1922; Japan forswore extrality in Manchukuo in 1932 and in China proper in 1938; the United States and Great Britain gave up extrality in China in 1943.

5. Morse cites sixteen cases in which foreigners were charged with killing Chinese and seven cases of Chinese assault against foreigners. Of these only one case, Terranova, is American. The Wabash case is not mentioned, and the Sue Aman case, which occurred in 1844, was, of course, beyond the terminal dates of his comment. International Relations of the Chinese Empire (London, 1910), I, 100-109.

6. The basic U.S. documents on the Terranova case are found in House Exec. Doc., 71, 26 Cong., 2 sess.; the Chinese account of the case is found in a memorial of Juan Yuan, November 8, 1821, in Ch'ing-tai Wai-chiao Shih-liao (Peking, 1932), Tao-kuang series, ch. 1, 7b-9b.

7. "Trade and Intercourse with China," The Quarterly Review (London), XLII (1830), 165-167; E. Everett, "Execution of an Italian at Canton," North American Review, XL (1835), 58-68.

8. Senate Doc., 58, 67, 28 Cong., 2 sess.

9. Ch'ing-tai Wai-chiao Shih-liao (State Papers of the Manchu Dynasty), 10 pen (Peiping, 1932).

10. See Tyler Dennett, Americans in Eastern Asia (New York, 1912), 120-121; Niles Weekly Register XIII (December 20, 1817), 266.

11. Wilcocks to Adams, House Exec. Doc., 71, 26 Cong., 2 sess., 7.

12. Ibid.

13. Ibid.

14. Translation by the Reverend Robert Morrison, Ibid., 9. The proclamation is dated June 6, 1817.

15. Cited by Dennett, 120.

16. National Register, 1818; Niles Weekly Register, XIII (February 21, 1818) 431; Ibid., IX (January 6, 1821), 308.

17. Ch'ing-tai Wai-chiao Shih-liao, Chia-ch'ing series, ch. 6, 43a-45b.

18. Ch'ing Shih Lieh Chuan (Shanghai, 1928), ch. 34, 16b-25b.

19. The other groups were occupational: criminals, barbers, and actors.

20. Couling, Encyclopaedia Sinica, 544.

21. Ch'ing-tai Wai-chiao Shih-liao, ch. 6, 43a-45b.

22. A British version definitely establishes the fact that the pirates spoke English, and supplies other details of interest: ". . . a Chinese Compradore's Boat went alongside the Wabash about 9 o'clock in the evening, and some of the Crew asserting in English that they were the Bearers of a Letter from the Captain (who had proceeded to Canton) they were permitted to come on board, when they suddenly attacked and quickly overpowered the Americans on deck; and having secured the rest of the Ship's Company, they plundered the vessel of valuable property and departed with their Booty, steering towards the Ladrone Islands. An officer and two seamen severly wounded in this attack were landed this morning and sent to the Portuguese Hospital." Quoted by Hosea B. Morse, The Chronicles of the East India Company, Trading to China, 1635-1834 (Oxford, 1929), III, 318.

23. Ch'ing-tai Wai-chiao Shih-liao, ch. 6, 43a-45b.

24. Ibid.

25. Ch'ing-tai Wai-chiao Shih-liao, Chia-ch'ing series, ch. 6, 45b-46a.

26. The Imperial endorsement is dated August 10, 1817, indicating a twenty-two-day interval between the dispatch of the memorial from Canton and its consideration at the court in Peking.

27. Ch'ing-tai Wai-chiao Shih-liao, Chia-ch'ing series, ch. 6, 47a-47b.

28. See Niles Weely Register, XIV (1818), 309; XXI (1822), 405; XXII (1823), 354-356.

Chapter 6: The Character of American Trade With
China, 1844-1860

1. William F. Seward in the Senate, March 11, 1850.
Works (New York, 1853), I, 60.

2. Hunt's Merchant's Magazine, X (1845), 77-80.
See also Ibid., XI, 104.

3. W. P. Stearns, "The Foreign Trade of the United
States from 1820-1840," Journal of Political Economy,
VIII (1900), 452-490.

4. E. R. Johnson, History of Domestic and Foreign
Commerce of the United States (New York, 1915), II,
31. Johnson characterizes the period, 1815-1860:
"The industries of the country were seeking a solid
basis, its transportation problems were being solved,
its commercial policy was being shaped. Meanwhile
the foreign trade experienced great fluctuations.
There were years of buoyancy and dullness, but each
advance reached a higher level than had previously
been attained, and each depression was less severe
than those proceding."

5. Statistics unless otherwise indicated are compiled
from the annual reports to the Secretary of the
Treasury, United States Bureau of Foreign and Domestic
Commerce, Commerce and Navigation Reports, 1844-1860.

6. The fur trade began in 1787 and was at its peak in
1802 when fifteen vessels were engaged in the trade.
Sturgess says that by 1844 it had ceased altogether,
which is true in the sense that no ships were trading
directly from the northwest to Canton. "Changes in
Our Trade With China," Hunt's Merchants' Magazine,
XII (1844), 298.

7. Sturgess, 298. As late as 1840 we find the
statement: "Nankeen still continues to be exported
in large quantities; and in point of strength,
durability, and essential cheapness, is unrivalled
by any of the cotton fabrics of Europe, an advantage
which it probably owes, in a good measure to the
excellence of the raw material." It had by this
time, however, ceased to be sent to the United States.
Hunt's Merchants' Magazine, III, 468-469; XI, 54-59.

8. The other period of increased importation of tea
had occurred in 1832 when the duty was removed. The
Americans used mostly green teas and the increased

demand, especially for the finer grades, hyson and hyson skin, could not be met in Canton. The Chinese merchants, being resourceful, treated damaged and poorer grades of black teas with tumeric powder, prussian blue, and gypsum (prussiate of iron and sulphate of lime), roasting the leaves and chopping them up to the proper appearance. Robert Fortune, Wanderings in China (London, 1847), 222-224.

9. Letter to Augustine Heard and Co., Canton, dated Boston, December 30, 1842. MS Appleton (Letter Books). All manuscript materials used are from the Baker Library, Graduate School of Business Administration, Harvard University.

10. January 13, 1845, MS Appleton.

11. To William Appleton, dated Canton, April 6, 1843. MS G. Dexter, II.

12. Russell and Co. to William Appleton, dated Macao, February 9, 1843; P.S. added February 14. MS G. Dexter, I

13. Ibid., Macao, February 13, 1843.

14. Augustine Heard to William Appleton, December to April. MS G. Dexter, II.

15. Ibid., April 14, 1843. MS G. Dexter, II.

16. Augustine Heard to William Appleton, dated Canton, February 24, 1843. MS G. Dexter, II.

17. Russell and Company to William Appleton, Canton, May 29, 1843. MS G. Dexter, II.

18. Augustine Heard and Company, January 13, 1844. MS G. Dexter, IV.

19. Augustine Heard to William Appleton, dated Canton, February 11, 1844. MS G. Dexter, IV.

20. Augustine Heard to William Appleton, dated Canton, September 19, 1844. MS G. Dexter, VI.

21. Wolcott Bates and Co. to William Appleton, dated Shanghai, January 20, 1845. MS G. Dexter, VII.

22. To William Appleton, dated Canton, January 8, 1845. MS G. Dexter, VII.

23. Hunt's Merchants' Magazine, XXIII, 159. There is a letter in the files from an opium firm in Smyrna soliciting the patronage of William Appleton and citing their 'friend F. B. Forbes, Esq.,' one-time American consul at Canton and member of Russell and Company, as reference. D. A. Langdon and Company, dated Smyrna, June 27, 1852. MS G. Dexter, XIX.

24. Nathan Allen wrote that the East India Company's revenue from opium for the season 1848-1849 was $10,967,662 from Calcutta alone, and that there were fifty ships engaged in the trade from India to China. He quotes from The Friend of India for 1849: "It is the most singular and anolmalous traffic in the world. To all appearances, we should find it difficult to maintain our hold on India without it; our administration would be swamped by its financial embarrassments. Its effect on Chinese finances must be as disastrous as it is beneficial to our own. The trade is not legalized in China, and the drug is paid for in hard cash. The annual drain of the precious metals from China, through this article, is, therefore, between five and six millions sterling. No wonder that the cabinet at Peking are struck dumb y this 'oozing' of silver, and that we hear from time to time of the most resolute determination to extinguish the trade. But with more than a thousand miles of sea-coast to guard, and so small a protective navy, and nine-tenths of the officers in it venal to a proverb, that cabinet is helpless." Hunt's Merchants' Magazine, XIII, 28-33; see David Edward Owen, British Opium Policy in China and India (New Haven, 1934).

25. "China and its Prospective Trade," Democratic Review, XVIII (May, 1846), 382-388. Many other such statements could be cited; for instance: "According to the present condition of the China trade, our exports must balance our imports from the nation. The surplus funds of the Celestial Empire now seem to be required to pay for the opium which is cultivated under the auspices of the East India Company and shipped to its ports. Were this trade abolished, substantial blessings would flow down upon that extraordinary people, and our own commerce, with that nation, would be placed on a more prosperous basis." "The China Trade," Hunt's Merchants' Magazine, XI (1845), 44-52. See also De Bow's Review, IX (1850), 441-442.

26. Chinese Repository, XV (June, 1846), 294-295.

27. To Russell and Company, dated Boston, January 28, 1845, MS Appleton.

28. George D. Carter to William Appleton, dated Canton, June 21, 1848. MS G. Dexter, XIII.

29. Russell and Company to William Appleton, dated Canton, February 24, 1846. MS G. Dexter, IX.

30. Augustine Heard to William Appleton, dated Canton, January 11, 1845. MS G. Dexter, VII.

31. MS G. Dexter, IX.

32. To William Appleton, dated Canton, July 1846. MS G. Dexter, X.

33. Augustine Heard to William Appleton, dated Canton, February 28, 1846. MS G. Dexter, IX.

34. Wolcott Bates and Company to William Appleton, dated Shanghai, May 1, 1846. MS G. Dexter, IX.

35. Augustine Heard to William Appleton, dated Canton, July 1846. MS G. Dexter, X.

36. Appleton to Russell and Company, dated Boston, October 3, 1848. MS Appleton.

37. Appleton to George D. Carter, dated Boston, December 26, 1848. MS Appleton.

38. Ibid., April 2, 1849.

39. Ibid., June 4, 1849.

40. To Appleton, dated Canton, November 26, 1851. MS G. Dexter, XVIII.

41. Augustine Heard and Company to Appleton, dated Canton, June 21, 1847. MS G. Dexter, XI. Richard P. Dana wrote from Shanghai in 1853: "The largest portion of the American trade with China must be carried on here, and it is my intention to pass a good portion of my time here." MS G. Dexter, XIX. See Hunt's Merchants' Magazine, XXXIV (1856), 393-394.

42. "American Trade with China," Hunt's Merchants' Magazine, XXVIII (1853), 742-743.

43. To William Appleton, dated Canton, July 21, 1852. MS G. Dexter, XIX.

44. Hunt's Merchants' Magazine, XXXIX, 224.

45. To William Appleton, dated Foochow, March 8, 1858. MS G. Dexter, XXIII. John Crawford, F. R. G. S. late governor of Singapore, wrote in 1859: "The constant cry of Chinese functionaries before 1842 was, 'the black dirt is always coming in, and the pure Sycee silver is always going out.' Not a word is now said about the 'black dirt.' Indeed, opium goes at present under the polite name of 'the foreign medicine,' and is a regular and open branch of trade as are silk and tobacco. A regular import duty is even levied o upon it as upon any other article of importation. The Chinese, in fact, have come to their senses, although the process was a painful and tedious one that brought it about. Hunt's Merchants' Magazine, XLI, 443.

46. Captain Cole to William Appleton, dated Foochow, January 21, 1858. MS G. Dexter, XXIII.

47. Ibid., June 13, 1858, XXIII.

48. William Appleton to Russell and Company, dated Boston, October 24, 1843. MS Appleton.

49. Ibid., October 3, 1848.

50. Augustine Heard to William Appleton, dated Canton, August 27, 1845. MS G. Dexter, VIII.

51. Dated Boston, June 12, 1842. MS Appleton.

52. To William Appleton, dated Canton, December 22, 1844. MS G. Dexter, VI.

53. Appleton to George D. Carter, dated Boston, September 24, 1847. MS Appleton. The amount of specie decreased from $1,046,045 in 1831 to $329,313 in 1851, while the total exports to China increased from $244,790 to $2,155,945 during the same period. Hunt's Merchants' Magazine, XXIX (1854), 104-105.

54. Appleton to Russell and Company, dated Boston, October 30, 1845. MS Appleton. Regarding increased insurance rates, see Ibid., June, 1846.

55. See Dane, Dana and Company's account with Baring Brothers. Statement dated London, September 21, 1852. MS Dane, Dana and Company.

56. Appleton to Augustine Heard, dated Boston, June 23, 1846. MS Appleton.

57. To Samuel T. Dana, dated Canton, September 25, 1852. MS Dane, Dana and Company.

58. To Samuel Dana, dated Canton, March 9, 1853. MS Dane, Dana and Company. Russell and Company wrote: "The table of imports shows a great increase in the consumption of American fabrics. It is to be noticed that all the supplies passed immediately into the country indicating a constant and continuous demand and as they went to various parts, the consumption in every direction and every province may fairly be considered as permanently increased and founded on an appreciation of the excellent wearing qualities of the cloth." To William Appleton, dated Shanghai, January 29, 1853. MS G. Dexter, XIX.

59. To William Appleton, dated June 27, 1858. MS G. Dexter, XXIII.

60. To F. Gordon Dexter, dated Boston, June 8, 1860. MS Appleton.

61. Appleton to Russell and Company, dated Boston, November 16, 1846. MS Appleton.

62. S. Hooper to F. Gordon Dexter, dated Boston, August 23, 1859. MS Appleton.

63. To William Appleton, dated Shanghai, May 10, 1858. MS G. Dexter, XXIII.

64. Hunt's Merchants' Magazine, XVIII (1848), 467-476.

65. Democratic Review, XXX (April, 1852), 319-332.

66. De Bow's Review, XV (1853), 199-200.

67. Hunt's Merchants' Magazine, XXIX (1853), 549-559.

68. J. J. Moore, "China and the Indies--Our 'Manifest Destiny' in the East," De Bow's Review, XV (1853), 541-571.

69. De Bow's Review, XVIII (1855), 11.

70. De Bow's Review, XX (1856), 66.

71. Russell and Company to William Appleton, dated Canton, April 22, 1849. MS G. Dexter, XIV.

72. Appleton to George D. Carter, Boston, February 5, 1849. MS Appleton.

73. Appleton to Captain William Cole of the Oxnard, dated Boston, December 4, 1849. MS Appleton.

74. Russell and Company to William Appleton, dated Canton, June 19, 1850. MS G. Dexter, XVI.

75. Appleton to Captain R. P. Holmes, dated Boston, July 9, 1850. MS Appleton. The use of gold in the China trade seems to have stopped about this time. "We notice by your circular of the 21st May you quote the value of California gold at $15.80 pr. oz.; the gold shipped here from California has realized from 17 3/4 to 18$ pr. oz.; if we understand your quotation of its value in China it would be best to send it to London or here and draw against it." Appleton to Russell and Company, dated Boston, August 6, 1850. Credit on London was resumed as the most convenient medium of trade in China. See Appleton to Richard P. Dana, dated Boston, May 3, 1851. MS Appleton.

76. To William Appleton, dated Canton, February 25, 1852. MS G. Dexter, XVIII.

77. Ibid., Canton, March 27, 1852. The Chinese were at this time welcomed in California. A San Francisco paper wrote: "From early morn until late in the evening, those industrious men are engaged in their occupation of housebuilders, a great number of houses having been exported from China, and the quietness and order, cheerfulness and temperance, which are observable in their habits, is noticed by everyone. Search the city through and you will not find an idle Chinaman, and their cleanliness exceeds any other people we ever saw." Quoted in the Chinese Repository, XIX, 511.

78. Richard P. Dana to William Appleton, dated Canton, April 22, 1852. MS G. Dexter, XVIII.

Chapter 7: Attitudes of Chinese Officials toward the
United States, 1841-1861

1. Translation by J.O.P. Bland, Annals and Memoirs
of the Court of Peking (London, 1914); quoted by
Harley F. MacNair, Modern Chinese History: Selected
Readings (Shanghai, 1923), 2.

2. Translation by Raymond Parker Tenney, MS in
National Archives, Washington, D.C., cited by Chu
Shih-chia, "Tao-kuang to President Tyler," Harvard
Journal of Asiatic Studies, VII (1942-1943), 172.

3. See, for example, the criticisms by Yuan Fu-hsun
of England's over-generous treatment by the Chinese
court, cited in MacNair, 12-13.

4. H. S. Brunnert and V. V Hagelstrom, Present Day
Political Organization of China (Shanghai, 1912), 160.

5. Ibid., 124.

6. IWSM. HF 25; 19a, 1.

7. IWSM. HF 69; 17b, 3-5.

8. IWSM. HF 17; 4b, 9.

9. IWSM. HF 22; 39b, 3-8.

10. IWSM. HF 31; 18a, 9-18b, 2.

11. IWSM. HF 13; 16b, 7.

12. IWSM. HF 22; 41a, 3-7.

13. IWSM. HF 18; 14b, 4-6.

14. Legge, Chinese Classics, I, 328.

15. Analects, III, 5; Legge, I, 20.

16. Mencius, IVa, 4; Legge, II, 129-130.

17. Mencius, Ib, 11; Legge, II, 47.

18. Stanley Lane-Poole, Life of Sir Harry Parkes
(London, 1894), I, 105.

19. Ibid., I, 77, 134.

20. Ibid., I, 280.

21. S. Wells Williams, <u>The Middle Kingdom</u> (London, 1883), II, 461-462.

22. <u>IWSM</u>. HF 7; 32a, 8.

23. <u>IWSM</u>. HF 8; 28a, 8.

24. <u>IWSM</u>. TK 71; 9a, 6-7.

25. <u>IWSM</u>. HF 23; 17a, 2.

26. <u>IWSM</u>. HF 21; 11a, 7.

27. <u>IWSM</u>. HF 72; 6a, 8.

28. <u>IWSM</u>. TK 26; 19a, 2.

29. <u>IWSM</u>. HF 32; 23a, 1.

30. <u>IWSM</u>. HF 23; 7a, 6.

31. <u>IWSM</u>. HF 36; 38b, 5.

32. <u>IWSM</u>. HF 9; 52b, 8.

33. <u>IWSM</u>. HF 32; 17a, 2.

34. <u>IWSM</u>. HF 36; 14a, 8.

35. <u>IWSM</u>. HF 9; 4a, 3.

36. <u>IWSM</u>. HF 20; 16a, 8-9.

37. <u>IWSM</u>. HF 18; 10b, 6-7.

38. <u>IWSM</u>. TK 65; 32b, 7.

39. <u>IWSM</u>. HF 31; 34b, 7-8.

40. <u>IWSM</u>. TK 59; 16a, 5-16b, 2.

41. <u>IWSM</u>. TK 41; 23b, 8-9.

42. <u>IWSM</u>. HF 39; 40b, 8-10.

43. <u>IWSM</u>. HF 72; 4a, 3.

44. <u>IWSM</u>. HF 21; 38a, 10-39a, 10.

45. IWSM. HF 9; 39b, 5-6.

46. IWSM. TK 21; 38b, 5; 28, 4a, 10.

47. IWSM. HF 42; 20a, 1.

48. IWSM. TK 26; 38b, 8.

49. IWSM. TK 26; 37b, 7.

50. IWSM. TK 58; 47a, 2; 59; 16b, 2.

51. IWSM. HF 19; 19b, 10-20a, 1.

52. Lane-Poole, I, 264-289.

53. IWSM. HF 10; 2b, 7-10.

54. IWSM. HF 41; 7a, 2-3.

55. IWSM. HF 11; 19a, 8-10.

56. IWSM. HF 69; 30a, 2-3.

57. IWSM. HF 22; 1b, 10-2a, 1.

58. IWSM. TK 23; 33b, 2.

59. IWSM. TK 73; 29a, 6.

60. IWSM. TK 74; 2b, 10.

61. IWSM. TK 73; 28b, 2-29a, 1.

62. IWSM. TK 73; 29a, 1-29b, 4; the letter to President Tyler was actually presented in both Manchu and Chinese texts. See Chu Shih-chia.

63. IWSM. TK 74; 17b, 2-18b, 4.

64. IWSM. TK 71; 24a, 3-5.

65. IWSM. HF 6; 25b, 2-9.

66. IWSM. TK 72; 3b, 8-4a, 1.

67. IWSM. HF 8; 21a, 1-3.

68. IWSM. HF 8; 34b, 8-9.

69. IWSM. HF 32; 5b, 10-6a, 2.

70. <u>IWSM</u>. HF 7; 30b, 8-10.

71. <u>IWSM</u>. HF 13; 14b, 4.

72. <u>IWSM</u>. HF 13; 11a, 8-11b, 4.

73. <u>IWSM</u>. TK 63; 30a, 4.

74. <u>IWSM</u>. TK 24; 36b, 8.

75. <u>IWSM</u>. TK 72; 34b, 2-3.

76. <u>IWSM</u>. TK 21; 23b, 1.

77. <u>IWSM</u>. HF 19; 2a, 8.

78. <u>IWSM</u>. TK 24; 37a, 3-4.

79. <u>IWSM</u>. HF 20; 7b, 3-5.

80. <u>IWSM</u>. TK 73; 20a, 3-8.

81. <u>IWSM</u>. TK 73; 18b, 6-19a, 1.

82. <u>IWSM</u>. TK 65; 33a, 3-4.

83. <u>IWSM</u>. HF 39; 14a, 7.

84. <u>IWSM</u>. HF 9; 47b, 9-10.

85. <u>IWSM</u>. TK 25; 42a, 10.

86. <u>IWSM</u>. HF 53; 43a, 2.

87, <u>IWSM</u>. HF 58; 43b, 4.

88. <u>IWSM</u>. HF 28; 48b, 8-10. Legge, II, 490.

89. <u>IWSM</u>. HF 53; 44a, 3-5.

90. <u>IWSM</u>. HF 30; 44a, 8-44b, 3.

91. <u>IWSM</u>. HF 62; 44a, 4-5.

92. <u>IWSM</u>. HF 54; 33b, 1-2.

93. <u>IWSM</u>. TK 65; 29a, 10-29b, 1.

94. <u>IWSM</u>. HF 7; 21a, 5-6.

95. <u>IWSM</u>. Hf 71; 10a, 5-6.

96. <u>IWSM</u>. HF 71; 11a, 8-11b, 1.

97. <u>IWSM</u>. HF 71; 12a, 2-4.

Chapter 8:   Chinese Barbarian Experts in Early
             Sino-American Relations

1. Teng Ssu-yu, <u>Chang Hsi and the Treaty of Nanking,</u>
<u>1842</u> (Chicago, 1944).

2. Ibid., 39.

3. Ibid., 35.

4. Ibid., 75.

5. Ibid., 84.

6. Ibid., 107.

7. Ibid., 87, 88 (Ch'en Po-ling).

8. Earl Swisher, <u>China's Management of the American</u>
<u>Barbarians</u> (New Haven, 1953), 32, 115, 155.

9. Ibid., 32-33, 155, 184, 186, 187; Hunter Miller
(ed.), <u>Treaties and Other International Acts of the</u>
<u>United States of America</u> (Washington, 1934), IV, 646.

10. Teng, 7, 24, 57.

11. Swisher, 155.

12. Miller, IV, 646.

13. Swisher, 33, 132, 133, 137.

14. <u>Ch'ing Shih Kao</u> (Peiping, 1928), ch. 499, 3b.

15. Tu Lien-che in Arthur Hummel, <u>Eminent Chinese of</u>
<u>the Ch'ing Period</u> (Washington, 1944), II, 851.

Chapter 9:   Chinese Representation in the United States

1. For standard accounts of this period, see Tyler
Dennett, <u>Americans in Eastern Asia</u> (New York, 1922,
1941, 1963), 3-64; W. C. Hunter, The "Fan Kwae" at
Old Canton (London, 1882); David <u>Abeel</u>, <u>Journal of a</u>
<u>Residence in Canton</u> (New York, 1836).

2. See Earl Swisher, <u>China's Management of the Amer-</u><u>ican Barbarians</u> (New Haven, 1953).

3. For a basic account of the American missions, and resulting treaties see Dennett, 292-346.

4. Fang Chao-ying in Arthur Hummel (ed.), <u>Eminent</u> <u>Chinese of the Ch'ing Period</u> (Washington, 1943), I, 382.

5. Ibid., 384.

6. See biography by Fang Chao-ying in Hummel, I, 428-430; descriptions by S. Wells Williams and W. A. P. Martin. Ibid., 384.

7. Biographer Fang Chao-ying in Hummel, II, 853-855.

8. <u>Hsien-feng Ch'ao-teng Ch'ou-pan I-wu Shih-mo</u> (Handling Barbarian Affairs in the Hsien-feng Period), ch. 71; 17-26.

9. Ibid., 19.

10. Ibid., 20.

11. Literally an "Office of Central Control"; full name Tsung-li Ko-kuo Shih-wu Yamen or "Central Foreign-countries Affairs Office," but always used in its abbreviated form.

12. Ibid., 21.

13. Ibid., 22-23.

14. Ibid., 25.

15. Ibid., 26.

16. Ibid., 26.

17. Charts prepared from Republic of China, Foreign Office Files, courtesy of Dr. George K. C. Wu (in Chinese, translated by the author).

18. H. S. Brunnert, <u>Present Day Political Organization</u> <u>in China</u>, 124.

19. Ibid., 160.

20. Republic of China, Foreign Office charts.

21. W. A. P. Martin, A Cycle of Cathay (New York, 1897); Awakening of China (New York, 1902); Lore of Cathay (New York, 1912).

22. The first Prince Ch'ing was the 17th son of the Ch'ien-lung Emperor. See biography in Hummel, I, 464-4?

23. Fang Chao-ying in Hummel, II, 965.

24. See biography by William J. Hail in Hummel, I, 464-471.

25. See Fang Chao-ying's biography in Hummel, II, 860-861.

26. Hummel, I, 380.

27. Republic of China, Foreign Office charts.

28. See Fang Chao-ying's biography in Hummel, I, 393-394.

29. Republic of China, Foreign Office charts.

30. See Knight Biggerstaff, "The Secret Correspondence of 1867-1868: Views of Leading Chinese Statesmen Regarding the Further Opening of China to Western Influence," The Journal of Modern History, XXII, No. 1 (March, 1950), 122-136.

31. Ibid.

32. Ibid.

33. See F. W. Williams, Anson Burlingame and the First Chinese Mission (New York, 1912); quoted from Dennett, 368.

34. Ibid., 368.

35. Knight Biggerstaff, "A Translation of Anson Burlingame's Instructions from the Chinese Foreign Office," Far Eastern Quarterly, I, No. 3 (May, 1943), 278.

36. Ibid., 279.

37. Knight Biggerstaff, "The Official Chinese Attitude Toward the Burlingame Mission," American Historical Review, 41, No. 4 (July, 1936), 685.

38. Ibid., 686-687.

39. Ibid., 694.

40. Ibid., 695.

41. Ibid., 701.

42. Knight Biggerstaff, "The Establishment of Permanent Chinese Diplomatic Missions Abroad," The Chinese Social and Political Science Review, XX, No. 1 (April, 1936), 13.

43. Yung Wing, My Life in China and America (New York, 1909), 181, 189.

44. Kuo T'ing-yee, Chin-tai Chung-kuo Shih-shih Jih-chih (Chronology of Modern Chinese History) (Taipei, 1963), II, Appendix, 64.

45. Yung Wing, 206.

46. Biggerstaff, Chinese Social and Political Science Review, 34.

47. Yung Wing, 198-199.

48. Biggerstaff, Chinese Social and Political Science Review, 35.

49. Republic of China, Foreign Office Roster.

50. Kuo T'ing-yee, II, Appendix, 64.

51. Tsung-li Yamen, Old Office Files, Chinese Ministers Residing in the United States, 1883, Item No. 1.

52. Ibid., Item No. 4.

53. Ibid., Item No. 2.

54. See below under Chang Yin-huan, note 59.

55. Hummel, I, 61.

56. Ibid., 62.

57. Ibid.

58. Chang Yin-huan San-chou Jih-chi (1896), 7v.

59. Chang Yin-huan, Diary.

60. Hummel, I, 62.

61. Ibid., 63.

62. Ibid., 62.

63. Kuo T'ing-yee, II., Appendix, 64-65.

64. Republic of China, Foreign Office Roster.

65. Ts'ui Kuo-yin, Ch'u-shih Mei-Jih-Pi Jih-chi (1894), 12v.

66. Republic of China, Foreign Office, Biographical List.

67. Herbert A. Giles, A Chinese Biographical Dictionary (London, 1897).

68. Yang Ju, compilor, Chung-O Hui-shang Chiao-shou Tung-san-sheng Tien-pao Hui ch'ao (Peiping, 1935).

69. Giles, 595-596.

70. Republic of China, Foreign Office Roster.

71. Ho Ch'ang, "Wu T'ing-fang Among the Devils," Ch'un-ch'iu Magazine, II, No. 4 (April, 1965), 19.

72. Tsung-li Yamen Files, Chinese Envoys to the United States, 1903.

73. Ibid.

74. Hummel, I, 404; Republic of China, Foreign Office Roster.

75. Tsung-li Yamen Files, Chinese Envoys to the United States, 1903.

76. Republic of China, Foreign Office Roster.

77. Kuo T'ing-yee, II, Appendix, 64-65.

78. Ibid.

79. Hummel, I, 60.

80. Wai Wu Pu, Chinese Envoys to the United States File, 1903.

81. Ibid., 1903 file.

82. Ibid.

83. Ibid.

84. Ibid., 1905 file.

85. Ibid.

86. Hummel, II, 780-782.

87. Wai Wu Pu, Chinese Envoys to the United States File, 1906.

88. Hummel, II, 780-782.

89. Wai Wu Pu, Chinese Envoys to the United States File, 1906.

90. Ibid.

91. Republic of China, Foreign Office Roster.